COFFEE

COFFEE

A GUIDE TO BUYING, BREWING, AND ENJOYING

FIFTH EDITION

Kenneth Davids

ST. MARTIN'S GRIFFIN

NEW YORK

www.stmartins.com

Production Editor: David Stanford Burr

Library of Congress Cataloging-in-Publication Data

Davids, Kenneth.
    Coffee : a guide to buying, brewing, and enjoying / by Kenneth Davids.—5th ed.
        p. cm.
    Includes bibliographical references and index.
    ISBN 0-312-24665-X
      1. Coffee.   I. Title.

TX415 .D38 2001
641.3'373—dc21   00-045857

First St. Martin's Griffin Edition: May 2001

10 9 8 7 6 5 4 3 2 1

CONTENTS

COFFEE

1 INTRODUCING IT

More than a wake-up pill

Filling the knowledge gap

Specialty vs. commercial coffees

When the first edition of this book appeared in the mid-1970s, finding a good cappuccino or a bag of freshly roasted specialty coffee was an act of esoteric consumerism often requiring miles of freeway travel and penetration into select corners of large American cities. Today there seems to be a specialty coffee store on every gentrified street corner (half of them Starbucks) and an espresso machine in every restaurant.

When I sold my caffè in Berkeley, California, in 1975, it was one of about five or six such establishments in the entire town and one of three putting out a decent cappuccino. Toward the end of the 1990s, there were over forty caffès on one side of the University of California campus alone, brewing close to 40,000 cups of Italian coffee a day, or 1.2 cups per student, per day, a figure that includes tea drinkers and various beverage puritans.

It would seem that the implicit theme of this book is on its way to prevailing: Coffee is a sensual experience as well as a wake-up pill, and if it is drunk at all, it should be drunk well and deliberately, rather than swilled half cold out of Styrofoam® plastic cups while we work. Enjoying good coffee may not save the world, but it certainly won't hurt.

The Knowledge Gap

Nevertheless, aspiration is not always fulfillment. Every Christmas large numbers of people purchase home espresso machines and, after several rounds of thin, overextracted espresso, sell their machines at a garage sale the following summer and go back to spending too much for too little at the corner caffè.

After picking, separating unripe coffee fruit from ripe in the Antigua Valley of Guatemala.

And at the corner caffè itself, mediocrity may reign, unchallenged by customers who lack sufficient knowledge and confidence to send back thin, bitter espressos, botched caffè lattes, and dead brewed coffee.

When we turn from espresso to single-origin coffees and fancy blends, the realm of Kenya AAs and Ethiopia Yirgacheffes, the gap between what most coffee-loving palates value and what their owners are able to turn up at their local coffee stores and supermarkets looms even deeper and broader. The media connoisseurship and consumer sophistication that has disciplined and given form to the fine wine industry is largely lacking for fine coffee. Charming small roasting companies spring up with wonderfully enthusiastic owners who proceed to destroy splendid green coffees by burning them. Supermarket chains replace the coffees of reputable, dependable specialty roasters with their own lines of specialty coffees that often prove to be, at best, mediocre.

Coffee lovers lack the language to impose their desires on the world, and even when they do, coffee sellers may not hear them. Recently I overheard a customer declare to a clerk in a coffee store that she did not care for acidy coffees. She then asked the clerk to recommend a less acidy coffee. These words are exactly the right words formed into the right question to get this coffee drinker exactly what she wanted. Nevertheless, the clerk could not come up with an adequate response, even though he had at least one superb low-acid coffee—a Brazil Santos—available in the bins behind him.

This book is addressed to those coffee drinkers who are interested in achieving their coffee aspirations, as well as to casual, unconverted readers who may doubt that coffee offers a world of pleasure and connoisseurship as rich and interesting as wine, although considerably more accessible. It is not another gift cookbook filled with recipes that you try once, during the week between Christmas and the New Year. It is a practical book about a small but real pleasure, with advice about how to buy better coffee, make better coffee, enjoy coffee in more ways, avoid harming yourself with too much caffeine, and, if you care to, talk about coffee with authority. Throughout, I have tried to blend the practical and experimental with the historical and descriptive, and to produce a book simultaneously useful in the kitchen and entertaining in the armchair.

A Bargain Luxury

A note on coffee cost: In the years since this book first appeared, coffee prices have fluctuated, often dramatically. But even at its most expensive, fine coffee has remained a bargain, perhaps too much of a bargain from the point of view of the growing countries. A cup of one of the world's premier coffees today costs less than the same amount of Pepsi-Cola, and is fifteen or twenty times cheaper than a wine of the same distinction.

I sometimes think that coffee has remained inexpensive because Americans want to keep it that way. They are willing to pay for quality in coffee, but not snobbery in coffee. Whereas wine carries with it an aristocratic culture of nostalgia, Americans have insisted on keeping coffee the people's drink, with the search for the "perfect cup" a quest for a holy grail that is accessible to everyone, no knighthood necessary. It often has been noted how consistently coffee has been associated with democracy in America's cultural history. From the defiant American embrace of coffee after the Boston Tea Party to the "good cup of Java" refrain on the cult television series *Twin Peaks*, coffee has represented an arena where plain folks can pursue and recognize quality without needing to put on airs or drop a lot of cash. Coffee offers connoisseurship at a good price, without pretension.

A Perfect Cup

I used to stay at a little run-down hotel in Ensenada, Mexico, overlooking the harbor. The guests gathered every morning in a big room filled with threadbare carpets and travel posters of the Swiss Alps, to sit on broken-down couches, sip the hotel coffee, and look out at the harbor through sagging French doors.

Nachita, the old woman who ran the hotel, made the coffee from very cheap, black-roasted, sugar-glazed beans. I assume the beans were carelessly picked and primitively processed because the coffee had the hard bitterness associated with such beans, a taste that, once experienced, is never forgotten. Nachita's tendency to lightly boil the coffee did not help much either. By the time the coffee got to us, it was dark, muddy, and sourly bitter, with a persistence no amount of sugar could overcome nor canned milk obscure.

By anyone's standards it was bad coffee. But—you can guess the rest—the morning, the sun on the sea, the chickens in the backyard, the mildewed smell of Nachita's carpets and the damp smell of old stone walls, the clumsy bilingual conversations, the poems about mornings and Mexico I never put on paper, got mixed up with that sour bitterness and turned it into something perfect. I loved it; I even loved the tinny sweetness of the condensed milk. After all, there was no other cup of coffee, and I was happy.

A cup of coffee is as much a moment caught in the matrix of time and space as it is a beverage: the "perfect" cup of coffee to whom and when?

The Perfect Cup

Of course, there are certain universals in good coffee making, which run through this book like comforting refrains: good water, good beans properly roasted and freshly ground, careful brewing, and so on. All of these fortunately do not depend on sleazily exotic mornings in Ensenada, and they work even at five o'clock on rainy Sundays in Cleveland.

There is plentiful indication, for instance, that the steady decline in coffee drinking in the United States (the near three cups a day the average American drank twenty years ago has shrunk to fewer than two cups today) results from the widespread use of instant coffees that lack both flavor and aroma. Why else would the consumption of quality coffees be increasing spectacularly, while the consumption of commercial coffees continues to decrease?

Nevertheless, those consumers of the average tasteless, thin-bodied instant who still have not tasted their first cup of one of the world's great, rich, full-bodied coffees may be in for a bit of a surprise when they do. If you are used to living in a studio apartment, a mansion may feel a little uncomfortable, at least for the first week.

Specialty vs. Commercial Coffees

All of the coffees recommended in this book are known as specialty coffees. The opposite of specialty is commercial coffee. From the consumer's viewpoint, the most immediately noticeable difference between commercial and specialty coffees is packaging: Commercial coffee usually comes in little jars of instant or is already ground and packed in a tin or a collapsed, plastic-encased brick. Specialty coffee is stored or delivered as whole beans, either in one-pound bags or in bulk, and needs to be ground before it is brewed.

Commercial coffee is usually roasted and packed in large plants, under nationally advertised brand names. Specialty coffee is usually roasted in small stores or factories, using traditional methods and technology, and is often sold where it has been roasted.

Specialty coffees offer considerably more choice than commercial coffees. You can buy coffee by the place where the bean originated (Kenya, Colombia), by roast (French roast, Italian roast), or by blend designed for the time of day, price, or flavor. Commercial coffees offer only a very limited selection of blend and roast, and little possibility of buying single-origin, unblended coffees.

Specialty coffees offer more opportunity for consumers to participate in the creation of their pleasure; commercial coffees are faits accomplis in tins or bags.

A Distinction Blurred

Admittedly, these once-clear distinctions have become a bit fuzzy. Because more and more consumers are buying specialty coffees and fewer and fewer are buying commercial coffees, commercial coffee companies have been attempting to co-opt the specialty market with a variety of compromise products, ranging from listless canned "French roasts" to decent whole-bean coffees sold under the private label of the supermarket chain.

Meanwhile, some large specialty roasters have invaded the commercial market with cans and two-ounce, single-serving bags of preground coffee. These products are usually superior to the corresponding commercial products because of the specialty roasters' tradition of quality and smaller scale of operation, but they still are a compromise product and do not represent the absolute best in specialty coffee roasting. The same can be said for Starbucks's foray onto the supermarket shelves: better than cans, but inferior even to the whole-bean coffees sold in Starbucks's own retail outlets.

In the larger picture, however, the essential distinction between commercial and specialty coffees remains. The best commercial, blended coffees are decent. The worst are atrocious. The best specialty coffees, bought fresh and brewed correctly, are more than good; they are superb, and superb in a variety of ways.

The Good, the Bad, and the Bland

Coffee buyers divide the world's coffee production into three very broad categories: high-grown milds, the misleadingly named category called Brazils, and robustas.

Both high-grown milds and Brazils come from trees that belong to the botanical species *Coffea arabica*. Arabica is the species that sold the world on coffee. It still grows wild in Ethiopia and was first cultivated in commercial quantities in Yemen at the southern tip of the Arabian peninsula. *Coffea arabica* was then carried around the world by coffee-hooked devotees, much as European wine grapes spread to form the basis of the world's wine industry.

The differences between the arabica coffees that make up the high-grown milds and the Brazils categories are twofold: growing altitude and how much care is taken in picking and preparation. The arabica tree will not tolerate frost, nor will it flourish in extremely high temperatures. This means it grows best in certain well-watered, mountainous regions of the tropics. High-grown mild arabica coffees are cultivated at altitudes over 2,000 feet above sea level, usually between 4,000 and 6,000 feet. They are produced from fruit that is picked only when ripe and are prepared with care. The responsible specialty-coffee roaster uses only the finest high-grown mild coffees.

Use of the term Brazils to describe the next most preferred group of coffees is misleading, since Brazil also produces excellent mild coffees. As a trade term, however, Brazils refers to lower-grade coffees that are grown at relatively low altitudes and are mass harvested and carelessly dried. Most of these mass-produced arabica coffees are grown in Brazil, but some are produced in East Africa and the Pacific. These coffees, at worse, taste harsh, sour, or fermented, at best they display a middle-of-the-road, neutral flavor with a flat aroma. Most decent supermarket canned blends contain large proportions of Brazils or similar coffees, with smaller additions of high-grown milds.

Many other species of coffee tree grow wild in Africa, and one, *Coffea canephora var. robusta,* has advanced to major importance in world markets. The main advantages of robusta, as it is generally called by coffee professionals, are that it resists disease and that it grows successfully at lower altitudes than *Coffea arabica.* The bean, however, does not have the fragrance or flavor of the best arabica, or even of a decent coffee from the Brazils category, and, in general, demands the lowest prices in the world market.

Tasting a good quality, pure robusta is an eerie experience for a coffee lover. It looks brown like coffee and hefts like coffee on the tongue, but it has no flavor whatsoever beyond a vague sweetness. It also packs 30 to 40 percent more caffeine than *Coffea arabica.* Robusta is used as a component in the cheapest American commercial coffees, especially instant coffees.

Coffee Processing and Coffee Quality

Coffee beans are not beans at all in a botanical sense. They are the twin seeds of a red (sometimes yellow) fruit that grows to about the size of the tip of your little finger. Growers call this fruit coffee "cherries." Before the coffee can be shipped and roasted, the bean or seed must be separated from the fruit. Nature has been lavish in its packaging of the coffee seed, and removing the three sets of skin and one layer of pulp from around the seed is a complex process. If done properly, the coffee looks better, tastes better, and demands a higher price.

The worst preparation or processing would be as follows: The coffee cherries, or berries, are stripped—leaves, unripe berries, and all—onto the ground. This mixture is then scooped up, sifted, and dried in the sun (and sometimes in the rain, which is one of the problems with such coffees). Later the dried, shriveled fruit is stripped of the bean. Some beans may be small and deformed, shriveled, or discolored. In very poorly prepared coffee all the beans, good and bad, plus a few twigs, a little dirt, and some stones, are shipped together. The various flavor taints associated with cheap coffee—sourness, mustiness, harshness, composty taste—all derive from careless picking, fruit removal, and drying.

The best preparation would run like this: The coffee cherries are selectively picked as they ripen. The same day they are picked, the outer skin is removed, exposing the pulp. The pulp-covered beans are then subject to controlled fermentation in tanks. The ferment-loosened, flabby pulp is then gently washed off the beans and they are dried, after which the last layers of skin, now dry and crumbly, are stripped from the bean by machine.

Between these two extremes—carelessly picked coffees simply put out into the sun to dry and selectively picked, wet-processed coffees—are coffees that have been dried in the old-fashioned way, with the fruit still clinging to the bean, but have been picked selectively and dried with care. These high-quality dry-processed or "natural" coffees can be superb, alive with fruity nuance.

Coffee is graded according to three basic criteria: quality of bean (altitude and species), size of bean, and quality of preparation. An additional criterion is simply how good the coffee tastes and smells, what coffee people call "cup quality."

Again, the responsible specialty coffee seller buys only the best grades of coffee, which means high-grown mild beans, carefully prepared, with high cup quality. When you buy from a responsible specialty coffee seller, you should be buying top quality, no matter what country of origin or roast you choose.

2 HOW IT STARTED

Dancing (and nondancing) goats

Coffee's economic paradox

Coffee snobs to the rescue

The favorite story about the origin of coffee goes like this: Once upon a time in the land of Arabia Felix (or in Ethiopia, if an Ethiopian is telling the story) lived a goatherd named Kaldi. Kaldi was a sober, responsible goatherd whose goats were also sober, if not responsible. One night, Kaldi's goats failed to come home, and in the morning he found them dancing with abandoned glee near a shiny, dark-leafed shrub with red berries. Kaldi soon determined that it was the red berries on this shrub that caused the goats' eccentric behavior, and soon he was dancing too.

Finally, a learned imam from a local monastery came by, sleepily, no doubt, on his way to prayer. He saw the goats dancing, Kaldi dancing, and the shiny, dark-leafed shrub with the red berries. Being of a more systematic turn of mind than the goats or Kaldi, the learned imam subjected the red berries to various experimental examinations, one of which involved parching and boiling. Soon, neither the imam nor his fellows fell asleep at prayers, and the use of coffee spread from monastery to monastery throughout Arabia Felix (or Ethiopia) and from there to the rest of the world.

Goats Put to the Test

Some centuries later, in 1998, I was visiting coffee farms in the mountains of Yemen, the home of Kaldi in the Arabia Felix version of the story. Central Yemen is an austerely beautiful landscape of steep, terraced mountains and stone villages. Yemen coffee is still produced in the simple, direct way it was hundreds of years ago, and it remains one of the finest of the world's coffees. I was curious about the Kaldi story, however, and persuaded a goatherd to bring his goats

into a coffee orchard. After having set up a video camera to document this dramatic reenactment of coffee myth, I asked the goatherd to offer the goats fresh coffee branches festooned with ripe coffee fruit.

The goats sniffed the coffee branches suspiciously, then began to munch some miserable dried grass growing around the foot of the trees.

I tried the same experiment later with what were advertised as much hungrier goats. This time I offered them three choices: fresh coffee branches, dry grass, and qat tree leaves, which Yemenis chew in the afternoon for their stimulant properties. Goat preference sequence: qat leaves number one, dry grass number two, coffee three.

Perhaps the goats I tried were just being perverse, as goats will. Perhaps myths are not supposed to be tested, only told. And I need to add that on a recent trip to Ethiopia I did see some goats happily munching on fresh coffee leaves a woman was feeding them. Perhaps Ethiopian goats are more prone to coffee eating than Yemeni goats, which could be taken as a goat vote for the Ethiopian claim that Kaldi was their goatherd not the Yemeni's.

Europeans Make the Wrong Assumption

In any event, Europeans initially assumed coffee originated in Yemen, near the southern tip of the Arabian peninsula, where Europeans first found it cultivated. But botanical evidence indicates that *Coffea arabica,* the finest tasting of the hundreds of species of coffee and the one that hooked the world on coffee, originated on the plateaus of central Ethiopia, several thousand feet above sea level. It still grows there wild, shaded by the trees of the rain forest.

How it got from Ethiopia across the Red Sea to Yemen is uncertain. Given the proximity of the two regions and a sporadic trading relationship that goes back to at least 800 B.C., no specific historic event needs to have been involved. But if one were to be cited, the leading candidate would appear to be the successful Ethiopian invasion of southern Arabia in A.D. 525. The Ethiopians ruled Yemen for some fifty years, plenty of time for a minor bit of cultural information like the stimulant properties of a small red fruit to become part of Yemeni experience and, eventually, its agricultural practices.

At any rate, *Coffea arabica* seems to have been cultivated in Yemen from about the sixth century on. It seems likely that cultures in the Ethiopia region cultivated the tree before it was transported to Yemen, but probably more as a kind of medicinal herb than as source of the beverage we know as coffee.

COFFEE CIRCUMNAVIGATES THE GLOBE

In Arabia coffee was first mentioned as a medicine, then as a beverage taken by Sufis in connection with meditation and religious exercises. From there it moved into the streets and virtually created a new institution, the coffeehouse. Once visitors from the rest of the world tasted it in the coffeehouses of Cairo and Mecca, the spread of *Coffea arabica,* by sixteenth-century standards, was extremely rapid.

The amazing odyssey of the arabica plant was pos-

sible only because of its stubborn botanical self-reliance. It pollinates itself, which means mutations are much less likely to occur than in plants that have a light pollen and require cross-fertilization. Most differences in flavor between arabica beans probably are caused, not so much by differences in the plants themselves, but by the subtle variations created by soil, moisture, and climate. The plant itself has remained extraordinarily true to itself through five centuries of plantings around the world.

Legend proposes that the Arabs, protective of their discovery, refused to allow fertile seed to leave their country, insisting that all beans first be parched or boiled. This jealous care was doomed to failure, however, and it was inevitable that someone, in this case a Muslim pilgrim from India named Baba Budan, should sneak some seeds out of Arabia. Tradition says that sometime around 1650, he bound seven seeds to his belly, and as soon as he reached his home hermitage, a cave in the hills near Chickmaglur in southern India, he planted them and they flourished. In

1928, William Ukers reported in his encyclopedic work *All About Coffee* that the descendants of these first seeds "still grow beneath gigantic jungle trees near Chickmaglur." Unfortunately, they do not grow there any longer, although the site has become something of a destination for twentieth-century coffee pilgrims.

The French, Dutch, and Portuguese all became interested in the money-making potential of coffee cultivation, but various attempts to propagate coffee in Europe failed because the coffee tree does not tolerate frost. The Dutch eventually carried coffee, perhaps the descendants of the first seven seeds of Baba Budan, to Ceylon (now Sri Lanka) and then to Java, where, after some effort, coffee growing was established on a commercial basis at the beginning of the eighteenth century.

At this point in history, coffee made its debut as the everyday pleasure of nobles and other Europeans rich enough to afford exotic luxuries. Coffee was available either from Mocha, the main port of Yemen, or from Java. Hence the famous blend of Mocha Java, which in those days meant putting together in one drink the entire world of coffee experience.

The Wayfaring Tree

Now comes one of the most extraordinary stories in the spread of coffee: the saga of the noble tree. Louis XIV of France, with his insatiable curiosity and love of luxury, was of course by this time an ardent coffee drinker. The Dutch owed him a favor and managed, with great difficulty, to procure him a coffee tree. The tree had originally been obtained at the Arabian port of Mocha, then carried to Java, and finally back across the seas to Holland, from where it was brought overland to Paris. Louis is said to have spent an entire day alone communing with the tree (probably thinking about all the money coffee was going to make for the royal coffers) before turning it over to his botanists. The first greenhouse in Europe was constructed to house the noble tree. It flowered, bore fruit, and became one of the most prolific parents in the history of plantdom.

This was 1715. From that single tree sprang billions of arabica trees, including most of those presently growing in Central and South America. But the final odyssey of the offspring of the noble tree was neither easy nor straightforward.

Coffee Hero de Clieu

The first sprouts from the noble tree reached Martinique in the Caribbean in about 1720, due to the truly heroic efforts of Chevalier Gabriel Mathieu de Clieu, who follows Baba Budan into the coffee hall of fame. De Clieu first had difficulties talking the authorities in Paris into giving him some trees (he finally stole them), but this was nothing compared with what he went through once at sea. First, a fellow traveler tried to rip up his trees, a man who, de Clieu writes, was "basely jealous of the joy I was about to taste through being of service to my country, and being unable to get this coffee plant away from me, tore off a branch." Other, more cynical, commentators suggest the potential coffee thief was a Dutch spy bent on sabotaging the French coffee industry.

Later, the ship barely eluded pirates, nearly sank in a storm, and was finally becalmed. Water grew scarce, and all but one of the precious little seedlings died.

Now comes the most poignant episode of all: de Clieu, though suffering from thirst himself, was so desperately looking forward to coffee in the New World that he shared half of his daily water ration with his struggling charge, "upon which," he writes, "my happiest hopes were founded. It needed such succor the more in that it was extremely backward, being no larger than the slip of a pink."

Once this spindly shoot of the noble tree reached Martinique, however, it flourished. Fifty years later there were 18,680 coffee trees in Martinique, and coffee cultivation was established in Haiti, Mexico, and most of the islands of the Caribbean.

De Clieu became one of coffee's greatest heroes, honored in song and story (songs and stories of white Europeans, that is; what the African and Indians working the new coffee plantations thought about coffee is not recorded). Pardon, in *La Martinique*, says de Clieu deserves a place in history next to Parmentier, who brought the potato to France. Joseph Esménard, a writer of navigational epics, exclaims:

With that refreshing draught his life he will not cheer;
But drop by drop revives the plant he holds more dear.
Already as in dreams, he sees great branches grow,
One look at his dear plant assuages all his woe.

The noble tree also sent shoots to the island of Réunion, in the Indian Ocean, then called the Isle of Bourbon. There, a combination of spontaneous mutation and human selection produced *var. bourbon*, a new variant or cultivar of *Coffea arabica* with a somewhat different pattern and smaller beans. The famed Santos coffees of Brazil and the Oaxaca coffees of Mexico are said to be offspring of the bourbon tree, which had traveled from Ethiopia to Mocha, from Mocha to Java, from Java to a hothouse in Holland, from Holland to Paris, from Paris to Réunion, and eventually back, halfway around the world, to Brazil and Mexico. Trees of the bourbon variety continue to produce some of Latin America's finest coffees.

For the concluding irony, we have to wait until 1893, when coffee seed from Brazil was introduced into Kenya and what is now Tanzania, only a few hundred miles south of its original home in Ethiopia, thus completing a six-century circumnavigation of the globe.

A Billion-Dollar Bouquet

Finally, to round out the roster of coffee notables, we add the Don Juan of coffee propagation, Francisco de Mello Palheta of Brazil. The emperor of Brazil was interested in cutting his country into the coffee market, and in about 1727, sent Palheta to French Guiana to obtain seeds.

Like the Arabs of Yemen and the Dutch before them, the French jealously guarded their treasure, and Palheta, whom legend pictures as suave and deadly charming, had a hard time getting at those seeds. Fortunately for coffee drinkers, he so successfully charmed the French governor's wife that she sent him, buried in a bouquet of flowers, all the seeds and shoots he needed to initiate Brazil's billion-dollar coffee industry.

What is the larger economic and social meaning of coffee's victorious march from obscure medicinal herb to the world's most popular beverage? Here are three stories that propose very different visions of coffee's impact on the world.

STORY 1: COFFEE AS THE WINE OF DEMOCRACY

The first story could be titled "How Coffee Created Western Civilization." It runs like this: Before coffee insinuated its way into European life by way of contact with the Turks, Europe was run by morose aristocrats in impractical clothing sitting around drafty castles wasting their mental energy digesting breakfasts consisting of warm beer, bread, and other weighty, thought-inhibiting substances. Then came coffee, tea, and coffeehouses; and fueled by caffeine and light breakfasts, Europe was energized and transformed. In due course democracy, individualism, modern culture, and the specialty coffee industry were born, and castles were turned into museums (with café attached).

Obviously an overstatement, but one with basis in fact. When it comes to the events of the seventeenth and eighteenth centuries: the scientific revolution, the Enlightenment, and the subsequent political and social revolutions in France and present-day United States, a strong case can be made for the contribution of coffee and coffeehouses. In fact, it is difficult to find a major paradigm-breaking intellectual movement since about 1700 that was not associated with coffeehouses and coffee drinking, from the Enlightenment and Paris's famous Procope, where Voltaire allegedly drank forty cups of coffee mixed with chocolate per day, to the coffeehouses of Addison and Steele's London, through the French Revolution and the Café Foy, where Camille Desmoulins supposedly made the speech that started the crowd on its way to storming the Bastille, to Boston's Green Dragon—according to Daniel Webster "the headquarters of the Revolution"—down to modern art movements, ranging from Dada through North America's Beat movement, first nurtured in the coffeehouses of San Francisco's North Beach neighborhood.

Coffee or Coffeehouse?

Given the consistent association of coffeehouses with intellectual innovation and iconoclasm, we might ask whether the connection is due to the effects of coffee or simply to the institution of the coffeehouse itself, one of the few places where a broke intellectual can find a place to read, talk, and carry on against the establishment for the price of a cup of coffee.

The great French historian Jules Michelet obviously thought it was the coffee. Here is his rhapsodic tribute to coffee-besotted Paris of the eighteenth century:

> Paris became one vast café. Conversation in France was at its zenith. . . . For this sparkling outburst there is no doubt that honor should be ascribed in part to the auspicious revolution of the times, to the great event which created new customs, and even modified human temperament—the advent of coffee.
>
> Its effect was immeasurable. . . . The elegant coffee shop, where conversation flowed, a salon

rather than a shop, changed and ennobled its customs. . . . Coffee, the beverage of sobriety, a powerful mental stimulant, which unlike spirituous liquors, increases clearness and lucidity; coffee, which suppresses the vague, heavy fantasies of the imagination, which from the perception of reality brings forth the sparkle and sunlight of truth; coffee anti-erotic . . .

I like to think that the reveries induced by caffeine are, as Michelet suggests, active and mental rather than emotional and sensuous, and so encourage an invidious comparison between what is and what could (or should) be.

STORY 2: COFFEE AS POISON OF THE TROPICAL POOR

There is, however, another coffee story. In this one coffee may have been the wine of democracy in Europe or North America, but for the rest of the world it was one more poison in the oppressive cup the developing world handed to the tropical poor to choke on for the next three hundred years.

Because, at the very historical moment that coffee-drinking intellectuals were shaking up politics and culture in Europe, floating the ideas that would turn into modern movements like abolition of slavery, socialism, and feminism, their more commercially inclined colleagues were setting up a global marketing machine. Together with sugar, tropical spices, and tobacco, coffee helped create history's first world market with Europe as its consuming, decision-making,

moneymaking hub. The same early plantation system that first produced sugar and tobacco later produced coffee for the elite of Europe, whether they hung out in palaces, like coffee-lover Louis XV, or in subversive coffeehouses, like Voltaire. Green coffee was a good cash crop for the new colonial entrepreneur. It stood up to long ocean voyages, had a splendid shelf life, and rapidly became one of those lucrative oxymorons, a necessary luxury.

The global economic network that was first created around sugar, coffee, tobacco, and other agricultural commodities is still with us, of course, the slaves of early coffee plantations having become free workers whose freedom largely consists of deciding whether to starve, work for a pittance, or head for the slums of the nearest big city.

A Few Chickens, Some Vegetables, and Coffee

Of course not all coffee is grown on large farms. Probably the majority of the world's coffee is raised by what economists innocently term "small holders," usually meaning a family in a shack on a couple of acres, augmenting a diet of chickens and vegetables with a little cash from coffee sold either to government agencies at predetermined prices or to small-time entrepreneurs cruising back roads in trucks ("coyotes" in Spanish-speaking Latin America), buying coffee for pennies a pound.

As poor as such small farmers may be, the fact that coffee early on escaped from the plantations and took root on the little plots of peasant farmers probably accounts for the fact that left-leaning historians have made it a lesser economic villain than, say, sugar, which is almost always grown on large farms or plantations.

Furthermore, coffee has entered the life and myth of many growing countries in such a fundamental way that it has become a difficult whipping boy. Poor Latin Americans, for example, love their coffee as much as Voltaire loved his, perhaps more so. This love is shared by the intellectual leaders of the Latin-American left, who are as reluctant to brand coffee an economic villain as North Americans might be to blame Santa Claus for materialism. I am told by Colombians, for example, that representatives of the National Federation of Coffee Growers of Colombia can pass as freely through rebel-held areas of Colombia as they do through those controlled by the government.

Nevertheless, from those forty cups that Voltaire drank at the Café Procope to the cup that Allen Ginsberg drank at the Caffè Trieste in 1956 to the caffè latte that you drank just yesterday, coffee has figured in exactly the sort of nasty economic exploitation that Voltaire, Allen Ginsberg, and (probably) you deplore.

So where does this leave coffee? Politically correct? Incorrect? Or just the usual don't-think-about-it-it's-too-complex kind of modern issue?

STORY 3: COFFEE SNOBS TO THE RESCUE

At this point a third history of coffee proposes itself, one that is closely linked with the theme of this book.

Until not very long ago, raw or "green" coffee beans arrived in North American ports wrapped in burlap and mystery. Most coffee was sold bulked in large lots according to various grading and market categories, its price driven by the same relentless (and faceless) supply-and-demand forces that have assured hard times for small (and often large) coffee growers ever since the eighteenth century. Even the dealers and roasters involved in the fledgling specialty coffee business of twenty-five years ago, when I researched the first edition of this book, seldom met a living, walking, talking coffee grower. They bought coffees based on how samples tasted, and they identified coffees in the often enigmatic language of the stencils on the burlap bags: Sumatra Lintong, Yemen Mocha Sanani, Mexico Oaxaca Pluma, Brazil Santos. No one even knew for certain what the more obscure of these traditional terms meant in regard to growing location and conditions. Gourmet coffee was a drama played out in the cup, rather than on the larger stage of the world and its social and economic issues.

The few coffees that did escape the impersonal leveling of the market and sold for a premium, like the famous Wallensford Estate Blue Mountain, did so on the basis of myth rather than direct contact between buyer and grower.

Global Market to Global Community

Now, however, a global coffee community has grown up around the global coffee market. And changes in how coffee is retailed and consumed means that coffees once buried in the general production of a country, continent, or region can be isolated and marketed separately, demanding a higher price per pound based on an interplay of factors ranging from the quality of the coffee to how it was grown (organically, sustainably, in the shade rather than in the sun) to how persistent a global networker the grower happens to be.

In 1950, North American coffee lovers had two choices for their Danish-modern-Chemexes: a cheap blend of coffees or a more expensive blend of coffees. The identity of the coffees making up either alternative and whatever human and gustatory stories lay behind them were lost in the vast apparatus of the market. To be fair, there was a third choice: Somewhere along the way Juan Valdez emerged from the coffee trees of Madison Avenue toting cans of Colombian coffee on the back of his well-groomed donkey. Colombia successfully positioned itself as the only unblended, single-origin coffee widely available in cans.

Today, however, those North American coffee enthusiasts, assuming they live in or near a large city, can choose from an enormous array of coffees whose human, botanical, and ecological stories are increasingly clear and accessible, at least for those willing to stop a moment and listen. And the expressive possibilities available to the coffee lover in turn create opportunities for the coffee grower.

Village in the 72heart of the Bani Mattar coffee-growing region of Yemen.

Commodity to Delicacy

I once sat on a committee of the Specialty Coffee Association of America, an industry association considerably (and increasingly) more international than its name implies, across from Jaime Fortuño, a bright and amiable young man who, with his wife, Susan, was leading a revival of Yauco, a once famous coffee from Puerto Rico.

Puerto Rico had stopped importing coffee years ago. Labor costs were too high in Puerto Rico for its coffees to compete in a global market driven largely by price, and Puerto Rico, like most of the rest of the coffee-growing countries of the world, could hardly afford an advertising campaign of the scope Colombia mounted to glamorize Colombia coffee and elevate its price.

However, taking advantage of the opportunities provided by the new American specialty coffee market, Jaime was able to work with other bright, amiable young men and women both in Puerto Rico and the United States, including the green coffee dealer David Dallis of New York City, to create a small, particularized market niche for coffees from a group of Puerto Rican farms. This revived Puerto Rico coffee not only would have been lost in the old, undifferentiated coffee market of thirty years ago, but it would not have existed in the first place, since the specialized market did not exist to support it and the high cost of growing it.

The farmers whom Jaime and Susan represent use the higher price their coffee commands to pay their workers better and take certain steps to ameliorate the environmental impact of their growing and processing endeavors. The environmental and social correctness of their coffee further justifies its higher price to environmentally and socially aware coffee lovers.

The Small-Holder Strategy

But what about the "small holders," the folks with their vegetables, chickens, and a few coffee trees up the hill? A variation of the same strategy is working for them, or at least for some of them. Cooperatives of small growers now market their coffees directly to sympathetic coffee dealers and roaster-retailers, exactly as Jaime Fortuño did with his coffee. Consumers can buy coffees produced by cooperatives of small growers located in places as various as Chiapas, Mexico; Haiti; northern Peru; Papua New Guinea; and East Timor. Furthermore, these small holders often hold an edge over larger farms in getting their coffees certified as organically grown, since they were never able to afford chemicals in the first place. By certifying their coffees as organically grown and identifying them as economically progressive, the small-grower cooperatives are able to separate their coffees from the crowd and obtain a higher price for them, a good deal of which actually makes it back to the growers rather than being swallowed up by exporters and dealers.

I do not want to make all of this sound more hopeful than it actually is. Most of the coffee of the world still gets fed into the faceless maw of the larger global market and comes out at the other end packed in cans, bricks, or glass jars. Many owners of larger farms attempting to take advantage of new, individualized marketing arrangements are substituting fancy brochures and hype for good coffee or may choose to spend the premium their coffee commands on mechanization or on themselves rather than on better wages and living conditions for their workers and more sustainable agricultural practices. Cooperative marketing efforts by associations of small growers often run into problems created by lack of capital and unfamiliarity with the North American market and its expectations.

Nevertheless, it is clear that the economic paradox of coffee and the old faceless relationships that supported it are dissolving in new and unpredictable ways.

Today, Voltaire would have E-mail, a fax, and a good travel agent. More to the point, his coffee dealer would have them too. Voltaire was a sincere humanist and cosmopolitan and probably would have chosen to drop a few extra francs a year on a coffee from, say, a cooperative in Chiapas. But even if he found him- self too distracted writing famous books and enter- taining amusing people to pay attention to coffee pol- itics, his palate would have made him a coffee progressive despite himself. Voltaire, I am sure, would always have his servants buy Puerto Rico Yauco Se- lecto in preference to generic in a can.

3   BUYING IT

Coffee stores, real and virtual
What all the names mean
Roast names and roast taste

A first decision in drinking coffee is how and where to buy it. The decision is complicated by roasted coffee's vulnerability to staling. Freshly roasted coffee is at its best about a day out of the roaster. If it is kept in an airtight container as whole, unground beans, it can remain splendid if ground and brewed in a week to ten days. But by three weeks out of the roaster, it is well on its way to listless mediocrity.

Roasted coffee beans constitute a natural package for the volatile, delicate oils that supply coffee's aroma and flavor. Storing coffee in whole-bean form and grinding it immediately before brewing is a first and essential step to experiencing it at its peak.

Delivering It Fresh

But strategies differ on how to deliver those whole beans to the consumer with minimum flavor loss. One way is to roast the coffee and sell it within a week after roasting. Freshly roasted coffee naturally degasses by emitting carbon dioxide. This slowly discharging gas protects the beans from penetration by oxygen and consequent staling. Roasters both small and large pursue this "roast it and move it" approach. When a coffee stays around too long owing to unexpected buying patterns, the store may start brewing it as the "coffee of the day" until it's gone or even donating it to a food bank or charity.

However, the roast-it-and-move-it strategy demands discipline and a deep commitment to coffee ethics. Other roasters take a less tricky route. Immediately after roasting, they seal the whole-bean coffee in bags that have been flushed with inert gas to chase out oxygen. Thereafter the carbon dioxide produced by the coffee slowly trickles out a one-way valve, further defending the coffee against staling.

Such gas-flushed valve bags are remarkably effective in preserving coffee freshness. Manufacturers of the bags claim that they preserve flavor and aromatics for up to three or more months. In fact, most responsible coffee sellers take no chances and aim at about six to eight weeks. The one problem with such bags: When the coffee first emerges from the bag, it tastes roaster fresh. But thereafter it seems to degrade in flavor a bit more rapidly than freshly roasted coffee.

The absolutely most responsible approach is pursued by roasters who pack their coffee in valve bags but date the bags and pull them off the shelves after about three weeks.

Simply because coffee is sold as whole beans in bins does not mean it has not seen the inside of a valve bag, by the way. Many large roasters, Starbucks included, ship their coffee to their stores in five-pound valve bags, which are then opened and dumped into the bins.

WHERE TO BUY: STORES AND INTERNET

In most metropolitan areas coffee aficionados can buy coffee from specialized coffee stores or from upscale (and sometimes some not-so-upscale) supermarkets. On the Internet coffees can be ordered directly from sites supporting by roasting companies (peets.com, for example; www.allegro-coffee.com; www.armeno.com; etc.) or through a handful of web sites (www.greatcoffee.com, www.gocoffee.com) that sell a variety of coffees from roasters across the country. See "Sending for It."

For freshness nothing beats buying coffee from places that roast the coffee in the same store where it is sold. In-store roasting, as it is called in the coffee business, is a growing, if still minor, component of the specialty coffee scene. Next up in size are small roasting companies with three or four stores, then medium-sized chains and wholesale roasters whose coffees appear in locations all around a given metropolitan area. Finally, a growing number of chains and franchises have spread themselves over an entire region or sometimes two or three regions. At this writing Starbucks is the only truly national specialty coffee chain.

Although single-store roasters appeal deeply to the coffee romantic in me, the best coffee being roasted in the United States today is produced by medium-sized, regional roasting companies, the kind with perhaps five to thirty stores or outlets. I wish this were not so, and that the single-store roasters were staying up with their somewhat bigger rivals in terms of quality, but at the moment few are. I have to assume that they lack both the resources to compete for the best coffees and the technical knowledge to produce the best roast. Their main edge, and a very significant one, is freshness and customer satisfaction at buying close to the source.

If you want to come to know coffee intimately and enjoy it as fresh as possible, you may want to consider roasting your own, an enjoyable and surprisingly simple procedure (see pages 109–11).

THE COFFEE LEXICON

Stores may carry as many as thirty varieties of coffee. Internet sites may offer even more. Each one has a name, plus a few aliases. The whole business is not quite as complicated as it may appear at first encounter, however. No matter how many names there are, they all refer to the degree to which the bean is roasted, the place the bean came from before it was roasted, the dealer's name for a blend of beans, or a flavoring that was added to the beans after they were roasted.

European Names

Suppose you are in a traditional specialty coffee store examining the beans in the glass-fronted bins. Some, you notice, are darker in color than others. You may also note that most names given these darker coffees are European: French, Italian, Viennese, Continental. These names do not refer to the origin of the beans. Rather, they refer to degree of roast, or how far along the beans have been brought from green to light brown to medium brown to dark brown to almost black. Something called an Italian roast, for example, usually is darker in color and has been carried deeper into the roast spectrum than something called a Viennese roast. If a dark-roast coffee comes from a single origin, it usually is given a double label such as Dark-Roast Colombia or Italian-Roast Mexican. In other cases, however, dark-roast coffees are a blend of beans from a variety of origins, in which case the name refers only to the roast, not to the origin of the bean.

Non-European Names

Next to the coffees with European names, you may note coffees that have a similar degree of darkness and carry non-European names, such as Sumatra, Kenya, or Mexican. Unlike the coffees with European names, these coffees are usually brought to about the same degree of roast or to what the roaster feels is the optimum roast to bring out the distinctive qualities of the coffee. The determining difference between these coffees is not the roast but the origin of the bean. A coffee labeled Sumatra, for instance, should consist entirely of beans from a single country, Sumatra. Since coffee can be grown successfully only in or very near the tropics, such single-origin coffees tend to carry names of an exotic and sultry timbre.

Single-origin coffees, in addition to the name of the country in which they originated, often carry qualifying names: Guatemala Antigua, Kenya AA, Brazil Bourbon Santos, Sumatra Mandheling, Costa Rica La Minita. Most of these qualifying terms are either grade designations (AA) or market names referring, directly or indirectly, to coffee-growing regions (Antigua, Mandheling, Santos). A few, such as Bourbon, describe a botanical variety of *Coffea arabica*. And more and more often, the specific name of a particular farm, estate, or cooperative (in this case La Minita) will appear.

Market Names

I discuss market names at length in Chapter 5, under the countries to which they refer. There are literally thousands in the coffee trade, but only the most famous find their way into the vocabulary of the

Three famous names in coffee. Top, a parade float in the Kona Coffee Cultural Festival, Kona, Hawaii. Middle, sign invoking the traditional name for Yemen coffee: Mokha or Mocha. Bottom, the town that gave its name to the famous Yirgacheffe coffee of Ethiopia.

specialty-coffee retailer. Some derive from the name of a district, province, or state; others from a mountain range or similar landmark; others from a nearby important city; and still others from the name of a port or shipping point. Oaxaca coffees from Mexico are named for the state of Oaxaca; the Kilimanjaro coffees of Tanzania for the slopes of the mountain on which these coffees are grown. The Harrar coffees of Ethiopia take their name from the province and city of Harrar; the Santos coffees of Brazil from the name of the port through which they are traditionally shipped.

Grade Names

Retailers may also qualify coffee labels by grade name. Grading is a device for controlling the quality of an agricultural commodity so that buyer and seller can do business without personally examining every lot sold. Coffee-grading terminology is, unfortunately, varied and obscure. Every coffee-growing country has its own set of terms, and few are distinguished by logical clarity. Kenya AA is an exception: Clearly AA is better than A or B. But through the Colombian terms *excelso* and *supremo* are both laudatory, one could hardly determine by reason alone that supremo is the highest grade of Colombian coffee, and excelso a more comprehensive grade consisting of a mixture of supremo and the less desirable extra grade. Although we may be aware that altitude is a prime grading factor in Central American coffees, one could hardly guess without coaching that "strictly hard bean" refers to Guatemalan coffees grown at altitudes of 4,500 to 5,000 feet, and "hard bean" to those at 4,000 to 4,500 feet. The higher the altitude, the

slower-maturing the bean, and the harder and denser its substance—hence, hard bean.

Estate Names

The latest development in the specialty coffee world is the marketing of coffee by estate, rather than by regional name, market name, or grade. A coffee estate is, properly speaking, simply a coffee farm, and an estate coffee is a coffee that has been kept separate from other coffees on its way from that farm to the consumer. "Estates" may range from tiny three-acre plots lovingly tilled by part-time farmers in the Kona district of Hawaii, to vast, technologically sophisticated farms in Brazil that stretch for tens of miles. Sometimes "estate coffees" may come from a cooperative of farms or from several farms in a district and may merit the estate designation only because they were collected and processed at the same mill.

The term *estate* has a long history in the coffee business, but its latest use in the specialty coffee trade is based on analogy with the wine industry's "estate-bottled" idea and was pioneered by William McAlpin of La Minita farm of the Tarrazu district of Costa Rica. Starting in the 1980s, McAlpin successfully established La Minita in the consciousness of the specialty coffee trade through careful and consistent preparation of the farm's coffee together with promotional efforts like a color brochure and a documentary video tape. La Minita's succees has led to an avalanche of other coffee farms attempting to imitate its successful strategies.

The marketing of a coffee by estate is clearly of advantage to the grower because an estate coffee commands higher and more consistent prices than coffees not similarly recognized and puts the grower less at the mercy of fluctuations in supply and other exigencies. Estate coffees also offer an advantage to roasters and importers because presumably these coffees will be more consistent in their character and quality than similar coffees of more vaguely identified origin.

Nevertheless, the opportunity for abuse remains, perhaps intensifies, with estate coffees. If a grower does succeed in creating a separate identity for a coffee, and if demand for that coffee eventually exceeds the possibility of supply, why not simply buy some cheaper coffee from somewhere over the hill and ship it as your own?

Furthermore, the estate concept lends itself to substituting hype for substance and myth for reality. For every farmer who, like William McAlpin, works just as hard on making his coffee taste good as he does on publicizing it, there may be others who decide to skip the taste part and just go for the publicity.

Still, buyers who handle specialty coffee always have their noses in the air sniffing for rats, and estates that do abuse their reputations risk losing them just as rapidly as they managed to establish them in the first place. Or let us hope so.

Estate coffees tend to share the cup characteristics of the growths in the region where the estate is located. The estate coffee, if it is a good one, typically is a better, more consistent exemplar of those characteristics.

There is little way of determining through deduction alone whether a given name is a general market name or a more specific estate name, unless retailers help you out by sticking "estate" into the description somewhere, which, fortunately, they usually do. I have noted a few of the better-known estates in the discussion of coffees by country in Chapter 5.

Flavored Coffee Names

Flavored coffees are good but inexpensive coffees, roasted to a medium to medium-dark brown, and mixed with liquid flavoring agents that soak into the beans. The flavorings are a modified version of those used throughout the food industry. You occasionally may see actual bits of nuts, fruit, or spice mixed in with the beans, but these components merely dress up the mix and give it a natural look. The real flavoring is done by the added liquids. Some specialty coffee sellers refuse to carry flavored coffees for various practical and philosophical reasons, but let us assume that our hypothetical coffee store does carry them. You will immediately notice that they bear names easily identified as part of the American pop gourmet lexicon. If it sounds like a name of a candy (hazelnut creme) or a bar drink (piña colada), for example, it is a flavored coffee. Or if its name includes the words creme, vanilla, chocolate, or the name of any nut, fruit, or spice, you can be certain it is a flavored coffee. To my knowledge, the only country to appear in the flavored-coffee lexicon is Ireland, and it should not require much reflection to deduce that Irish Creme does not describe a coffee grown in Ireland. I discuss flavored coffees in detail in Chapter 5.

Surmounting the Confusion

To return to the traditional coffee lexicon, the average specialty coffee retailer's use of terminology in labeling coffees is seldom logical or consistent, even when dealing with single-origin coffees. Ideally, we ought to be made aware of the country and region where a coffee originated, its grade, its botanical variety, its market name, when it was harvested, and the name of the farm or cooperative where it was grown and processed. Some of this information may not be known to the retailer; what is known tends to be communicated in sincere but rather arbitrary fashion.

The labels attached to coffees in signs and lists are particularly vague. We usually are given the name of the country and one or two qualifying adjectives. Some retailers may choose the most significant qualifying adjectives, others the most romantic, but the end result is still confusion. Readers of Chapter 5 should be able to manage the terminology fairly well, however, and at least be in a position to make intelligent deductions.

Coffe-Speak: A Test

To find out how capable you are of surmounting the confusion at this point, try this: Kenya. A tropical name, therefore a single-origin coffee from Kenya. Kenya AA. The qualifying adjective, AA, does not sound like a place and has a superlative ring to it, so you conclude it is a grade. Correct. Sumatra Mandheling. A tropical name, therefore a single-origin coffee from Sumatra. Since Mandheling does not sound like a grade, nor have you heard it mentioned as a botanical variety, you assume it is a market name referring to a specific coffee-growing region in Sumatra. You have deduced correctly. Mexico Altura Coatepec. Another single-origin coffee, this one from Mexico. Coatepec sounds like a regional name. Altura has the superlative ring associated with grades, and if you are at all famil-

iar with Spanish, you know it refers to height, so you infer that it is the name of a grade based on the altitude at which the coffee is grown. Correct. Murasaki Estate Kona. Everybody knows Kona is a place in Hawaii, and Hawaii is tropical; therefore, you conclude that this is a single-origin coffee from the Kona district of Hawaii, specifically from an estate or farm called Murasaki. Sound deduction. Passion fruit. Passion fruit is definitely a tropical name, but it remains the name of a fruit and not a place, so you assume that this is a coffee of unspecified origin, roasted medium brown, and flavored with something that tastes like passion fruit. Absolutely correct. French. Coffee is not grown in France, so this must be a roast, darker than usual. Pick any prize on the lower shelf. French-Roast Mexico Oaxaca Pluma. First of all, a single-origin coffee from Mexico roasted darker than usual. Since Oaxaca is a city in Mexico, you figure (correctly) that Oaxaca refers to the region in Mexico where the coffee was grown. That leaves Pluma, which must be either a botanical variety or a grade; you guess grade and you are right. Any prize on the top shelf, including the pandas.

Traditional Blend Names

Deduction is even more in order when dealing with blended coffees. Blends, of course, are mixtures of two or more single-origin coffees. There are two basic reasons to blend beans: One is to create a coffee with a flavor that is either better and more complete than, or at least different from, the flavor produced by a single-origin coffee. The other is to cut costs while producing a palatable drink.

Nearly all commercial coffees sold preground in

cans or bags are blended. Commercial roasters might want to market a pure Sumatra coffee, for instance, but they cannot count on obtaining an adequate supply of the same coffee month after month to warrant the risk of offering a name that is not immediately recognized and valued by consumers.

With many blends found in specialty coffee stores, the name gives some clue to the origin of the coffees involved. The simplest to interpret is the famous combination of Yemen Mocha and Java, the Mocha Java of tradition. Such a blend is not designed to save money but rather to combine two coffees that complement one another. Yemen Mocha is a sharp, fruity, distinctive, medium-bodied coffee, whereas Java (usually) is smoother, deeper toned, and richer. Together the two coffees make a more complete beverage than either one on its own. Although even here blend ambiguity reigns: Harrar, a similar coffee from Ethiopia, is often substituted for the Yemen in Mocha Java blends, and coffees from Sumatra may be substituted for the Java. The philosophy of the blend remains the same, however.

Other blends are named after the dominant single-origin coffee and combine an inexpensive coffee with a more costly name coffee. Thus we have Jamaica Blue Mountain blends or Hawaii Kona blends. Ideally, the characteristics of the name coffee still come through, less intensely than in a single-origin coffee, but distinctively enough. There is also a savings for the consumer (and a profit for the seller). In other cases, the blender may use lesser-known coffees to mimic the characteristics of a more famous and expensive coffee, producing Blue Mountain–style or Kona-style blends.

Another tendency in blend nomenclature might be called the generally geographical. We find a Central America blend, or a Caribbean blend. Or, we meet blends named for the time of day we presumably might drink them: Breakfast blend usually means a blend of brisk, medium-bodied coffees roasted more lightly than afterdinner blends, which generally consist of heavier-bodied, heavier-flavored coffees carried to a darker roast.

Mysteriously Named House Blends

At this point we reach the ultimate test: names for house blends, the beloved children of the proprietor or roaster, baptized with names of his or her personal fantasy. A specialty roaster may have one such child or a dozen. Some of these offspring may have been a tradition in a coffee-roasting family for two or three generations; others may have been born yesterday. A few may be unique, but most are standard blends well known in the coffee business, with slightly different proportions and fanciful names. Occasionally the name gives us a clue to content, but most often we are faced with the romance of the proprietor, whose preferences may run from mountaineering (Tip of the Andes Blend) to the elegantly British (Mayfair) to the darkly Latin (Orsi).

I harbor mixed feelings about vaguely named blends. Romance and imagination are marvelous qualities and should be encouraged, but I also think the consumer deserves to be informed in a direct and unpatronizing way. Fortunately, responsible specialty coffee roasters increasingly do offer descriptions of their blends. Although these one-liners are sometimes colored by wine label romance, they do at least name the constituent coffees, if not their proportions and precise origin.

Organic and Cause Coffees

Coffee, grown in relatively poor countries and largely consumed in richer ones, is well suited to partnerships between producers and consumers aimed at achieving a variety of ecological, economic, and social goals.

Organic coffees are certified by various international monitoring agencies as having been grown without the use of potentially harmful chemicals, thus supporting the health of consumer, producer, and environment. Shade Grown and Bird Friendly are epithets for coffees, particularly coffees from Central and South America, that are grown under canopies of native trees that provide shelter and sustenance for migrating birds. Fair-Traded coffees are purchased (usually from small holder farmers) at a "fair" price, one that should permit farmers to adequately sustain their families and their farms. This price is determined by international formula and is always higher than the typically brutally low prices paid small holders by the local market. ECO-O.K. coffees are certified by an arm of the Rainforest Alliance to meet a range of balanced environmental and economic criteria intended to assure the long-term health of both land and people. An even broader set of criteria is in process of being defined under the general term *sustainable,* although at this writing that term, like shade grown, is not distinguished by any mechanism for definition and certification. In other words, it currently means whatever the user wants it to mean. Finally, individual roasting companies have developed their own social and economic programs. A percentage of the retail purchase price of a given coffee may go directly to support projects that help the growers of that coffee, for example.

Such organic and cause coffees should be identified by origin and roast like any other single-origin coffee. I discuss organic and cause coffees in detail in Chapter 6 and take up related consumer health concerns in Chapter 13.

Brand Names

A few commercial-style brand names for blends or single-origin coffees are beginning to slip into the specialty-coffee lexicon. These names are catchy, evocative, always accompanied by a logo, and usually appear on well-designed bags in more sophisticated supermarkets and gourmet and natural food stores. Some have been developed in an effort to create an identity for various certified, organically grown coffees. I could say, only partly facetiously, that if a name is vague, poetic, Latin American, and comes with a good but sincere-looking logo, it is probably a brand name for an organic coffee. Some brand names try to piggyback on the fame of Jamaica Blue Mountain: Haitian Bleu is a revived, socially progressive coffee from Haiti and Blue de Brasil an organic estate coffee from—where else—Brazil.

Caffeine-Free Coffee Names

Decaffeinated, or caffeine-free, coffees have had the caffeine soaked out of them. They are sold to the roaster green, like any other coffee. Roasters in most metropolitan centers offer a variety of decaffeinated single-origin coffees, roasts, and blends. The origin of the bean and the style of the roast, when relevant, should still be designated: Decaffeinated French Roast Colombia, for instance.

The names used for the various methods of decaffeination may cause some confusion. Water-only or Swiss Water Process decaffeinated coffees have had the caffeine removed from them by first soaking the green beans in hot water, then removing the caffeine from the water by means of activated charcoal filters, then restoring the remaining chemical constituents to the green beans by reimmersing them in the same hot water.

Conventional process, traditional process, or European process all refer to methods in which the caffeine has been removed from the beans with the help of a solvent, rather than by charcoal filters. In the indirect solvent method, the solvent is used in place of charcoal filters to remove the caffeine from the hot water. The solvent never touches the beans themselves. In the direct solvent method, the solvent is directly applied to the beans, and solvent residues are removed by steaming the beans. Typically, if a process is not named for a decaffeinated coffee, it has been treated by either the direct or indirect solvent methods. If you are curious about whether a coffee has been decaffeinated by the direct or indirect method you can try asking, although most likely the clerk or order taker will not know. Solvents used in decaffeination are either methylene chloride or ethyl acetate. Ethyl acetate is derived from fruit, so you may see beans decaffeinated by processes using it described as "naturally decaffeinated" coffees.

Finally, coffees are beginning to appear that have been decaffeinated by direct treatment of the bean with a compressed, semiliquid form of carbon dioxide (CO_2 process). For a detailed discussion of decaffeination processes and the health and quality issues involved, see Chapter 13.

Some Last Slipperty Terms

A few terms are particularly ambiguous: Turkish coffee refers to neither coffee from Turkey nor roast. The name designates grind of coffee and style of brewing. Turkish is a common name for a medium- to dark-roast coffee, ground to a powder, sweetened (usually), boiled, and served with a sediment still in the cup. Viennese is a slippery designation. It can mean a somewhat darker-than-normal roast or a blend of roasts (part dark and part medium) or, in Great Britain, a blend of coffee and roast fig. New Orleans coffee is usually a dark-roast coffee mixed with chicory root or a dark-roast, Brazilian-based blend without chicory.

Coffee Roasts and Coffee Flavor

Given a good-quality bean, roasting is probably the single most important factor influencing the flavor of coffee. The most significant variable is degree, or darkness, of roast. The longer coffee is held in the roaster and/or the higher the roasting temperature, the darker the bean. The darker the bean, the more tangy and bittersweet the flavor. When this flavor settles onto the uninitiated coffee drinker's palate, the usual response is to call it strong.

However, strength in coffee properly refers to the proportion of coffee to water not the flavor of the bean. The more coffee and the less water, the stronger the brew. So you could make a light-roasted, mild-flavored coffee very strong and brew a dark-roasted, sharp-flavored coffee very weak.

I would rather call this dark-roasted flavor dark, pungent, bittersweet, or tangy. This flavor occurs in degrees, depending on how dark the bean is roasted and how the bean is roasted (quickly at high temperatures, slowly at lower, etc.). It peaks when the bean is roasted to a very dark brown and eventually vanishes entirely to be replaced by a charred, carbon taste when the bean is roasted almost black. To understand the chemistry behind the changes in taste, we need to examine what happens when a coffee bean is roasted.

Roasting Chemistry

The green coffee bean, like the other nuts, kernels, and beans we consume, is a combination of fats, proteins, fiber, and miscellaneous other substances. The aroma and flavor that make coffee so distinctive are present only potentially until the heat of roasting simultaneously forces much of the moisture out of the bean and draws out of the base matter of the bean fragrant little beads of a volatile, oily substance variously called coffee essence, coffee oil, or "coffeol." This substance is not properly an oil, since it (fortunately) dissolves in water. It also evaporates easily, readily absorbs other less desirable flavors, and generally proves to be as fragile a substance as it is tasty. Without it, there is no coffee, only sour brown water and caffeine, yet it constitutes only 0.5 percent of the weight of the bean.

The roasted bean is, in a sense, simply a dry package for this oil. In medium- or American-roasted coffee, the oil gathers in little pockets throughout the heart of the bean. As the bean is held in the roaster for longer periods and more moisture is lost, the oil develops further and some begins to rise to the surface of the bean, giving dark roasts their characteristic lightly slick to oily appearance.

Beneath the oil, the hard matter of the bean begins to develop a slightly burned flavor while the sugars carmelize, which together help create the bittersweet tones so attractive to dark-roast aficionados. Eventually, the sugars are burned off almost entirely and the woody matter of the bean turns dry and brittle. This ultimately roasted coffee is variously called dark French, Italian, or Spanish and tastes thin and charred.

Dark roasts also contain a touch less caffeine than lighter roasts, and lack the dry snap coffee people call acidy. Some dark-roast coffees may taste unpleasantly bitter, but this bitterness is the result of poor quality coffee or clumsy roasting technique. This disagreeable bitterness or sharpness should not be confused with either the dry-wine bite of a good, medium-roast, acidy coffee or the rich bittersweetness of a good dark roast.

Roast Terminology

Returning to terminology, coffee drinkers are so habitual that entire nations march from coffee initiation to grave knowing only one style of roast. This uniformity accounts for the popular terminology for describing roasts: French roast, usually the darkest; Italian roast, a little less dark; and Viennese or light

French, only slightly darker than the traditional American norm.

This assigning of national names to coffee roasts is a bit arbitrary but has some basis in fact. French roasters, particularly those in parts of northern France, do roast coffee very darkly, justifying the epithet French for the very darkest roast style. And, very generally, southern Europeans roast their coffee darker than northern Europeans. I will leave the question of whether darkness of roast correlates to the relative intensity of nocturnal habits among the various nations of coffee drinkers to those who may want to consider the issue over their second cup of dark-roast coffee.

However, the "standard" roast, against which the French and Italian roasts of America are implicitly measured, varies both by region and by roaster. Berkeley-based Peet's Coffee & Tea, which initiated the current American fashion for very dark roasting, brings all of its coffee to an extremely dark degree of roast. Consequently, the "regular" Peet's roast is far darker than many other roasters' French roasts. Traditionally, the American West Coast prefers a darker roast standard than the East Coast, with the Midwest appropriately somewhere between. Some of the darkest roasting in the world goes on in the American Southwest.

The success of Starbucks, with its darker-roast style, has, in part, altered this regional pattern. Many newer roasting companies, regardless of region, are now attempting to imitate the original Starbucks's dark-roasting style. Unfortunately, many of these newcomers tend to be clumsy in their imitation, resulting in dried-out, burned coffees. Meanwhile, Starbucks itself has pulled back from its original dark-roasting position. And, being Starbucks, has come up with its own copyrighted terms for various degrees of roast as they interact with the coffees being roasted. In Starbucks-speak, 2000 edition, a traditional American medium roast is Milder Dimensions; a slightly darker roast, Lively Impressions; a moderately dark roast, Rich Traditions; and a dark roast, Bold Expressions.

The Specialty Coffee Association of America (SCAA) has gone in the opposite naming direction from the fanciful route taken by the Starbucks's publicists. The SCAA has promulgated a straightforward, no-nonsense terminology for roast and related that terminology to objective, instrument-determined criteria for degree of roast. The SCAA terminology, which is as practical as a Volvo station wagon (and about as exciting), runs from Light Brown for the lightest roast, through Medium Brown for the middle of the range, to Very Dark Brown for the darkest, with various intermediate stages defined by inspiring terms like Light Medium Brown and Moderately Dark Brown. Despite its blunt simplicity, the SCAA system probably gives the specialty coffee buyer the clearest available set of guidelines for describing roast.

The only way to really understand roast is to associate flavor with the color and appearance of the bean rather than with name alone, but for reference I have condensed most of what an aficionado needs to know about the names of roasts in a table on page 34.

Roast color	Bean surface	Common names	Notes
Light Brown	Dry	**Light** **Cinnamon** New England	Can taste sour and grainy. Typically used only for inexpensive commercial blends.
Medium brown	Dry	**Medium** **American** Regular City	The traditional American norm. Flavor is fully developed; acidity is bright; characteristics of green coffee are clear.
Medium dark brown	Dry to tiny droplets or patches of oil	**Viennese** **Full City,** **Light French** **Espresso** Light espresso, Continental	The normal or regular roast for the West and for many newer specialty roasters. Acidity and the characteristics of the green coffee begin to mute and sweetness and body increase. The norm for northern Italian–style espresso.
Dark brown	Shiny surface	**French** **Espresso** Italian Turkish Dark	The normal or regular roast for many roasters in the West and Southwest. Acidity is backgrounded; the characteristics of the green coffee muted. Bittersweet tones dominate. The norm for most American-style espresso.
Very dark brown	Very shiny surface	**Italian** **Dark French** Neapolitan Spanish Heavy	The normal or regular roast for Peet's Coffee and its imitators. Acidity is gone. In tactful versions of this roast, muted but clear characteristics of the green coffee survive; in aggressive versions all coffees taste the same: bittersweet with hints of burned or charred tones.
Black-brown	Shiny surface	**Dark French** Neapolitan Spanish	All differentiating characteristics of the green coffee are gone; burned or charred notes dominate. Body is thin. Flavor is reduced to faint sweet tones.

4   TASTING IT

What to taste for
The cupping ritual demystified
Grace notes and ambiguities

Learning to distinguish roast is a first, relatively simple step in learning to taste and buy coffee expressively. Once we move from distinguishing roast to discrimination among coffees by country or region of origin, we enter a more ambiguous realm. Signs, brochures, and web sites bombard us with light and full bodies; mellow, acidy, bright, and distinctive flavors; rich and pungent aromas; and on into the mellow, full-bodied tropical sunset.

Most stores carry fifteen to thirty varieties of single-origin coffee, all of which have to be described somehow on a sign or brochure or package. Web sites may carry even more coffees. By the middle of the list, you sense a certain strain; by the end, the writer sounds desperate: "stimulating and vibrant," writes one; "an exotic coffee with a lingering aftertaste, full-bodied and provocative," writes another; "stands apart in its own special way," adds still another. Perhaps. Is the emperor wearing his new clothes? Do these coffees really taste different?

They do and they do not. Broad differences stand out on a coffee-educated palate as clearly as do sugar and salt. It would be difficult for even a half-trained palate to mistake a Kenya for a Sumatra, for example, or a Yemen for a Guatemala. On the other hand, subtler differences can be striking but are difficult to communicate and, above all, may not be consistent from crop year to crop year or from farm to farm. No sane coffee professional would pretend, for example, to be able to consistently describe the difference between a Guatemala Antigua and a Guatemala from another part of the country, or between an estate Costa Rica and an estate Panama, or even,

as was clear in a recent scandal in which Panama and Costa Rica coffees were sold in place of Hawaii Kona, between a Panama, a Costa Rica, and a Hawaii Kona.

Coffee Language, Coffee Clichés

The problem is twofold and has to do with communication. First, the public does not understand coffee language—that is, does not associate terms in brochures with sensations in the mouth. Second, in their effort to make every coffee sound absolutely different from every other coffee, copy writers often resort to mealymouthed romanticisms and wine label clichés in place of genuine description.

The comedian George Carlin once pointed out that there is no name for the two little ridges under the nose. The world is full of unnamed phenomena, and the closer we get to the heart of what it means to be alive, the more unnameable things become. The subtle differences in flavor and aroma among coffees are as real as the chair you are sitting in, but the words do not exist to describe them. We sling a word at a flavor and feel like a Sunday painter trying to capture a misty morning with a tar brush. So we are back to the same old refrain: The only thing to do is taste.

Less Than Specific

Coffee tasting is in many ways more crucial to buying quality coffee than wine tasting is to buying quality wine. The reason: Wine is labeled fairly specifically, whereas coffee is labeled vaguely. For instance, we can learn from its label that a given wine is from

France, a country; from Beaujolais, a region; and from Moulin-à-Vent, a village in Beaujolais whose vineyards produce a particularly sturdy and rich red wine. Finally, the bottle tells us what year the grapes were grown and the wine bottled.

Suppose, however, that we buy a coffee from Ethiopia. More than likely it will simply be labeled Ethiopia or Ethiopian. This tells us nothing and would be analogous to simply labeling all wines from France, from the cheapest everyday wine to aged Lafite-Rothschild, as French.

Some specialty roasters might go further and label a coffee Ethiopia Harrar. Harrar, like Beaujolais, is a region or market name, so we are getting closer. But few spcialty roasters will tell us more. Only occasionally are we told what plantation, estate, cooperative, or village a coffee comes from, for example, even though this may be the most important piece of information of all. Nor are we told when the coffee was harvested or how long the coffee was held in warehouses before roasting.

So a wine book can be much more specific in its recommendations than can a coffee book, not only because wine labels are themselves more specific, but also because coffee is a continuous work in progress, a collaborative endeavor involving creative and crucial contributions from many individuals, starting with the grower, moving from there to the mill operator, the exporter, the importer, the roaster and blender, and finally, the consumer who actually brews the beverage.

A bottle of wine can be affected by how it is stored, transported, and handled, but the fact remains that it is bottled and ready to be enjoyed (at however remote a date) when it leaves the winery. Coffee is subject to three crucial operations—roasting, grinding, and brewing—by parties who are thousands of miles away from the tree on which the bean originated. Thus, coffee even from the same crop and estate may taste different after having been subjected to the tastes of different roasters and a variety of grinding and brewing methods.

A Few More Imponderables

Furthermore, conditions in growing countries change in ways beyond the control of any roaster or importer. A coffee from a certain heretofore reliable estate, cooperative, region, or even country may become unavailable or suddenly deteriorate in quality, sending a buyer scurrying for a substitute that may be sold under the same name as the now unavailable original.

Finally, there is always the question of whether a coffee actually is a Sumatra Mandheling, or a Yemen Mattari, or a Jamaica Blue Mountain. Particularly with high-priced coffees, a temptation exists at every step, from the exporter to the importer to the roaster, to substitute lower-priced or more readily available coffees for those represented in signs and brochures. Or, as may be the case with Jamaica Blue Mountain, to expand the definition of Blue Mountain to include lower-grown coffees that would not have merited that designation ten or twenty years ago. Thus, coffee thrusts the consumer into a more active, and possibly more satisfying, role than does wine but frustrates those who might prefer memorizing to tasting.

LEARNING TO TASTE

For all of these reasons, anyone interested in coffee must learn to taste. There is no traditional tasting ritual for the lay coffee drinker as there is for the wine drinker. Professional tasters, or "cuppers" as they are called, slurp coffee loudly off a spoon, roll it around in their mouths, and spit it into a bucket, which is not common afterdinner behavior. I suggest when you are tasting that you make coffee in your ordinary way, sample the aroma, taste some black, and then enjoy it. If you normally add cream and/or sugar, do so after the first sampling.

You may well want to compare samples of various coffees at the same sitting, however, so you have an idea of what coffee terminology actually describes. Remember that dark roasting mutes or eliminates distinctions in flavor, so make certain you taste coffees that have been roasted to traditional North American taste: medium to medium–dark brown, with a dry or vaguely slick bean surface. It is best to buy all of your samples from the same supplier, so that your palate will not be confused by differences in style of roast. You can either make individual samples with a small French press pot or a one-cup filter cone, or brew the way professional cuppers do. In either case, use the same amount of each coffee, ground the same and brewed identically.

I suggest you start with three coffees: a good Costa Rica Tarrazu (if possible a La Minita Estate Tarrazu); a Kenya AA, and a Sumatra Mandheling or Lintong.

The Professional Cupping Ritual

If you want to proceed as professional cuppers would, assemble identical clean cups or shallow, wide-mouthed glasses (capacity 5 to 6 ounces) for each coffee to be sampled; a soup spoon with a round bowl; a glass of water in which to rinse the spoon between samplings; and something to spit into.

Put one standard measure (2 level teaspoons) of each coffee to be sampled, freshly and finely ground, in each cup; pour 5 to 6 ounces of not-quite-boiling water over each sample. Some of the grounds will sink to the bottom of the cup, and some will form a crust on the surface of the coffee.

Wait a couple of minutes for the coffee to steep, then test each coffee for aroma. Take the spoon and, leaning over the cup, break the crust. Virtually stick your nose in the coffee, forget your manners, and sniff. The aroma will never be more distinct than at this moment. If you want to sample the aroma a second time, lift some of the grounds from the bottom of the cup to the surface and sniff again.

After you have broken the crust, most of the grounds should settle to the bottom of the cup. Use the spoon to scoop up froth and whatever grounds remain floating on the surface and dump them into the improvised spittoon. Top off the cup with fresh hot water. Now take a spoonful of each coffee, lift it to a point just below your lips, and suck it violently into your mouth while taking a breath. The purpose is to spray coffee all over your tongue while drawing it into your nasal passages in order to experience a single, comprehensive jolt of flavor.

Top, coffee sample prepared for cupping. Bottom, Minabu Fujita cupper at work, Hawaii.

This inhaling of coffee spray should give you a notion of the nose of the coffee or the pure aromatic elements of its flavor. Now roll the mouthful of coffee around your tongue, bounce it, chew it even. This exercise should give you a sense of both the body or mouth-feel of the coffee, as well as its flavor as influenced by both aromatics and fundamental tastes, particularly sweetness and acidity. Also note how the sensation of the coffee develops after the first impression. Note whether it changes and deepens, or whether it becomes weaker or flatter; whether it sweetens and softens or hardens. After all this, spit out the coffee, noting the aftertaste.

Continue this procedure until you can distinguish the qualities I discuss in the following pages. Take your time, and feel free to simply take mouthfuls and experience them without the often distracting inhaling business. It is a good idea to concentrate successively on each of the broad, tasting categories: taste all three samples for acidity; then taste all three for body; then for flavor and finish; and finally for aftertaste. Always continue to taste as the coffee cools. Some characteristics reveal themselves most clearly at room temperature. If your palate becomes jaded or confused, sip some water or nibble on a bit of unsalted soda cracker.

COFFEE-TASTING WORDS AND CATEGORIES

Whether you taste the coffees after brewing them as you usually do, or set up a little cupping exercise along the lines I just described, here are some words and concepts that may help you feel your way into the rich and complex sensory world of fine coffee.

Acidity

Taste those high, thin notes, the dryness the coffee leaves at the back of your palate and under the edges of your tongue? This pleasant tartness, snap, or twist, combined with an underlying sweetness, is what coffee people call "acidity." It should be distinguished from sourness or astringency, which in coffee terminology means an unpleasant sharpness. The acidy notes should be very clear, powerful, and transparent in the Costa Rica; rich and wine- or berry-toned in the Kenya; and deeper-toned and muted in the Sumatra. They should be drier in the Costa Rica and perhaps a bit sweeter in the Kenya. Robustas and some lower-grown arabica coffees may display virtually no acidity whatsoever and consequently taste flat.

You may not run into the terms *acidity* or *acidy* in your local coffee seller's signs and brochures. Many retailers avoid describing a coffee as acidy for fear consumers will confuse a positive acidy brightness with an unpleasant sourness. Instead you will find a variety of creative euphemisms: bright, dry, sharp, brisk, vibrant, etc.

An acidy coffee is somewhat analogous to a dry wine. In some coffees the acidy taste actually becomes distinctly winy; the winy taste should be relatively clear in the Kenya. In promotional tags you may find the tones that I call winy described with other terms: fruity, dry fruit, and various specific fruit names, particularly berry and black current. The main challenge is to recognize the fundamental complex of fruit and winelike sensations; once you do that, you can call them anything you like.

Body, Mouth-feel

Body, or *mouth-feel*, is the sense of heaviness, tactile richness, or thickness when you swish the coffee around your mouth. It also describes texture: oily, buttery, thin, etc. To cite a wine analogy again, cabernets and certain other red wines are heavier in body than most white wines. In this case wine and coffee tasters use the same term for a similar phenomenon. All of the sample coffees I recommend should have relatively substantial body; either the Costa Rica or the Sumatra will be the heaviest, and the Kenya—usually a medium-bodied coffee—the lightest. In terms of texture or mouth-feel, the Sumatra may display the most interest—perhaps an oily or gritty sensation. But avoid inventing something you fail to taste. None of these coffees will be thin-bodied or anemic.

Aroma

Strictly speaking, *aroma* cannot be separated from acidity and flavor. Acidy coffees smell acidy, and richly flavored coffees smell richly flavored. Nevertheless, certain high, fleeting notes are reflected most clearly before the coffee is actually tasted. There is frequently a subtle floral note to some coffee that is experienced most clearly in the aroma, particularly at the moment the crust is broken in the traditional tasting ritual. Of the three coffees I recommend for your tasting, you are most likely to detect these fresh floral notes in the Kenya; but depending on the roast and freshness of the coffee, you could experience it in any of the three samples. Latin-American coffees brought to a medium roast, like the Costa Rica, may display a sweet vanilla-nut complex in aroma. The Sumatra also may exhibit smoky, pungent, earthlike, or spicy notes. Finally, if your Costa Rica is a La Minita, the aroma should have a sort of echoing, resonant depth to it.

The same should be true of the Kenya, whereas you may find that the aromatic sensations of the Sumatra are rather immediate and limited, without a sense of dimension opening behind and around them.

Finish

If aroma is the overture of the coffee, then *finish* is the resonant silence at the end of the piece. Finish is a term relatively recently brought over into coffee tasting from wine connoisseurship. It describes the immediate sensation after the coffee is spit out or swallowed. Some coffees develop in the finish—they change in pleasurable ways. All three of the sample coffees I recommend should develop in the finish. I would predict that the pungent tones of the Sumatra may soften toward cocoa or chocolate in the finish, and the dry wine or berry tones of the Kenya turn sweeter and fruitier.

Flavor

Flavor is a catch-all term for everything we do not experience in terms of the categories of acidity, aroma, and body. In another sense, it is a synthesis of them all. Some coffees simply display a fuller, richer flavor than others, are more complex, or more balanced, whereas other coffees have an acidy tang, for instance, that tends to dominate everything else. Some are flat, some are lifeless, some are strong but monotoned. We also can speak of a distinctively flavored coffee, a coffee whose flavor characteristics clearly distinguish it from others.

The following are some terms and categories often used to describe and evaluate flavor. Some are obvious, many overlap, but all are useful.

Richness. *Richness* partly refers to body, partly to flavor, at times even to acidity. The term describes an interesting, satisfying fullness.

Range. This is one of my favorite tasting concepts. Imagine that the sensations evoked by a mouthful of coffee are a musical chord. Then take note of the *range*—where the main interest and complexity of sensation are concentrated. The Kenya will have great complexity throughout, but particularly in the higher ranges, the equivalent of treble notes. The Sumatra, if it is a good one, will be very complex in the lower ranges, the equivalent of bass notes. The Costa Rica will be more integrated and total, perhaps with sensation more concentrated in the middle range.

Complexity. I take *complexity* to describe flavor that shifts among pleasurable possibilities, tantalizes, and does not completely reveal itself at any one moment; a harmonious multiplicity of sensation. The Kenya is probably most complex; if the Sumatra is a good one, it may also be complex, though perhaps less balanced. If the Sumatra is not a particularly good one, it may feel hard and monotoned on the palate. The Costa Rica is probably more like a singular bellcap—perfect, resonant, contained, and complete.

Balance. This is a difficult term. When tasting coffees for defects, professional tasters use *balance* to describe a coffee that does not localize at any one point on the palate; in other words, it is not imbalanced in the direction of some one (often undesirable) taste characteristic. As a term of general evaluation, balance appears to mean that no one quality overwhelms all others, but there is enough complexity in the coffee to arouse interest. It is a term that on occasion damns with faint praise. The Costa Rica sample should be most balanced, although it probably has less idiosyncrasy to balance than the other two coffees. The Kenya should be both complex and balanced; the Sumatra may be imbalanced by overbearing pungent tones and may be a bit rough.

Varietal Distinction or Character

If a coffee displays characteristics that both set it off from other coffees yet identify it as what it is, it has *varietal distinction*. In one sense, all of our three samples are distinctive, because they probably embody the best and most characteristic traits of the growing region from which they came. In another sense the Kenya and the Sumatra could be seen as more distinctive than the Costa Rica simply because the Costa Rica embodies what for North Americans is a normative coffee taste, whereas the Kenya and Sumatra display characteristics that set them off from that norm. The rich, winy acidity of the Kenya immediately suggests that it is an East Africa coffee, probably a Kenya. The Sumatra may be less distinctive, but it also may, depending on how it was handled after picking, exhibit pungency or mustiness or earthiness, all (hopefully) combined with a softening sweetness. On the other hand, it would be difficult to distinguish the Costa Rica La Minita conclusively from other high-quality, high-grown Central America coffees except in its power and perfection.

BAD TASTES, GOOD TASTES: FLAVOR TAINTS

How the fruit is removed from the coffee beans and how they are dried dramatically affects how the coffee finally tastes in the cup. Among professionals and aficionados there are two schools of thinking (or tasting) in regard to how fruit removal and drying should affect coffee flavor.

Clean Cuppers. One school, whom I call "clean cuppers," feels that fruit removal and drying should not affect taste in any way and should be as transparent and unobtrusive as possible. This school of thinking prefers that all coffees be wet-processed, meaning that the fruit is removed from the bean immediately after picking so that it does not affect the taste of the bean, and the drying is done as decisively and cleanly as possible. If the wet-processing is conducted with care and precision, and the drying is impeccable, the coffee will taste clean, bright but cleanly sweet, without murky ambiguities. For this school, any deviation from this clean, transparent cup, in other words, any taste characteristic that is added to the coffee through some idiosyncrasy of fruit removal or drying, is called a taste defect.

Romance Cuppers. For these coffee folks certain flavor taints and twists given the bean by deviations

The origin of the earthy taste in some Sumatra coffees: Freshly pulped coffee beans dry directly on the clay in front of a farmer's house in the Mandheling region of Sumatra. This practice is atypical. Most Sumatra coffee is dried on tarpaulins rather than directly on clay.

from the orthodox wet method of fruit removal and drying may be desirable. "Romance cuppers" consider coffee a product of culture as well as nature, and feel that various taste twists and taints given coffee by traditional ways of removing fruit from the bean are part of the full expression of coffee and worthy of attention and enjoyment.

Specific Flavor Taints and Defects

Here are some of the more common (and controversial) flavor taints given coffee by deviations in fruit removal and drying.

Soft or Sweet Ferment. Often the sugars in the coffee fruit begin to ferment before the fruit is removed from the bean, and the fermented taste is transferred to the bean. (This inadvertent fermentation needs to be distinguished from the controlled kind of fermenting that is used to remove fruit residues from the beans during wet-processing and which, properly conducted, does not negatively affect taste.) Soft ferment often gives a vaguely rotten taste to the cup, as though you had stuck the beans in the compost for a while before brewing them. This rotten taste can range from a slight, not entirely unpleasant undertone, to flat-out barnyard nasty.

If this sort of composty ferment is intense, it is considered a flavor defect by both clean cuppers and romantics, but with some coffees it may be tolerated as part of a larger positive taste package. A slight fermented, composty tone haunts all Yemen Mocha coffees, for example, but most cuppers tolerate or even enjoy this taste in the context of the remarkable spectrum of complex fruit tones in Yemens. Similarly, some Central America and Colombia coffees may be pleasantly fruity, but the fruit tones may "flirt with ferment," as my colleague Mane Alves of Coffee Lab International says. We may tolerate this hint of ferment for the sake of the rich fruitiness that comes with it.

Hard, Musty, or Moldy Ferment. If various microorganisms enter the coffee during inadvertent ferment, the taste imparted to the affected beans can be hard, harsh, medicinal, pondy, or moldy. Personally, I do not like hard ferment, whereas I tolerate some soft, sweet ferment. To my palate the hard or harsh tones blot out other positive flavor characteristics, whereas ferment that is sweet tends to allow other characteristics of the coffee to continue to flourish.

Other coffee lovers are quite tolerant of hard ferment, and may even like it. The most extreme example of this difference in attitude are conflicting reactions to the medicinal tasting coffees of Brazil. North American coffee drinkers typically dislike the harsh, iodinelike taste of these coffees, whereas coffee drinkers in parts of the Middle East and Eastern Europe value the taste and are willing to pay a premium for such tainted coffees.

Closer to home (and to our tasting exercise), your Sumatra sample may embody a hard, musty taste, something like the odor of old shoes left in a damp closet. Many American coffee drinkers enjoy this taste and consider it part of the attractive character of Sumatras. Some of the current versions of aged coffees, considered a delicacy by some sophisticated coffee drinkers, carry a hard, musty pungency into the cup along with the pleasing heaviness of the aged profile.

Earthiness. If coffee is dried on earth, rather than on dirt-free concrete, stone, brick, or wood, the coffee will pick up a distinct earth taste. Again, some consider any earthy taste whatsoever a flavor defect, whereas others enjoy earthiness and consider it an idiosyncratic delicacy. A Brazilian farmer I know supplies coffee to a Japanese buyer who insists that he dry coffee for him every year on earth patios to obtain the earthy tones his customers admire.

Your Sumatra sample may be earthy. The taste is easy to recognize: the odor of fresh earth carried into the cup. A few aficionados even go as far as to distinguish between various kinds of earth taste: red earth (Brazils), yellow clay (some Sumatras), and so on. For my part, I enjoy some earthiness in coffees like Sumatras if the earth taste is sweet, free of the hardness imparted by micoorganisms.

Greenness, Astringency. This taint presents itself as absence of sweetness and a thin, vegetal tone to the cup. It is not a dramatic taint, but no one has anything good to say about it. It is caused by the coffee fruit having been picked too soon, before the fruit is fully ripe and sweet and the sugars fully developed in the bean. It is not a typical taint in any of the three coffees I recommend you taste, although it could turn up in the Sumatra as a background lack of sweetness.

A Final Exhortation

With coffee, the dialogue between palate and product is truly global in nature, more so than almost any other beverage. It reaches from our brewing apparatus through roasting rooms into the heart of mountain remoteness and exotic cultures. It as much a dialogue with culture and history as with a beverage. Learning to enjoy coffee's range of sensory possibility and the remarkable collaboration between culture and nature it embodies is one of those acts of knowledge and connoisseurship that is as pleasurable in the act of learning as it is in the reward of understanding.

5 TASTING PLACE IN IT

Choosing coffee by origin
Blending and blends
Flavored coffees

Anyone who reads a newspaper is aware of how arbitrary the concept of nation-state can be. National boundaries often divide people who are similar and cram together those who are different. A Canadian from Vancouver has considerably more in common culturally with an American from across the border in Seattle than with a fellow Canadian from across the continent in Quebec, for example.

The concept of country often plays a similarly arbitrary and misleading role in understanding coffee. Countries tend to be large and coffee-growing areas small. Ethiopian coffee that is gathered by hand from wild trees and processed by the dry method hardly resembles coffees from the same country that have been grown on larger farms and processed by the wet method. On the other hand, some families of taste-alikes transcend national boundaries. In the big picture, for example, high-quality coffees from Latin American countries generally resemble one another, as do coffees from East Africa and the Arabian Peninsula. And both tend to differ from coffees from the Malay Archipelago: Indonesia, New Guinea, and Timor.

But the notion of generally labeling coffee by country of origin is inevitable and well established. Hence the organization of the next section of this chapter by continent and country. It is well to keep in mind, however, that in tasting coffee, as in thinking about history, the notion of country is no more than a convenient starting point.

Mexico: Coatepec, Oaxaca, Chiapas

Most Mexico coffee comes from the southern part of the country, where the continent narrows and takes a turn to the east. Veracruz State, on the Gulf side of the central mountain range, produces mostly lowland coffees, but coffees called Altura (High) Coatepec, from a mountainous region near the city of that name, have an excellent reputation. Other Veracruz coffees of note are Altura Orizaba and Altura Huatusco. Coffees from the opposite, southern slopes of the central mountain range, in Oaxaca State, are also highly regarded and marketed under the names Oaxaca or Oaxaca Pluma. Coffees from Chiapas State are grown in the mountains of the southeasternmost corner of Mexico, near the border with Guatemala. The market name traditionally associated with these coffees is Tapachula, from the city of that name, but coffee sellers now usually label them Chiapas. Chiapas produces some of the very best and highest-grown Mexico coffees.

The typical fine Mexico coffee is analogous to a good light white wine—delicate in body, with a pleasantly dry, acidy snap. If you drink your coffee black and prefer a light, acidy cup, you will like these typical Mexico specialty coffees. However, some Mexico coffees, particularly those from high, growing regions in Chiapas, rival the best Guatemala coffees in high-grown power and complexity.

Mexico is also the origin of many of the certified organically grown coffees now appearing on North American specialty menus. These are often excellent coffees certified by various independent monitoring agencies to be grown without the use of pesticides, fungicides, herbicides, or other harmful chemicals.

Coffee from many of the most admired Mexican estates seldom appears on the United States market but is sold almost exclusively in Europe, particularly

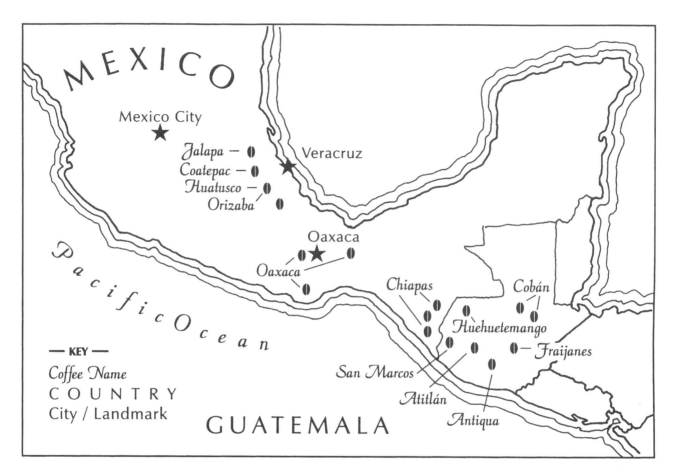

Germany. Some of these names, should they ever become relevant for the North American aficionado, include Liquidambar, Santa Catarina, Irlandia, Germania, and Hamburgo.

Guatemala: Antigua, Cobán, Huehuetenango, Atitlán, San Marcos, Fraijanes

The highlands of Guatemala produce several of the world's finest and most distinctive coffees. The mountain basin surrounding the austerely beautiful colonial city Guatemala Antigua produces the most distinguished of these highland coffees: Guatemala Antigua, a coffee that combines complex nuance (smoke, spice, flowers, occasionally chocolate) with acidity ranging from gently bright to austerely powerful. Fraijanes displays similar cup characteristics. Other Guatemala coffees, perhaps because they are more exposed to wet ocean weather than the mountain-protected Antigua basin, tend to display slightly softer, often less powerful, but equally complexly nuanced profiles. These softer Guatemalas include Cobán, admired for its fullish body and gentle, deep, rounded profile, chocolaty and fruity; Huehuetenango from the Caribbean-facing slopes of the central mountain range; and San Marcos coffees from the Pacific-facing slopes. Coffees from the basin surrounding Lake Atitlán in South-Central Guatemala typically offer the same complex nuance as Antiguas but are lighter in body and brighter in flavor.

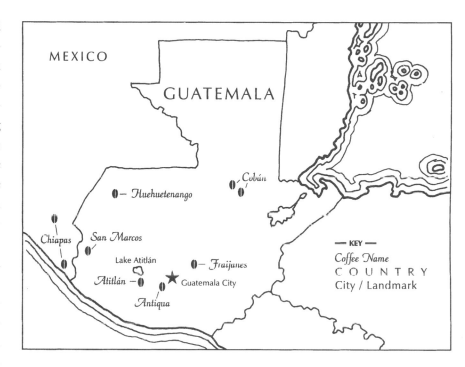

There are many excellent Guatemalan estates. To name just a small selection: in the Antigua Valley, San Sebastián, La Tacita, San Rafael Urias, Pastores, El Valle, and Las Nubes. In Huehuetenango, Santa Cecilia, Huixoc, and El Coycgual. In the Coban region, Yaxbatz, Los Alpes, and El Recreo. In San Marcos, Dos Marias.

Small-holder coffees predominate in Huehuetenango and Cobán, but transportation difficulties and wet weather during harvest may compromise quality. Perhaps the best small-holder Guatemala coffees come from peasant farmers in the Lake Atitlán basin, who are organized into cooperatives that run their own mills and turn out meticulously prepared coffee. A cooperative near the town of San Juan La Laguna markets its excellent coffee under the poetic name "La Voz que Clama en el Desierto." This cooperative practices coffee production at the ultimate end of en-

vironmental correctness: organically grown in a dense, bird-sheltering, shade canopy of native trees and plants. The coffee is processed with passion and precision, although delays in getting the freshly picked coffee fruit down the mountainside to the cooperative mills sometimes impart a slight, giddily fermented twist to the cup. Atitlán cooperative coffees are a perfect choice for those in search of both cup quality and a coffee grown in exquisite harmony with earth and the aspirations of people on it.

The highest grade of Guatemala coffee is Strictly Hard Bean (SHB). The regionally designated coffees (Antigua, Atitlán, Cobán, etc) are tasted and approved as meeting flavor profile criteria established for these regions by Anacafé, the Guatemalan Na-

A stage in the wet method of processing coffee fruit in Guatemala. After natural fermentation has loosened the sticky fruit mucilage clinging to the beans, the mucilage is washed off in channels of running water like this one.

tional Coffee Association. Those coffees that do not meet regional flavor profile criteria are only allowed to be sold as SHB without regional designation.

Generally, Guatemala has preserved more of the traditional *typica* and *bourbon* varieties of arabica than many other Latin American growing countries, which may account for the generally superior complexity of the Guatemala cup. Most Guatemala coffee is grown in shade, ranging from rigorously managed shade on large farms to the serendipitous thickets of small growers.

El Salvador

Like Guatemala, El Salvador is recovering from a terrifying civil war brought about in part by the now abandoned Cold War policies of the United States. And, as in Guatemala, the terrors of the civil war ironically preserved many of the traditional varieties of arabica like *bourbon* from replacement with more modern, sun-grown, hybrid coffee varieties.

However, El Salvador apparently lacks the typography that produces the complex, authoritative coffees of the Antigua growing region in Guatemala and Central Costa Rica. Most El Salvadors are soft, ingratiating coffees with relatively subdued acidity, much like many Mexico and Central America coffees grown on ocean-influenced slopes and valleys. Nevertheless, these El Salvador coffees can be fine, if gentle: fragrant and seductive. Occasionally an El Salvador appears that is powerful, deep, and acidy like the finest Guatemalas.

A few El Salvador farms and cooperatives, including Los Ausoles and Larin, grow the intriguing hybrid variety *pacamara*, a tree that produces a large bean that is a cross between the extremely large-beaned *maragogipe* and a local strain of the *caturra* variety called *paca*. Los Ausoles markets its pacamara coffee under the name Tizapa. From an aficionado point of view, pacamara is a fascinating hybrid because it is superior in cup quality to either of its parent varieties. From a coffee drinker's point of view, the large bean makes an interesting curiosity and the soft but complex cup gives some sensual support to the conversation-invoking potential of the bean size.

Also making an effective push into the American specialty market is a large cooperative that markets its pleasantly sweet, nutty, certified organic coffee as Café Pepil. Pepil is the name of one of the Native American cultures that dominated El Salvador at the time of the arrival of the Spanish.

The best grade of El Salvador coffee is Strictly High Grown (SHG). Most El Salvador coffee is grown in various degrees of shade.

Honduras: Marcala

Recently Honduras has been plunged into a horrific period of suffering, starting with the almost otherworldly devastation of Hurricane Mitch in 1998 and continuing through the floods and storms of 1999. These events cut off a promising entry of a small number of Honduras growers and exporters into the American specialty market.

Honduras also suffers from having most of its coffees produced by small holders who are forced to perform the fruit removal and drying of the coffee themselves owing to poor coffee infrastructure. These small lots of coffee are then mixed together, producing understandably inconsistent quality. Coffees from the Marcala region near the El Salvador border have the best reputation of Honduras origins. Strictly High Grown is the highest grade.

When Honduras coffees do return to the specialty market, most probably will prove to be rather gentle, low-key coffees of medium body, with occasionally brighter, more acidy coffees from the Marcala region.

Nicaragua: Jinotega, Matagalpa, Segovia

Like Guatemala and El Salvador, Nicaragua too is recovering from the brutality of civil war followed by the ravages of Hurricane Mitch. In the case of Nicaragua, its coffees are only now becoming known again in the United States owing to the long interruption of the Cold War years when Nicaraguan coffee was not allowed to be imported into the United States.

The distinctive genius of some Nicaragua coffees is a round, deep, yet resonant, chocolaty fullness. The typical acidity of Central American coffees makes itself felt but only enveloped inside the almost fatty fullness of the cup. Look for coffees from the Prodocoop cooperative mill in the Segovia region for an example of this subtly distinctive variation on the Central America theme.

Other Nicaragua coffees offer a cup in the more familiar Central America mode: fragrant, complex, with a nut and vanilla bouquet, moderately acidy and medium in body. Jinotega, Matagalpa, and Segovia are the best-known growing regions. Most Nicaragua coffee is shade grown. The highest grade is Strictly High Grown.

Costa Rica: Tres Ríos, Tarrazu, Dota, Herediá, Volcán Poás

Central Costa Rica is one of those classic coffee origins that is respected but not fawned over. Although Costa Rica produces a variety of coffees, those that reach American specialty coffee menus usually are very high-grown Strictly Hard Bean coffees from regions near the capital of San José in the central part of the country: Tarrazu, Herediá, Tres Ríos, Volcán Poás. At best Costa Rica coffees from these regions are distinctive in a way that defies simple, romantic description. When good they are clean, balanced, and resonantly powerful. When ordinary they are clean, balanced, and rather inert.

The relative lack of innuendo in Costa Rica coffees ironically may be owing to the advanced state of the Costa Rican coffee industry. They tend to come from trees of relatively recently selected or developed cultivars of arabica like *caturra* or *catuai* and usually are impeccably wet-processed using technically advanced techniques that eliminate the oddities of flavor that derive from traditional or regional variations in processing.

Among estates, La Minita has become particularly prominent owing to the quality of its almost fanatically prepared coffee and the skillful publicity efforts of its owner, William McAlpin. The La Minita coffee appearing in specialty stores is likely to be so labeled: Costa Rica La Minita, La Minita Tarrazu, etc. Bella Vista can be almost as remarkable, although recently it has been available only from Starbucks.

Coffees from the Dota area of Tarrazu are the exact opposite of the classic-at-best, boring-at-worst Costa Ricas. Apparently owing to a local variation in fermenting technique, Dotas walk a thin, wild edge between disturbing overripeness and exciting fruit and chocolate and are a good choice for those who prefer romantic risk to perfection.

Panama: Boquete

Panama is a rising star, an up-and-coming contender among Central America coffee origins. All premium Panama coffees are produced on large, family-owned farms in Chiriquí Province in the western part of the country near the border with Costa Rica. At least five growing regions are clustered around Barú volcano: Boquete (the best known), Paso Ancho (also admired), Volcán, Piedra de Candela, and Renacimiento. The elevations are impressive (3,600 to 5,200 feet, 1,100 to 1,600 meters), the soil volcanic, the wet-processing state-of-the-art. Although some traditional *typica* and *bourbon* varieties are grown, most Panama specialty coffee appears to come from *caturra* (a twentieth-century selection) and the respected hybrid *catuai*.

Many well-run estates (Lerida, Berlina, La Torcaza, Los Alpes, El Túcan, Las Victorias, Don Bosco, Bajo Mono, Boutet, La Florentina, among others) produce meticulously prepared coffees that range from lively but gently acidy and round to others that are rich, complexly nuanced, and boldly acidy. In short, Panama is a superior Central America wet-processed coffee with all of the range and potential virtues of those coffees.

Jamaica: Blue Mountain

The central Blue Mountains of Jamaica are an extraordinary landscape. The higher reaches are in almost perpetual fog, to which the tropical sun gives an otherwordly internal glow, as though the light itself has come down to settle among the trees. The fog slows the development of the coffee, producing a denser bean than the relatively modest growing elevations (3,000 to 4,000 feet) might produce elsewhere. Coffee grown in the Blue Mountains of Jamaica is the world's most celebrated, most expensive, and most controversial origin.

Jamaica Blue Mountain has been an admired cof-

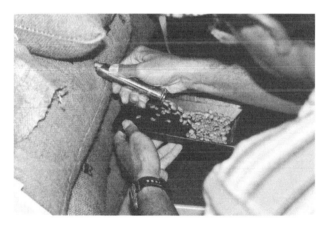

Protecting the identity of high-priced coffee in Jamaica and Kona, Hawaii. Top, barrels of Jamaica Blue Mountain coffee waiting to be shipped. Bottom, an agricultural official drawing a sample from a bag of Kona coffee waiting State of Hawaii certification.

fee since the early nineteenth century when, for a brief time, Jamaica led the world in coffee production. After World War II the British colonial government, alarmed that undisciplined production was on the verge of ruining the Blue Mountain reputation, instituted a rigorous program of regulation and quality control under the leadership of the newly established Coffee Industry Board of Jamaica. After Jamaica achieved its independence from Britain, the new Jamaican government continued that coffee policy, requiring that all Blue Mountain be wet-processed at government-sanctioned mills and dried, dry-milled, cleaned, and graded at centralized facilities.

Volume Increases, Quality Decreases. In the mid-1970s, when I first tasted Jamaica Blue Mountain from a mill that exported a famous mark called Wallensford Estate, it was indeed a splendid coffee, without drama perhaps, but extraordinarily rich, balanced, resonant and complete. In the 1970s and 1980s, however, the Coffee Industry Board began investing in Jamaica Blue Mountain with money provided by Japanese interests. New mills were constructed that use a short-cut version of the wet-processing method called aquapulping or mechanical demucilaging, and volume increased dramatically while quality decreased despite the Coffee Industry Board's efforts to maintain it.

The famous Wallensford mark now has become close to meaningless: It simply describes coffee wet-processed at a mill that pretty much resembles all of the other government mills. (True, the Wallensford mill is located in the central part of the Blue Mountains, which may give its coffees a slight edge in altitude over coffees produced by some of the other mills.) Most Blue Mountain coffees now are a decent to mildly impressive version of the Caribbean taste profile: fairly rich, soft, with an understated acidity that is sometimes gently vibrant, other times barely sufficient to lift the cup from listlessness.

Blue Mountain Estate Coffees. At this writing a prolonged recession in Japan (Japan supported Jamaica coffee prices by buying Blue Mountain heavily) and a general, worldwide plunge in coffee prices has the Jamaica Blue Mountain industry in trouble. At the same time, the Coffee Industry Board of Jamaica has embarked on an unprecedented experiment by allowing several farmers to wet-process their Blue Mountain on their farms and export their coffees as separate and distinct estate coffees, rather than as generic Blue Mountain. These new estate Blue Mountains include Alex Twyman's Old Tavern Estate, and the RSW Estates, a group of three family-owned farms that wet-process their coffees at a common mill. All of these estate coffees are processed using the traditional ferment-and-wash technique, rather than the mechanical demucilage method used to process generic Blue Mountain.

I do not have sufficient experience with RSW Estates to evaluate its coffees. However, I am very familiar with Alex Twyman's Old Tavern Estate Jamaica Blue Mountain and can vouch that it often approaches the original Wallensford Blue Mountain in its combination of gentleness and deep, vibrant power. However, Old Tavern currently suffers from inconsistency: A slight, almost undetectable hardness sometimes haunts its bouillonlike richness. Time will tell whether Old Tavern becomes a consistently exceptional coffee and whether it, the RSW Estate cof-

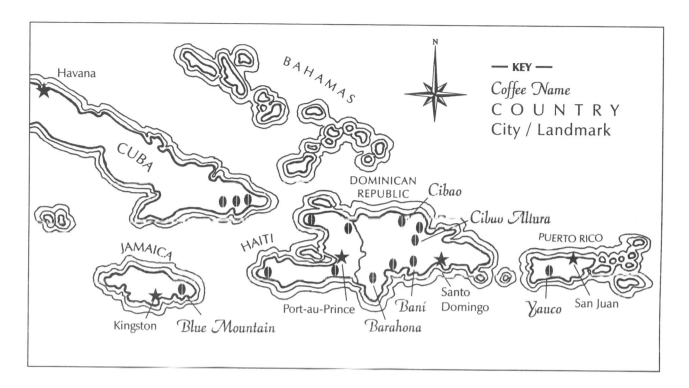

fees, and more vigorous leadership from Jamaica coffee officials can help lead the Jamaica Blue Mountain industry generally out of its quality doldrums.

Jamaica Blue Mountain's fame and high prices have encouraged the usual deceptive blender creativity: Blue Mountain blends that contain very little actual Blue Mountain or Blue Mountain–"style" blends that contain no Blue Mountain whatsoever. These coffees may be excellent, but they are not Blue Mountain.

Puerto Rico: Yauco Selecto, Alto Grande

In the nineteenth century, Puerto Rico was one of the world's leading coffee origins. In 1896, for example, the island was the sixth largest coffee producer in the world. But in the twentieth century coffee apparently became lost in the complex political and economic shuffle that marked Puerto Rico's passage from agricultural economy and Spanish colony to developing American commonwealth. In the late 1980s, however, a consortium of farmers led by Harvard-educated marketing expert Jaimé Fortuño revived Puerto Rico as a specialty coffee origin.

Puerto Rico Yauco Selecto is produced at elevations above 3,000 feet in the southwestern mountains from trees of the admired *bourbon* variety and other traditional local Puerto Rican cultivars. At best it is a superb example of the Caribbean taste, soft yet powerful, with a fragrant, fruity sweetness. At this writing Yauco is not what it has been in the recent past, however, with a hard, flavor-dampening edge often insinuating itself into the Caribbean sweetness. Hopefully, quality will pick up again. Other Puerto Rico coffees, including Alto Grande, are only occasionally sold in the American specialty market.

Dominican Republic: Santo Domingo, Cibao, Bani, Ocoa, Barahona

Coffee from the Dominican Republic is occasionally called Santo Domingo after the country's former name, perhaps because Santo Domingo looks romantic on a coffee bag and Dominican Republic does not. Coffee is grown on both slopes of the mountain range that runs on an east-west axis down the center of the island. The four main market names are Cibao, Bani, Ocoa, and Barahona. All tend to be well-prepared wet-processed coffees. The last three names have the best reputation. Bani leans toward a soft, mellow cup much like Haiti; Barahona toward a somewhat more acidy and heavier-bodied cup, closer to the better Jamaica and Puerto Rico coffees in quality and characteristics.

Haiti: Haitian Bleu

Haiti, which shares the island of Hispaniola with the Dominican Republic, is one of many countries in which coffee has been called upon to help heal the scars of war and alleviate poverty. During the mid-1990s, conditions in Haiti were so dire owing to a United States–led embargo against the prevailing dictatorship that many farmers burned their coffee trees to produce charcoal for sale in local markets. Haiti coffee, another Caribbean origin with a long and distinguished tradition, virtually disappeared from the specialty coffee menu. Decades of disorder had so depressed the quality of this once celebrated origin that few in the coffee world probably even noticed or regretted its absence.

Today, however, with the help of an international development agency, a cooperative of over seven thousand farmers called Cafeieres Natives produces and markets a revived specialty coffee from Haiti trademarked Haitian Bleu. At its best, Haitian Bleu is rich, opulent, and sweetly low-toned, another fine example of the Caribbean cup. It is difficult to control quality with seven thousand participating farmers, however, and Haitian Bleu can be very inconsistent. Nevertheless, if you like rich, full coffees with dry tones well balanced by sweetness, as many American coffee drinkers do, and if you want to make your dollars count to help the Western Hemisphere's most impoverished farmers, Haitian Bleu is worth trying.

Colombia

Colombia is the paradox of the specialty coffee world. Its 100 percent Colombia campaign, featuring the ubiquitous Juan Valdez, is a model of successful coffee organization and marketing. Colombia remains the only premium single-origin coffee able to compete successfully in the arena of canned supermarket blends. Although it ranks second to Brazil in total coffee production—with about 12 percent of the world's total coffee production compared to Brazil's 30 to 35 percent—most of Colombia's 12 percent is excellent coffee, grown at high altitudes on small peasant holdings, carefully picked, and wet-processed. The Colombian Coffee Federation ranks among the world's most thorough-going and successful efforts at organizing and supporting small-holder coffee farmers. For seventy-five years the federation has maintained fair, stable coffee prices for the over 550,000 small holder farmers, helped build over 200,000 neat, sturdy little houses for them, constructed over 200 hospitals, and provided an impressive range of other technical and social services.

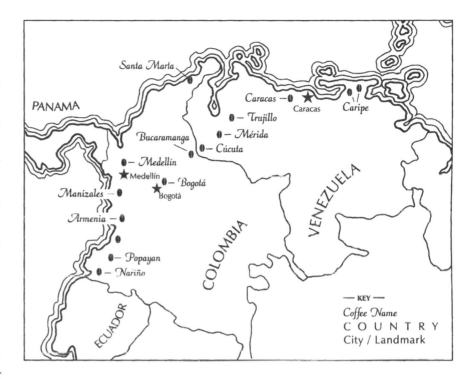

Nevertheless, for most specialty coffee afficionados and professionals, Juan Valdez is Rodney Dangerfield's Latin cousin. Colombias carry nowhere near the insider panache of the coffees of Kenya, Guatemala, even of Papua New Guinea and Zimbabwe. Colombia sells well in specialty stores only because it is the sole name on the menu that coffee neophytes recognize.

It would appear that Colombia's remarkable success at producing large and consistent enough quantities of decent-quality coffee to position it at the top of the commercial market has doomed it as an elite origin. The Colombian Coffee Federation has evolved a system wherein hundreds of thousands of small producers wet-process their coffee on or close to their farms and deliver it to collection points and eventually to mills operated by the federation, where the coffee is sorted and graded according to rigorous national standards.

There is an inherent leveling effect in such an arrangement. One farmer's wet-processing and microclimate may be exceptional and another's may be mediocre, but both end up mixed in the same vast sea of coffee bags in which the only discriminations are the broad ones imposed by grading criteria. The regional origins famous in the earlier part of the twentieth century—names like Armenia, Manizales, Medellín—are now lost in a well-organized but faceless coffee machine.

Private Mill Colombias. In fact, until recently the only viable specialty coffees to come out of Colombia were developed by private mills and exporters operating largely outside the institutional structure of the coffee federation. These "privates" often supply coffees from single farms and cooperatives or from relatively narrowly defined growing regions. They may offer coffees produced exclusively from traditional, heirloom varieties of *Coffea arabica* like *typica* and *bourbon*, rather than from a mixture of varieties including newer, federation-sponsored hybrid cultivars like the controversial *var. colombia*.

By contrast, the standard Colombia coffees exported by the coffee federation are distinguished by grade only. Origin is not specified. Supremo is the highest grade, Extra second. The two are often combined into a more comprehensive grade called Excelso. If the only qualifying adjective you see bestowed on a Colombia is a grade name like Supremo or Excelso, you are almost certainly contemplating a standard Colombia from the Colombian Coffee Federation. Nevertheless, these standard Colombias will not all taste the same. Some lots will display much more quality and character than others, and skillful coffee buyers will find them for their customers.

However, if a Colombia coffee is identified by a regional or market name rather than grade name, it may be either a private-mill coffee or one of a new group of specialty coffees developed by the Colombian Coffee Federation. Most of these regionally specific coffees come from traditional cultivars, either *bourbon* or *typica*, and most display more character than standard lots of Colombia. Those with the most character and distinction tend to be produced in the southwestern part of the country, in the departments of Nariño, Cauca (market name Popoyan), and Southern Huila.

At this writing the Colombian Coffee Federation is busy attempting to revive the specialty coffee concept in Colombia by systematically identifying coffees with distinctive cup characteristics and marketing them to specialty coffee buyers as separate regional origins. Given the technical and marketing savvy of the coffee federation and the diversity of the coffee environment in Colombia, I expect this program to be a success.

Colombia coffee at its finest is, like Costa Rica, a classic. No quality is extreme. The body tends to be medium, the acidity vibrant but not overbearing, and the cup lively and nuanced by understated fruit tones.

Venezuela: Maracaibo, Táchira, Mérida, Caripe

At one time, Venezuela ranked close to Colombia in coffee production, but in the 1960s and '70s, as petroleum temporarily turned Venezuela into the richest country in South America, coffee was relegated to the economic back burner. Today Venezuela produces less than 1 percent of the world's coffee, and most of it is drunk by the Venezuelans themselves. However, some interesting Venezuela coffees are again entering the North American specialty market.

The most admired Venezuela coffee comes from the far western corner of the country, the part that borders Colombia. Coffees from this area sometime are called Maracaibos, after the port through which they are shipped, and may include one coffee, Cúcuta, which is actually grown in Colombia but may be shipped through Maracaibo. The best-known Maracaibo coffees, in addition to Cúcuta, are Mérida,

Trujillo, and Táchira. Mérida typically displays fair to good body and an unemphatic but sweetly pleasant flavor with hints of richness. Táchira and Cúcuta resemble Colombias, with rich acidity, medium body, and occasional fruitiness.

Coffees from the coastal mountains farther east are generally marked Caracas, after the capital city, and are shipped through La Guaira, the port of Caracas. Caripe comes from a mountain range close to the Caribbean and typically displays the soft, gentle profile of the island coffees of the Caribbean.

Regardless of market name, the highest grade of Venezuela coffee is Lavado Fino.

Ecuador

Ecuador produces substantial amounts of coffee but little seems to appear in specialty stores in the United States. By reputation it is a generally unremarkable coffee, with thin to medium body and occasional bright acidity.

Peru: Chanchamayo, Urubamba

Generally a mildly acid coffee, light-bodied but flavorful and aromatic, Peru is considered a good blender owing to its pleasant but understated character. Peru also is widely used in dark-roast blends and as a base for flavored coffees. But the best Peru coffees are subtly exceptional: light and levitating with a vanilla-nut-toned sweetness that deserves appreciation as a distinctive specialty origin.

Wet-processed coffee from the Chanchamayo Valley, about two hundred miles east of Lima in the high Andes, has the best reputation of the Peru coffees.

The Cuzco region, particularly the Urubamba Valley, also produces respected, wet-processed coffee. The highest grade is AAA. Certified organic coffees from cooperatives of small farmers in northern Peru are often excellent, and represent the socially progressive side of specialty coffee at its most admirable.

Brazil: Santos, Bourbon Santos, Estate Brazils

Brazil is not only the world's largest coffee producer, it is also the most complex. It turns out everything from mass-produced coffees that rank among the world's cheapest to elegant coffees prized as the world's finest origins for espresso brewing. In Brazil, fruit is removed from the bean using four different processing methods, and it is not uncommon for all four methods to be used on the same farm during the same harvest.

For one thing Brazil coffee is not is high-grown. Growing elevations in Brazil range from about 2,000 to 4,000 feet, far short of the 5,000-plus elevations common for fine coffees produced in Central America, Colombia, and East Africa. Lower growing altitudes means that Brazil coffees are relatively low in acidity. At best they tend to be round, sweet, and well-nuanced rather than big and bright.

Santos Brazils, Estate Brazils. The most traditional Brazil coffee, and the kind most likely to be seen in specialty stores, has been dried inside the fruit (dry-processed) so that some of the sweetness of the fruit carries into the cup. It also sometimes comes from trees of the traditional Latin American variety of ara-

KEY
Coffee Name
C O U N T R Y
City / Landmark

include Ipanema, Monte Alegre, and Boa Vista, all of which produce excellent coffee. Respected smaller fazendas include Lagoa, Lambari, Fortaleza, Corcampo, and many others. The farms operated by Ottoni and Sons, particularly Fazenda Vereda, produce very fine coffees. Improving organic coffees are produced by an increasing number of farms, including Fazenda Cachoeira and a farm that markets its coffees as Blue de Brasil.

The premium coffees arriving in the United States from these farms are usually dry-processed or "natural" coffees. However, estate Brazils also may be wet-processed, which turns them a bit lighter and brighter in the cup, or they may be what Brazilians call pulped natural or semiwashed coffees, which have been dried without the skins but with the sticky fruit pulp still stuck to the beans. Typically these pulped natural coffees absorb sweetness from the fruit pulp and are full and sweet in the cup like their dry-processed brethren.

Risks and Rewards of Dry-Processing. When coffee is dried inside the fruit, as most classic Brazil coffees are, lots of things can go wrong. The seed or bean inside the fruit is held hostage, as it were, to the general health and soundness of the fruit surrounding it. If the fruit rots, the coffee will taste rotten or fermented. If microorganisms invade the fruit during that rotting, a hard or medicinal taste will carry into the cup. At the most extreme medicinal end of this taste spectrum are the notorious rio coffees of Brazil, which are saturated by an intense iodinelike sensation that American coffee buyers avoid but which coffee

bica called *bourbon*. The best of these coffees are traded as Santos 2, or, if the coffee comes exclusively from trees of the *bourbon* variety, Bourbon Santos 2. Santos is a market name referring to the port through which these coffees are traditionally shipped, and 2 is the highest grade. On specialty coffee menus the 2 is usually dropped, so you will see the coffee simply described as Brazil Bourbon Santos or Brazil Santos.

Some years ago the Brazilian government deregulated the coffee industry, allowing large farms to market their coffees directly to consuming countries without regard to government-mandated grading structures. Consequently, coffees similar to Santos or Bourbon Santos also reach the American market directly from large farms (*fazendas*). Names of very large fazendas that you may see on specialty menus drinkers in parts of Eastern Europe and the Near East seek out and enjoy. In fact, in some years these intensely medicinal-tasting coffees fetch higher prices in the world market than sound, clean-tasting Brazil coffees.

Brazilian Growing Regions. Three main growing areas provide most of the top-end Brazil coffees. The oldest, Mogiana, lies along the border of São Paulo and is famous for its deep, richly red soil and its sweet, full, rounded coffees. The rugged, rolling hills of Sul Minas, in the southern part of Minas Gerais State northeast of São Paulo, is the heart of Brazil coffee country and home of two of the largest and best-known fazendas, Ipanema and Monte Alegre. The Cerrado, a high, semiarid plateau surrounding the city of Patrocinio, midway between São Paulo and Brasilia, is a newer growing area. It is the least picturesque of the three regions with its new towns and high plains but arguably the most promising in terms of coffee quality, since its dependably clear, dry weather during harvest promotes a more thorough, even drying of the coffee fruit.

An Espresso Treasure. The very finest of Brazils are a coffee treasure, so spicy sweet and smooth that even a sugar fanatic can drink them black with pleasure. They particularly come into their own in espresso brewing, which puts a premium on mellow sweetness.

Yemen: Mocha, Mattari, Hirazi, Ismaili, Sanani

Mocha is one of the more confusing terms in the coffee lexicon. The coffee we call Mocha (also spelled

Moka, Moca, or Mocca) today is grown as it has been for hundreds of years in the mountains of Yemen at the southwestern tip of the Arabian Peninsula. It was originally shipped through the ancient port of Mocha, which has since been replaced by a modern port and has fallen into picturesque ruins. The name Mocha has become so permanently a part of coffee vocabulary that it stubbornly sticks to a coffee that today would be described more accurately as Yemen or even Arabian.

Complicating the situation are coffees that closely resemble Yemen in cup character and appearance from eastern Ethiopia, near the town of Harrar. These dry-processed Ethiopia Harrar coffees often are sold under the name Mocha or Moka. They are typically lighter bodied than their Yemen namesakes but otherwise very similar.

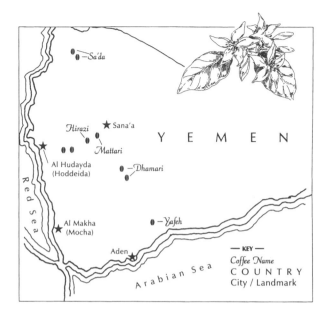

Still another possibility for confusion derives from the occasional chocolate tones of Yemen Mocha, which caused some enthusiast to tag the name onto drinks that combine hot chocolate and coffee. So Mocha is an old-fashioned nickname for coffee itself, a common name for coffee from Yemen, a name for a similar coffee from the Harrar region of Ethiopia, and the name of a drink made up of coffee and hot chocolate.

The World's Most Traditional Coffee. True Arabian Mocha, from the central mountains of Yemen, is still grown as it was over five hundred years ago, on terraces clinging to the sides of semiarid mountains below ancient stone villages that rise like geometric extensions of the mountains themselves. In the summer, when the scrubby little coffee trees are blossom-

ing and setting fruit, misty rains temporarily turn the Yemen mountains a bright green. In the fall the clouds dissipate and the air turns bone dry as the coffee fruit ripens, is picked, and appears on the roofs of the stone houses, spread in the sun to dry. During the dry winter, water collected in small reservoirs often is directed to the roots of the coffee trees to help them survive until the drizzles of summer return.

Yemen coffees are processed as they have been for centuries. All Yemen Mochas are dry or natural coffees, dried with the fruit still attached to the beans. After the fruit and bean have dried, the shriveled fruit husk is removed by millstone, which accounts for the rough, irregular look of Yemen beans. I have been told that some of these millstones are still turned by camels or donkeys, although I never managed to witness this spectacle. But even millstones turned by little gasoline engines are fascinating and nostalgic for the coffee historian, since they represent the oldest and most fundamental of coffee technologies.

The husks of the dried coffee fruit, neatly broken in half by the action of the millstones, are used to make a sweet, light drink Yemenis call *qishr*. The husks are combined with spices and boiled. The resulting beverage is cooled to room temperature and drunk in the afternoon as a thirst quencher and pick-me-up. Yemenis drink roast-and-ground coffee only in the morning, when, after bathing and prayers, they line up at coffeehouses for a quick morning cup of coffee boiled with sugar in Middle Eastern fashion.

Almost all Yemen coffee comes from ancient varieties of *Coffea arabica* grown nowhere else in the world except perhaps in eastern Ethiopia. Yemenis have scores, perhaps hundreds, of names for their local coffee varieties. Most of these names and the trees to which they refer have never been documented and are identified only within the rich and complex set of oral traditions that make up Yemeni coffee lore. At least one variety is widely recognized (and admired) across Yemen, however: Ismaili, which produces tiny, rounded beans resembling split peas.

Mysterious Market Names. Market names for Yemen coffee are as irregular as the beans themselves. Many names refer both to variety of tree and to growing district. For example, to an outsider it is never entirely clear when a coffee seller says he has an Ismaili coffee available whether he is describing a coffee from the Bani Ismail growing district, beans from the Ismaili variety of coffee tree, or both.

Given that caveat, this much can be said about market names for Yemen coffee. Mattari, originally describing coffee from Bani Mattar, a very high-altitude growing district just west of the capital of Sana'a, is the most famous of Yemen coffees. Despite the fact that most exporters mix true Mattari coffees with other, similar coffees, coffee sold by that name still is likely to be the most acidy, most complex, most fragrantly powerful of Yemen origins. Hirazi, from the next set of mountains west of Sana'a, is likely to be just as acidy and fruity, but a bit lighter in the cup. Ismaili, regardless of whether the name describes cultivar or region, is also likely to be excellent but a bit gentler and less powerful than Mattari. The market name Sanani describes a blend of coffees from various regions west of Sana'a and is typically more balanced, less acidy, and

Winnowing chaff from coffee beans after removing the dried fruit by millstone, Yemen.

less complex than coffees marketed as Mattari, Hirazi, or Ismaili. Sanani usually includes somewhat lower-grown coffees from districts like Rami.

History in the Cup. No matter what market name modifies it, Yemen is one of the most distinctive coffees in the world and one of the finest. It literally em-

65

bodies coffee history. When you drink a Yemen, you are drinking the exact coffee, picked from the same variety of trees, grown on the same terraced fields, dried on the same rooftops, as Sufis drank in Cairo in 1510, as Europeans first discovered in Constantinople, and as Diderot and Voltaire enjoyed in Paris in the eighteenth century.

It also is an excellent alternative for those who wish a coffee grown without chemicals. Yemen Mocha is as organically grown as it was five hundred years ago when the first trees from Ethiopia were established.

When I conduct a coffee tasting with nonprofessionals, the participants almost always prefer Yemen to other samples. The reason: Yemen is acidy but sweet, it is distinctively dry and fruity, and it is satisfyingly rich and full-bodied. Coffee professionals, on the other hand, often criticize Yemen owing to a very faint off-taste that probably derives from an endemic microorganism that the coffee fruit picks up during drying. This aftertaste, a very muted ferment tone, apparently is an inevitable component of the rich, luxurious Yemen flavor package. The similar-tasting coffees from the Harrar region of eastern Ethiopia share it. Those of us who love Yemens either learn to love this odd aftertaste or simply put up with it for the sake of the rest of what this explosively flavorful, historical coffee brings to the cup.

Ethiopia: Harrar, Yirgacheffe, Sidamo, Limu, Jima

Coffee was first developed as a commercial crop in Yemen, but the arabica tree originated across the Red Sea in western Ethiopia on high plateaus where country people still harvest the wild berries. Today Ethiopia coffees are among the world's most varied and distinctive, and at least one, Yirgacheffe, ranks among the very finest.

All display the wine- and fruit-toned acidity characteristic of Africa and Arabia coffees, but Ethiopias play a rich range of variations on this theme. These variations are in part determined by the processing method. Ethiopia coffees neatly divide into those processed by the dry method (the beans are dried inside the fruit) and those processed by a sophisticated, large-scale wet method, in which the fruit is immediately removed from the beans in a series of complex operations before the beans are dried.

Ethiopia Casual Dry-Processed Coffees. In most parts of Ethiopia dry-processing is a sort of informal, fall-back practice used to process small batches of coffee for local consumption. Everywhere that even a single coffee tree grows, someone will pick the fruit and put it out to dry. I recall driving along a seemingly uninhabited road in western Ethiopia and suddenly coming upon a slice of pavement that had been walled off with a row of rocks to protect a patch of drying coffee! Such informally dry-processed coffee is seldom exported, but simply hulled, roasted, and drunk on the spot or sold into the local market.

Instead, the best and ripest coffee fruit is sold to wet-processing mills, called washing stations, where it is prepared for export following the most up-to-date methods. Only the leftovers, the unripe and overripe fruit, is put out to dry, usually not on roads, but on raised, tablelike mats in front of the farmers' clay and thatched houses. This dry-processed coffee may reach export markets, but only as filler coffees for inexpensive blends.

Ethiopia Dry-Processed Harrar. The exception to dry-processed coffee's second-class status in Ethiopia is the celebrated and often superb coffee of Harrar, the predominantly Muslim province to the east of the capital of Addis Ababa. In Harrar, all coffee fruit, including the best and ripest, is put out in the sun to dry, fruit and all. Often, the fruit is allowed to dry directly on the tree. The result is a coffee much like Yemen, wild, fruity, complexly sweet, with a slightly fermented aftertaste. This flavor profile, shared by both Yemens and Ethiopia Harrars, is often called the Mocha taste and is one of the great and distinctive experiences of the coffee world. For this reason Harrar often is sold as Mocha or Moka, adding to the confusion surrounding that abused term. Some retailers cover both bases by calling the Ethiopian version of this coffee type Moka Harrar. (Harrar may be spelled Harari, Harer, or Harar.)

Yirgacheffe and Other Wet-Processed Ethiopias. The first wet-processing mills were established in Ethiopia in 1972, and three decades later more and

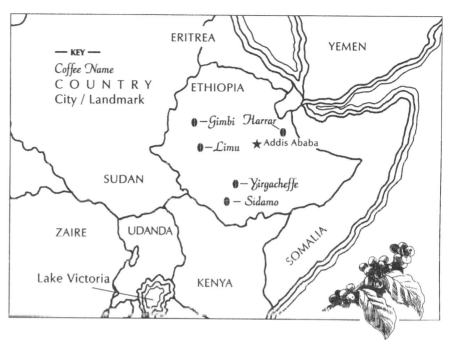

more coffees in the south and west of Ethiopia are being processed using a sophisticated version of the wet method. The immediate removal of fruit involved in wet-processing apparently softens the fruity, winelike profile of dried-in-the-fruit coffees like Harrars and turns it gentle, round, delicately complex, and fragrant with floral innuendo.

In the wet-processed coffees of the Yirgacheffe region, a lush, deep-soiled region of high rolling hills in southwestern Ethiopia, this profile reaches a sort of extravagant, almost perfumed apotheosis. Ethiopia Yirgacheffe, high-toned and alive with shimmering citrus and flower tones, may be the world's most distinctive coffee. Other Ethiopia wet-processed coffees—Washed Limu, Washed Sidamo, Washed Jima, and

Selective coffee picking, Sidamo region of Ethiopia.

others—are typically soft, round, floral, and citrusy, but less explosively fragrant than Yirgacheffe. They can be very fine and distinctive coffees, however.

Most Ethiopia coffees are grown without use of agricultural chemicals in the most benign of conditions: under shade and interplanted with other crops. The only exceptions are a handful of wet-processed coffees produced by large, government-run estates in southwestern Ethiopia that make discreet use of chemicals. Harrars and Yirgacheffes in particular are what Ethiopians call "garden coffees," grown on small plots by villagers using completely traditional methods.

Poorest Country, Richest Coffee Culture. Economically Ethiopia is one of the globe's poorest countries, but it embodies one of the world's richest coffee cultures. The Ethiopian coffee ceremony is a communal event practiced across Ethiopia and neighboring Eritrea. It gathers neighbors for an hour or two of food and gossip while the hostess roasts, grinds, brews, and serves coffee and can be one of the most moving tributes to the art of coffee the world has to offer. These ceremonies are often mounted in restaurants and hotels for tourists and visitors. These public, contrived versions of the ceremony may unfold with less authenticity than the countless gatherings carried out in coffee-growing villages, but the reassurance for a coffee lover is how good the coffee always turns out, even when the so-called ceremony is conducted, as it once was for me, in a roadside hotel by a well-dressed bar girl. If there is one culture in the world that thoroughly incorporates the wisdom of coffee in all of its aspects, from seed to cup, that culture is Ethiopia.

Kenya

Of all contemporary coffee origins, Kenya is doubtless the most universally admired. Coffee growing came late to this mainly tea-drinking nation, introduced in 1900 by the British. When the Kenyans achieved independence, they structured their coffee industry with what, in retrospect, seems admirable foresight. They maintained a technically sophisticated research establishment, made use of the most advanced techniques in fruit removal and drying, developed efficiently run cooperatives of small holders, and organized their export industry around an open auction.

The auction system in particular may be the key to Kenya's coffee success. The buyer who offers the highest price for a given lot of coffee at the weekly government-run auction gets that coffee. No insider deals can be cut. Samples of lots of coffee up for auction are distributed to licensed exporters, who evaluate them and distribute them to their customers for their evaluation. The exporters bid for the coffees based on their own evaluations and on the preferences of their customers.

This simple, transparent system tends to reward higher quality with higher prices. Kenya coffee growing also has the advantage of consistently high altitudes and whatever imponderables of soil and climate contribute to the heady fruit and wine tones that embellish the best East Africa and Arabia coffees.

The main growing area stretches south from the slopes of 17,000-foot Mt. Kenya almost to the capital, Nairobi. There is a smaller coffee-growing region on the slopes of Mt. Elgon, on the border between Uganda and Kenya. Most Kenya coffee sold in specialty stores appears to come from the central region around Mt. Kenya and is sometimes qualified with the name of the capital city, Nairobi. Grade desig-

nates the size of the bean: AA is largest, followed by A and B.

The Kenya Cup. Kenya is both the most balanced and the most complex of coffee origins. A powerful, wine-toned acidity is wrapped in sweet fruit. Although the body is typically medium in weight, Kenya is almost always deeply dimensioned. Sensation tends to ring on, resonating like a bell clap rather than making its case to the palate and falling silent. Some Kenyas display dry, berryish nuances, others citrus tones. The berry-toned Kenyas are particularly admired by some coffee buyers. Finally, Kenya coffees are almost always clean in the cup. Few display the shadow defects and off-tastes that often mar coffees from other origins.

Like many origins, Kenya is under fire from specialty buyers for introducing new hybrid varieties of *Coffea arabica* that successfully resist disease but, according to the buyers, do not taste as good as the older hybrid varieties, like SL28, on which the Kenya coffee industry was built. Perhaps the criticism is particularly intense in the case of Kenya because we fear losing one of specialty coffee's greatest treasures.

Uganda: Bugisu

Uganda, situated in the Great Lakes region of central Africa at the headwaters of the Nile, is the original home of *Coffea canephora*, or robusta. The main part of Uganda coffee production continues to be dry-processed robusta used in instant coffees and as cheap fillers in blends. Uganda also produces excel-

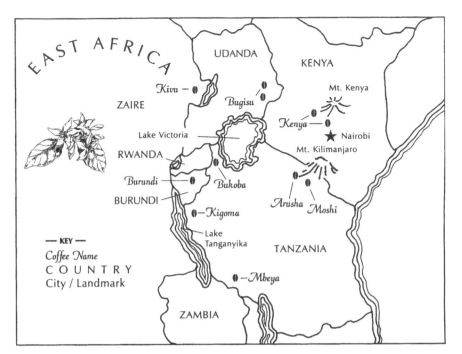

EAST AFRICA

UDANDA

KENYA

ZAIRE

Kivu —

Bugisu

Mt. Kenya

Lake Victoria

Kenya —

★ Nairobi

RWANDA

Mt. Kilimanjaro

Burundi —

Bukoba

BURUNDI

Arusha *Moshi*

— KEY —

Coffee Name

COUNTRY

City / Landmark

Kigoma

Lake
Tanganyika

TANZANIA

Mbeya

ZAMBIA

auction to exporters in a system resembling the Kenya auction system. Burundi is still another organically grown coffee owing to the fact that the farmers cannot afford chemicals. Most is grown in full shade. At best, when not spoiled during drying, storage, or transportation, it is a floral and brightly acidy version of the East Africa style.

Tanzania

Most Tanzania arabicas are grown on the slopes of Mt. Kilimanjaro and Mt. Meru, near the Kenyan border. Those from Mt. Kilimanjaro usually are called Kilimanjaro or Moshi; those from Mt. Meru are marked Arusha. The Moshi and Arusha designations derive from the respective main towns and shipping points. Smaller amounts of arabica are grown much farther south, between Lake Tanganyika and Lake Nyasa, and are usually called Mbeya, after one of the principal towns, or Pare, a market name. In all cases, the highest grade is AA, followed by A and B. Owing to tradition, most Tanzania coffee sold in the United States is peaberry, a grade made up entirely of coffee from fruit that produces a single, rounded bean rather than twin flat-sided beans.

Most Tanzania coffees share the characteristically sharp, winy acidity typical of Africa and Arabia coffees. They tend to be medium- to full-bodied and fairly rich in flavor. Other Tanzania coffees may exhibit soft, floral profiles reminiscent of washed Ethiopia coffees.

lent wet-processed arabicas, however, virtually all grown by villagers on small plots.

Coffee marketed as Wugar is grown on mountains bordering Zaire along Uganda's western border. More admired is Bugisu or Bugishu, from the western slopes of Mt. Elgon on the Kenya border. Bugisu is another typically winy, fruit-toned African coffee, usually a rougher version of Kenya.

Burundi: Ngoma

Tucked between Tanzania and Congo in central Africa, Burundi is a relative newcomer on the American specialty stage. Its coffees are produced on small plots by villagers in the northern part of the country and wet-processed at small mills. The coffee is sold at

Malawi

Malawi is a relatively small country whose borders meander on a north-south axis between Mozambique and Zambia in southeastern Africa. Although there are many subsistence growers in Malawi organized into cooperatives, Malawi specialty coffees currently reaching North America are produced by estates. These estate Malawis embody the softer, more floral style of East Africa coffee: sweet, delicate, shyly bright.

Zambia

Zambia coffee currently appearing in North America specialty stores is produced by large estates. The most prominent are Terranova and Kapinga. At their very best, these are coffees in the classic East Africa tradition: medium-bodied, floral in aroma, with a wine-toned, resonantly acidy cup.

Zimbabwe

Zimbabwe, formerly Rhodesia, has been exporting an excellent coffee to the United States for some years. It is a wet-processed coffee grown on medium-size to large farms, mainly in the mountainous Chipinge region in eastern Zimbabwe bordering Mozambique. It is still another variant on the acidy, winy-toned coffees of East Africa. Some importers rank Zimbabwe with the best Kenya coffees. Samples

I have tasted over the years are not so deeply dimensioned or rich, but it is a fine medium-bodied, complexly wine- and berry-toned, African-style coffee. The best grade is AA. Smaldeel and La Lucie currently are the most prominent estate names.

India: Niligris, Baba Budan, Sheveroys, Monsooned Malabar

India has a long and deep coffee culture. Coffee was first brought to India around 1600 by the Muslim pilgrim Baba Budan, who smuggled seed

has made some impact on American specialty menus of late.

India has eight main coffee-growing regions, all in the southern part of the country. Those with the highest elevations—Baba Budan, Niligris, and Shevaroys—produce the most admired specialty coffees. They are all wet-processed or washed coffees; Arabica Plantation A is the highest grade.

Currently the most distinguished India coffees to reach the American market come from estates in the Sheveroys district: Pearl Mountain, Arabadicool, and others. These are bright yet gentle coffees, with a buoyant body and an intriguing bouquet of spice notes. The spice is subtle yet explicit: tantalizing suggestions of nutmeg, clove, and cardamon. Since these farms typically grow, process, and store coffee in close proximity to crops of spices, the coffee probably picks up its spice tones during drying and storage in an atmosphere redolent with those scents.

Aside from high-grown estate coffees, India arabica tends to be full, round, sweet, occasionally spicy or chocolaty, but usually a bit listless. Relatively low, growing elevations and the use of disease-resistant hybrids that often have been back-crossed with robusta probably contribute to this full but often inert profile. Nevertheless, India coffees' sweetness and full

out of Mecca. Coffee growing for export was not started until 1840 by the British, however. India now claims to be the fifth-largest producer of coffee in the world, after Brazil, Colombia, Mexico, and Ethiopia.

Much of India's production is consumed at home, and India has never achieved a reputation as a fancy coffee origin among North Americans. However, mainly through the efforts of Joseph Johns of Josuma Coffee, a specialized importer of India coffee, India body recommend them to espresso blenders, who may use them as a base component in Italian-style blends.

Monsooned Malabar. India's most unusual coffee is the famous Monsooned Malabar, a dry-processed coffee that has been exposed for three to four months in open-sided warehouses to the moisture-laden winds of the monsoon. The monsooning process swells and yellows the bean, fattens body, and reduces acidity, imparting a heavy, deep, syrupy sweetness to the cup. Unfortunately, many monsooned coffees also acquire a sharp, hard, mustiness that overlays and dampens the attractive sweetness.

Monsooning was originally devised by Indian exporters to produce a cup similar to Old Brown Java coffees, which were similarly transformed in taste by exposure to salt air and moisture in the hulls of wooden sailing ships on the voyage from Java to Europe. If you can find a monsooned coffee that is free of mustiness (a version exported as Coelho's Gold often is), you may enjoy a cup as sweetly sultry as the name, the history, and the exotic process.

Sumatra: Lintong, Mandheling, Aceh, Gayo Mountain, Kopi Luak

Sumatra is one of the great romance coffees of the world. It is not simply that the Indonesian island of Sumatra embodies a Conradian romance of the unfamiliar. When it is at its best the coffee itself suggests intrigue, with its complexity, its weight without heaviness, and an acidity that resonates deep inside the heart of the coffee, enveloped in richness, rather than confronting the palate the moment we lift the cup.

Sumatra Lintong and Mandheling. This praise applies mainly to the finest of the traditional arabica coffees of northern Sumatra, the best of those sold under the market names Lintong and Mandheling. Lintong properly describes only coffees grown in a relatively small region just southwest of Lake Toba in the kecamatan or district of Lintongnihuta. Small plots of coffee are scattered over a high, undulating plateau of fern-covered clay. The coffee is grown without shade, but also without chemicals of any kind, and almost entirely by small holders. Mandheling is a more comprehensive designation, referring both to Lintong coffees and to coffees grown under similar conditions in the regency of Diari, north of Lake Toba.

Sellers often label Lintong and Mandheling coffees dry-processed. In fact, the fruit usually is removed from the bean by a variety of hybrid methods. The most prevalent is a backyard version of the wet method. The farmers remove the skins from their little crops of coffee cherries immediately after picking using rickety pulping machines ingeniously constructed from scrap metal, wood, and bicycle parts. The skinned, slimy beans are then allowed to ferment overnight in woven plastic bags. In the morning the fruit pulp or mucilage, loosened by the overnight fermentation, is washed off the beans by hand. The coffee (now in its parchment skin) is given a preliminary drying on sheets in the farmer's front yard. The parchment skin is then removed by machine at a middleman's warehouse and the coffee is further dried. Finally, the coffee is trucked down to the port city of Medan, where it is dried a third and last time.

I am told that elsewhere in the Mandheling area

Pulping (removing the skins from freshly picked coffee fruit), Mandheling region of Sumatra. The pulping machine is entirely made by hand from improvised components. The fly wheel consists of a slab of truck tire and the axle and handle are constructed from recycled bicycle parts.

drying, first at the middleman's warehouse, then at the exporter's facility in Medan.

Processing and Sumatra Character. I go into these procedures in such detail because it is not clear how much of the unique character of Lintong- and Mandheling-style coffee derives from soil and climate and how much from these unusual processing techniques and the prolonged three-step drying. One thing is certain: These procedures produce a sporadically splendid yet extremely uneven product, and only relentless hand sorting at the exporters' warehouses in Medan assures that the deep body and unique, low-toned richness of the Lintong/Mandheling origins emerge intact from the distractions of dirty-tasting beans and other taints.

Some admirers of Sumatra enjoy certain of these flavor taints. Earthy Sumatras, which pick up the taste of fresh clay from having been dried directly on the earth, are popular among some coffee drinkers. Musty Sumatras, which acquire the rather hard, mildewy taste of old shoes in a damp closet, are also attractive to some palates.

Sumatra Gayo Mountain, Aceh. Less famous than Lintong and Mandheling are arabicas from Aceh, the province at the northernmost tip of Sumatra. Aceh coffees are grown in the lovely mountain basin surrounding Lake Tawar and the town of Takengon. All are grown in shade and almost all without chemicals.

Processing methods vary widely with Aceh coffees, however, as do flavor profiles. Some are processed by

the mucilage is simply allowed to dry on the bean after the skins have been removed, much as is done with the semiwashed coffees of Brazil. Thereafter the dried mucilage and parchment skin are removed by machine and the coffee subjected to the same two-phase small farmers using the traditional Sumatran backyard washed method. These coffees resemble Lintong/Mandheling coffees, and probably often are sold as such by the Medan exporters.

But the Aceh coffees most likely to reach North American specialty stores come from a large mill near Takengon. The mill's Gayo Mountain Washed Arabica is processed by a meticulous wet method following international standards and is certified organic by a Dutch agency. Gayo Mountain Washed is sweet and subtly rounded, a higher-toned, lighter-bodied version of the Lintong/Mandheling flavor profile.

The Gayo mill also markets coffees that have been processed by the semidry method, in which the outer skin of the coffee fruit is removed and the beans, still covered with sticky mucilage, are sun-dried. These often excellent coffees offer an attractive compromise between Gayo Mountain Washed and the resonant weight of the traditional Lintong/Mandheling. Such coffees are marketed as Gayo Unwashed. The last term is a bit misleading. (Did the beans forget to take a bath?) A more accurate description might be Gayo Semidry.

The Infamous Kopi Luak. Luak coffee is one of those snicker-rich stories beloved of newspaper writers and party raconteurs. This gourmet curiosity consists (ostensibly) of coffee beans that have been excreted by a smallish animal called a luak or palm civet after the luak has consumed (and digested) the coffee fruit that previously enveloped those beans. Apparently villagers in parts of Sumatra gather the beans from wild luak excrement as well as feed coffee fruit to luaks kept in cages.

Owing to a production method that is clearly limited in volume, Kopi Luak is a rare coffee that demands by far the highest price of any coffee on the world market—currently around $300 per pound retail roasted.

Note that the luak-assisted method of picking and processing coffee is not so outlandish as it at first may sound. Presumably the luak, like any good coffee picker, chooses only ripe cherries to eat. And recall that in the classic wet method of coffee preparation, one step involves allowing natural enzymes and bacteria to literally ferment or digest much of the fruit from the beans.

Although the odor kopi luak produces while roasting dramatically reminds us of its intestinal journey from fruit to bean, the taste in the cup does not. The kopi luak I have tasted is a rather pleasant, low-key, full-bodied, earthy Sumatra coffee.

As for authenticity, I suspect that, amazing as it sounds, most kopi luak is actually produced as advertised. The beans in the lots I have examined are irregular in size and shape, have little nicks and nibbles taken out of them, and seem saturated with intestinal nuance rather than simply rubbed in it. Nevertheless, only the luak knows.

For those well-heeled gastronomical adventurers interested in sampling a luak-prepared coffee, see Sending for It.

Sulawesi or Calebes: Toraja, Kalossi

The Indonesian island of Sulawesi, formerly Celebes, spreads like a huge four-fingered hand in the middle of the Malay Archipelago. The Sulawesi coffee most likely to be found in specialty stores today comes from a mountainous region near the base of the southwestern finger of the island, north of the port of Ujung Padang. The region and the coffee, Toraja, are named after the colorful indigenous people of the region. The coffee is also called Kalossi, after a regional market town.

Whether we call it Sulawesi Toraja or Celebes Kalossi, coffee from this region can range from a plantation-grown, wet-processed coffee with a smooth, vibrant, but relatively low-acid, medium-bodied profile to small-grower coffees that resemble the Mandheling coffees of Sumatra both in virtues (when they are good they are deep, resonant, and pungently complex in the lower registers) and in vices (off-tastes range from earth through musty hardness to an odd stagnant water or pondy taste).

Java: Estate Arabica

The Dutch planted the first *Coffea arabica* trees in Java at the beginning of the eighteenth century; and before the rust disease virtually wiped out the industry, Java led the world in coffee production. Most of this early acreage has been replaced by disease-resistant robusta, but under the sponsorship of the Indonesian government, arabica has made a modest comeback on several estates originally established by the Dutch at the turn of the century and situated in the dramatic mountains of East Java. In many of these estates the original machinery the Dutch introduced is still in use, maintained perfectly and as neat as a museum display but infinitely more useful.

Java coffees share some of the low-key vibrancy of the best Sumatra and Sulawesi coffees but tend to be lighter, cleaner, and brighter in the cup owing to having been subjected to sophisticated wet-processing and drying methods on large farms. At best they can be astoundingly sweet, buoyantly fragrant, and alive with nut, spice, and vanilla tones. At worst they can display hardness or mustiness owing to the same moisture-interrupted drying that plagues all Indonesia coffees. Nevertheless, a really fine Java is a coffee treasure: restrained in acidity, yet light-footed, spirited, and complex with nuance.

Of the four revived "old" estates that provide most of the good Java arabica—Jampit (or Djampit), Blawan, Kayumas, and Pancur—Jampit and Blawan are the most likely sources of the Java coffee in American specialty stores.

Old Government, Old Brown, or simply Old Java describe Java arabica that has been held in warehouses for two to three years. Such matured coffee turns from green to light brown, gains body, adds pungency, and loses acidity. Old Java was a celebrated gourmet coffee until it disappeared from the market after World War II. It has been revived, although it remains difficult to obtain in the United States. A somewhat similar taste is offered by aged Sumatra and India Monsooned Malabar coffees.

Timor: East Timor

Timor is another do-good, feel-good coffee that is gradually becoming taste-good as well. As any newspaper-reading adult knows, over the decades of the 1980s and '90s, East Timor—a former Portuguese colony—underwent a bloody war of resistance to Indonesian occupation, and eventually, at the end of the 1990s, a brief but even bloodier spasm that led to independence from its much larger neighbor. During the 1990s, international assistance organizations helped the East Timorese revive their once famous coffee industry. Like most small-holder coffees from the Malay Archipelago, East Timor coffees are grown without chemicals, but Timors have the advantage of being internationally certified as organic. They are wet-processed at recently established wet mills or washing stations. Buying a Timor coffee at this moment in history means making a small but valuable gesture of support for one of the many peoples of the world caught up in sectarian and political conflict.

In terms of taste, most current versions of Timor are typical for small-holder, wet-processed coffees from the islands of the Malay Archipelago: low-key, sweet, with a musty pungency that can range from soft and intriguing to hard and oppressive. However, the very best and cleanest-tasting Timors can be extraordinary: full, round, smooth, sweet, and deliciously cocoa-toned. These coffees, already promising, may continue to improve as the first decade of the new century unfolds.

New Guinea: Papua New Guinea

Coffee labeled New Guinea comes from Papua New Guinea, often abbreviated PNG, which occupies the eastern half of the island of New Guinea. Like Indonesia coffees, New Guineas come in two versions: estate coffees that have been meticulously wet-processed in large-scale facilities and small-holder, peasant coffees that usually are wet-processed

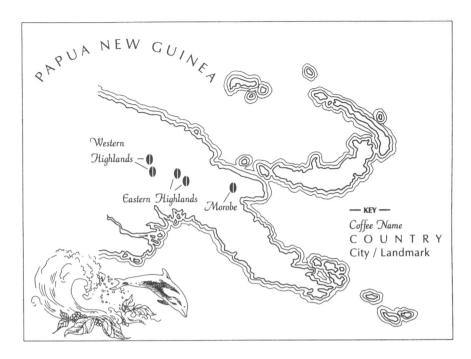

PAPUA NEW GUINEA

Western
Highlands —

Eastern Highlands
Morobe

— KEY —
Coffee Name
C O U N T R Y
City / Landmark

Papua New Guinea small-holder coffees often are certified organically grown. They share the problem faced by all small-holder coffees worldwide. If hundreds or thousands of small-holders do their own wet-processing and drying, quality is erratic. Many of these New Guineas arrive in North America musty, hard-tasting, earthy, or fermented. When they are clean-tasting, however, they too express the coffee genius of the Pacific: low-key, vibrant, luxuriously deep. Efforts are being made to control the processing and grading of some of these coffees and establish them as recognized origins. Village Premium Morobe from Morobe Province in the East-Central part of the country represents one of these efforts.

by the farmers using the simplest of backyard methods.

Most New Guineas sold in North American specialty stores are estate coffees. Most prominent are Sigri, grown in Western Highlands Province near the town of Mount Hagen, Madan, also in Western Highlands Province, and estate coffees from the Eastern Highlands Province exported as Arusafa or Arona.

Depending on year and harvest, Sigri, Arona, and other New Guinea estate coffees range from pleasant to splendid, at best displaying the authority of a high-grown coffee together with the transparency of a carefully wet-processed coffee while retaining the fragrant, low-key luxuriousness characteristic of all coffees of the Malay Archipelago.

Hawaii: Kona, Kaanapali Coffee, Malulani Estate, Kauai Coffee

Hawaii Kona. The tiny Kona growing district on the southwest coast of Hawaii, the "Big Island" of the Hawaiian chain, produces the most famous and the most traditional of Hawaiian coffees. Entirely hand-picked, wet-processed, and from trees of a splendid local strain of *typica* called Guatemala, Kona is grown on clusters of tiny farms above the Pacific on the lower slopes of Mount Hualalai and Mauna Loa.

The coffee trees are shaded by a cloud cover that appears regularly most afternoons, followed by tourist-discouraging drizzles that often escalate into downpours. The combination of regular rain and cloud cover, the temperature-moderating influence of the Pacific, and very porous soil (sometimes the trees grow straight out of the volcanic rubble) seems to mimic the effect of higher growing altitudes. Although grown at altitudes of 800 to 2,500 feet, very low for arabica, Kona often displays the powerful acidity of much higher-grown coffees.

But it is the gently acidy, fragrant, sometimes wine- and fruit-toned cup of the more typical Konas that made Kona's reputation as one of the world's premier coffee origins. In the late 1990s, the soft, aromatic cup, tourist-inspired demand, limited supply, and palms-and-sand romance made Kona the highest priced coffee in the world, with prices exceeding even those attracted by Jamaica Blue Mountain.

Kona Deceptions and Evasions. At this writing Kona prices have moderated somewhat, but the extremely high prices paid for Konas in the 1990s apparently encouraged one mill owner and supplier to sell Costa Rica and Panama coffees in Kona bags. After a few years of successful deceit he was uncovered and indicted for fraud. The resulting scandal shook the little world of passionate, outspoken Kona growers and mill owners. The end result seems to be positive, however, as the growers work with authorities toward clearer control of the Kona coffee identity.

However, retail sales of Kona coffee continue to be rife with dubious marketing practices. Commercial roasters produce Kona-style coffee, Kona-blend cof-

Young girl helping with family coffee picking in the Kona district of Hawaii.

fee, and Hawaiian hotels brew coffee vaguely labeled Kona that probably consists in large part of (often low-grade) Central America beans. In fact, it is difficult to find a good cup of Kona coffee in Kona, and flat-out impossible in hotels. The colorful bags of Kona coffee sold in Hawaiian supermarkets and airport gift stores are almost always poor quality and

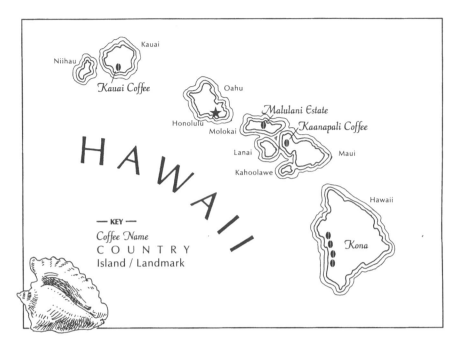

buy Kona coffee is to visit Kona in person, find an estate or mill that produces a coffee you like, and arrange to buy that coffee, custom-roasted, on a regular basis by mail.

Visiting Kona farms and mills can be a delight. The current Kona coffee industry largely was founded by Japanese immigrants fleeing the regimentation of work at the large sugar plantations. They established tiny family farms in the rugged countryside, one of which, the D. Uchida Farm, has been restored for visitors by the Kona Historical Society. The ongoing theme of individualism and independence was given a boost in the 1960s and '70s by back-to-the-land hippie types from the mainland, who settled in to grow coffee next to the Hawaiians and Japanese. Today, you can arrange tours, led by the owners themselves, of tiny farms that produce excellent coffee or visit the wonderful Bayview Farms or Greenwell mills, where from late August to early December you can watch coffee being fastidiously wet-processed.

stale. Tourists who visit Kona often do come across that one splendid cup, however, and driven by its fragrant memory, plus recollections of the warm air insinuating itself under their newly purchased aloha shirts and muu-muus, spend the next six months trying to find a comparable coffee experience through mainland supermarkets and specialty stores. Most, I suspect, give up and buy something else.

Buying and Visting Kona. One way to enjoy a good, bona-fide Kona on the mainland is to find a roaster who sells a Kona from a single, designated estate, and who does not destroy it by roasting it too dark. If there is no one who fits that description in your area, consult Sending for It. An even better way to

"Other Island" Hawaiis: Maui, Molakai, Kauai. Today, Kona is no longer the only coffee grown in Hawaii. Visitors to the "other" major coffee-growing islands—Maui, Molokai, and Kauai—now encounter an entirely different coffee spectacle. In place of Kona's family plots shoehorned in among rocks and rusting cars, long, regular lines of coffee trees undulate like gleaming dark-green hedges over low coastal plains where sugar and pineapple once grew. Rather than isolated groups of pickers balancing their way over rocks, ingenious harvesting machines roll across the nearly flat terrain, coaxing ripe cherries off the trees with hundreds of fiberglass rods vibrating through the branches like tireless fingers. The soil is deep and red, and rainfall, less frequent than in Kona, is supplemented by meticulously managed drip-irrigation systems.

These coffee farms—Kaanapali Coffee with 450 acres on Maui, Malulani Estate with 460 on Molokai, and Kauai Coffee with an astonishing 4,000 on Kauai—are revivals of earlier efforts to grow coffee on a commercial scale on the coastal plains of Hawaii. In the nineteenth century, these coffee farms gave way to the more profitable crops of sugar and pineapple, and coffee growing survived only in rugged Kona, where the rocky terrain discouraged large-scale agriculture.

Today, however, cheap-labor competition from other parts of the world has shut down the less productive of the big pineapple and sugar plantations, and growers and the state of Hawaii are scrambling to find replacement crops that will prevent rural Hawaii from turning exclusively into a playground for tourists and a bedroom community for hotel maids and helicopter tour operators.

Experiment and Innovation. Coffee is one such crop. Coffee romantics may entertain existential atti-

tude problems with these highly technified coffees and their corporate sponsors. For some afficionados, however, the experiment and innovation they represent can be as engaging as Kona's tradition. All three farms are among world leaders in the effort to maximize quality and offset extremely low growing altitudes through superior processing and seed selection.

All have succeeded to some degree. Pioneer Mill, just outside Lahaina, markets its excellent Kaanapali Estate coffees by botanical variety: *moka* or *mocha*, a very old, traditional variety that arrived in Hawaii from Yemen via Brazil; *yellow caturra*, a more recent selection; *red catuai*, a good hybrid; and the traditional Kona strain of *typica*. All are subtly different. The *typica* has proven to be something of a failure in the Maui growing conditions, but any of the other three varieties can produce oustanding coffee in any given crop year. The *moka* produces a particularly interesting cup. Kaanapali offers it roasted and packaged as (of course) Maui Gold.

All Molokai coffee is grown at the Coffees of Hawai'i plantation in the central part of the island at around 850 feet. Most comes from trees of the hybrid (but admired) *red catuai* variety. The wet-processed Malulani Estate and the dry-processed Moloka'i Muleskinner coffees are medium-bodied, sweet, low-acid coffees with complex, attractive bouquets that often include unusual herbal tones.

Kauai Coffee produces a highly selected coffee called Kauai Estate Reserve from trees of the hybrid *yellow catuai* and the *typica* varieties. These are consistent, agreeable coffees that will please those who prefer a full-bodied, sweet, low-acid cup.

Maragogipe (Elephant Bean)

Maragogipe (also called *elephant bean*) is a variety of arabica that produces an extremely large, rather porous bean. It is a mutant that spontaneously appeared in Brazil, almost as though the giant of Latin America thought regular beans were too puny and produced something in its own image. It was first discovered growing near the town of Maragogipe, in the northeastern state of Bahia. Subsequently it has been carried elsewhere in Latin America and generally adopts the flavor characteristics of the soil to which it has been transplanted.

Opinions differ about the special qualities of the Maragogipe. William H. Ukers, one of the world's great authorities on coffee, found it tasted "woody and disagreeable" in 1928. Others have called it the finest coffee known and claim it has a heavier body than a comparable arabica coffee from the same region. Current opinion, which I share, is that it produces a thinner and less acidy cup than other traditional arabica varieties grown under the same conditions. This weakness in the cup coupled with low productivity has discouraged farmers from replanting Maragogipe, and it has become a rather rare, difficult-to-find coffee. Most Maragogipes sold in North America are grown in Mexico, Nicaragua, or Guatemala. Those from Chiapas, Mexico, and the Cobán district of Guatemala have the best reputation.

Maragogipe is a romantic's coffee curiosity, and deserves respect on that ground alone. An alternative for those aficionados who have trouble finding a Maragogipe, or who want a dramatically large bean with more consistent cup quality, might try the *pacamara* variety, a large-bean Maragogipe hybrid grown in El Salvador on Los Ausoles and Larin estates and impressively soft and full in the cup.

Peaberry (*Caracol*)

Throughout the world, the coffee fruit occasionally produces a single, rather than a double, bean. It grows to be small and round, with a tiny crevice that splits it halfway down the middle. Called *peaberry* in English and *caracol* in Spanish, these beans are often separated from normal-shaped beans and sold as a separate grade of the same coffee.

According to coffee folklore, peaberry grades are considered superior to normal grades from the same crop, apparently on the basis that, in peaberries, the good stuff that ordinarily goes into a double bean goes into only one bean. I am not sure peaberry tastes better than normal beans from the same crop, but it does taste different. Typically, peaberry is more buoyant and more brightly acidy, more complex in the upper aromatic ranges of the profile but somewhat lighter in body than comparable normally shaped beans.

Peaberry coffee should be sold by country and market or estate name like any other coffee. If you read a notice that simply says peaberry, you should inquire about the origin of the coffee.

Aged Coffees

As green coffee ages, its flavor characteristics change. If it is stored in cool darkness, it may change very little over the course of years, at most losing some acidity. However, coffees stored in warehouses located in hot, humid, tropical port cities can change in flavor dramatically and rapidly.

Coffee delivered for roasting soon after harvest and processing is called new crop. Coffee that has been held in warehouses for a period before delivery is called old crop. The differences between new and old crop may be minor. Sometimes the old crop is better because it displays more depth and less immature grassiness. In other cases new crop may be better because it is brighter and fresher tasting, whereas old crop may taste dull or woody. At times roasters combine old and new crop of the same coffee, aiming at a more complete version of the same flavor profile.

Aged or vintage coffees, however, are a different matter. Traditionally aged coffees, which are rare, may have been held in warehouses for anywhere from three to ten years, and can be superb: sweet, full almost to a fault, syrupy but clean-tasting.

However, a kind of accelerated aging is now performed in Indonesia, wherein the beans are deliberately exposed to moist air, much like India's Monsooned Malabar (page 73). These aged coffees lose acidity and gain body, but they often also gain a kind of hard pungency, which I do not care for but which some coffee drinkers find attractive.

If an aged coffee originates in Latin America, most likely it has been aged in the traditional way. In fact, it may have been inadvertently aged. An importer or grower may have found he had too much coffee to sell, stored it, and trotted it out some years later as a special delicacy. As conceptually sloppy as this practice sounds, it often produces the best aged coffees, with a sweet heaviness unmarred by hard tastes.

Today, however, most aged coffees come from Sumatra and Sulawesi, and most are aged quickly by deliberate exposure to humid air in port cities. If you're lucky, you may run across one that is sweet, deep, resonant, and free of musty hardness. If you're not lucky, you may still enjoy the heavy sweetness overlaid with a sharp twist of mustiness. Many coffee drinkers do.

BLENDS AND BLENDING YOUR OWN

Since blending is the ultimate proof of coffee expertise and since it gives consumers a chance to participate in the creation of their own pleasure, specialty coffee customers often blend their own coffees. The only drawback to such a rewarding practice is impatience: Consumers may decide to begin blending coffees before they know enough to do it right, and sellers may get frustrated if they have to stop to make a blend of five coffees for a customer when there are ten more customers waiting in line. But few storekeepers will object if they feel the customer is really blending, rather than just showing off or demanding attention.

Different roasts, coffees with different caffeine contents, or single-origin coffees from different countries can be blended. One of the more common practices is to blend dark and light roasts to maximize the complexity of roast taste. Another reason to blend is to cut caffeine content. If you drink only decaffeinated coffee, you may get bored, since specialty shops carry a limited number of caffeine-free coffees. An excellent compromise is to blend a caffeine-free coffee with your favorite single-origin coffees, thus cutting your caffeine intake while fulfilling your sense of coffee adventure.

Blending Coffees from Different Origins

The art of blending coffees from a variety of origins brought to approximately the same degree of roast is a subtler business, but hardly difficult once the basic principles are understood. Blenders who work for large commercial coffee companies need to be highly skilled because their goals are more complex than our simple efforts to blend a coffee that suits us better than would a single-origin coffee taken alone. The commercial blender blends to cut costs while maintaining something resembling quality and wants to assemble a blend with consistent taste even though the single-origin coffees that make up the blend may differ. Certain coffees are not always available; some coffees may be cheaper than others at certain times of the year, and so on. But in an economy dominated by highly advertised brand names, the blend has to taste more or less the same every time. So blenders may find themselves amid a shifting kaleidoscope of prices and availabilities, con-

stantly juggling coffees in an attempt to keep the taste the same and the cost down.

A good commercial blend may take an acidy, aromatic coffee such as a Colombia, Costa Rica, or Mexico and combine it with a decent grade of Brazil coffee to cut costs, plus some bland robustas to cut costs still more and add body. If it is a premium blend, the blender might combine more than one quality coffee with the Brazil: a rich, full-bodied coffee to balance a bright, acidy coffee, for instance. Low-cost blends might decrease the proportion of high-grown and Brazil coffees and make up the difference with robusta. The cheapest blends eliminate the high-grown coffee entirely and simply combine a decent grade of Brazil with the robustas.

With blends found in specialty-coffee stores, the blender's main goal is to produce a distinctive and consistent coffee, rather than simply to cut costs. A typical specialty roaster may have only one blend, a house blend, or a dozen for all pocketbooks, tastes, brewing methods, and times of day. Some larger specialty roasters, like their commercial counterparts, also may blend for price, although (one hopes) with less urgency and compromise.

Personal Blends

Coffee lovers who create their own blends have less to consider than either commercial or specialty blenders. They should not have to worry too much about consistency, and they cannot use blending to bring the price down much, since most single-origin coffees sold through specialty stores are already premium coffees with premium prices. Blending for price would be like trying to save money by cutting caviar with truffles. Commercial coffee concerns can save money on their blends because they are able to buy large quantities of cheap coffee at bargain prices. As I indicate in Chapter 7, a more effective way to save money would be to buy green coffee in bulk and learn to roast it yourself.

So you will be blending for taste. The way to go about this is simple: Combine coffees that complement one another with qualities the others lack. The world's oldest and most famous blend, for instance, combines Yemen Mocha and Java. Part of the reason for its fame is tradition. The blend originated when Mocha and Java were the only coffees the world knew. Nevertheless, it embodies the sound principle of balancing extremes or complements. Yemen is an acidy, fruity, winy coffee; Java is rounder and deeper-toned. Together they make a coffee that is both less and more—less striking and distinctive, but more balanced and comprehensive.

The first, pleasurable task in assembling a personal blend is to learn to taste coffee attentively, to distinguish acidity, body, and flavor and some of the more individual quirks: the floral tones of Ethiopia wet-processed coffees, the pungent tones of Sumatra, the dry fruit tones of Kenya. You should also know what qualities you prefer in a coffee and what to blend for. You may simply want an all-around coffee with the best of all worlds, or a heavy, mellow coffee with only a little acidy brightness, or a brisk, light coffee with plenty of body as well.

Blending Families

Always proceed the same way. If you have a favorite coffee that seems to lack something, combine it with a coffee that provides what your favorite lacks.

- For brightness, briskness, and acidity, add a Costa Rica, Colombia, Guatemala, or any high-grown Central America coffee.
- For body and richness, add a dry-processed Brazil Santos or estate coffee or a good Sumatra Mandheling.
- For body and sweetness, add a dry-processed Brazil Santos or a high-grade India.
- For flavor and aroma, add a Kenya, Guatemala, New Guinea, Yemen Mocha, or Zimbabwe.
- To add aromatic intrigue at the top of the profile, add an Ethiopia Yirgacheffe or Kenya. To add complexity near the bottom of the profile add a Sumatra Mandheling or traditionally processed Sulawesi.
- To add wine or fruit notes, make the acidy/highlight coffee a Yemen, an Ethiopia Harrar, or a Kenya.

The only real mistake you can make blending is to combine two coffees that are distinctive or extreme in the same way. Two coffees with similar bright, winy acidity, such as a Kenya and a Zimbabwe, might produce a pointless blend. On the other hand, coffees such as Brazil Santos are so congenially understated that they get along with everything. Others, such as Yemen Mocha, wet-processed Ethiopias, and most good Central America coffees, are like easygoing individualists who manage to mix with almost everybody, yet still maintain their distinction.

BLENDING WITH CHICORY OR FIG

Dark-roast coffee is sometimes blended with chicory, particularly in northern France, parts of Asia, and the southern United States. Chicory is an easily grown, disease-resistant relative of the dandelion. The young leaves, when used for salad, are called endive. The root resembles the dandelion root and, when dried, roasted, and ground, produces a deep brown, full-bodied, almost syrupy beverage that has a bitter peppery tang and does not taste at all like coffee. In fact, it tastes as if someone put pepper in your herbal tea mixture. It is almost impossible to drink black; sweetened with milk, it makes a fairly satisfying hot beverage, though it leaves a bitter, cloying aftertaste.

According to Heinrick Jacob in *Coffee: The Epic of a Commodity*, some Germans first exploited the use of chicory as a coffee substitute around 1770. The Germans adopted chicory because it lacked caffeine and (possibly most important) because it eluded the tariffs imposed on such foreign luxuries as coffee. Jacob describes the trademark on eighteenth-century packets of chicory: "A German farmer sowing chicory seed, and waving away ships freighted with coffee beans. Beneath was the legend: 'Without you, healthy and rich.'" But it was under Napoleon's Continental System, a reverse blockade aimed at cutting England off from its European markets and making conquered Europe self-sufficient, that chicory came into its own. The French developed the sugar beet to replace sugar cane, but the chicory root was the best they could come up with for coffee. It was not much of a substitute, since it has neither caffeine nor the aromatic oils of coffee. After the collapse of the Napoleonic Empire, most of the French went back to coffee, but some never totally lost their taste for chicory.

New Orleans Coffee. The famous New Orleans–style coffee, which came to the southern United States with French colonists, tastes the way it does for three reasons: it has chicory in it (or should), the beans are dark-roasted, and (usually but not always) some cheap, naturally processed Brazilian coffee has been added to give the brew that old-time sour twist. If you like New Orleans–style coffee and want to carry your taste to more refined levels, you first need to determine which components account for what you like about the flavor: the chicory, the dark roast, or the twisty-tasting beans.

I assume by now you have tried dark-roast coffee. The classic choice to mix with chicory would be a rather sweet coffee, like a Haiti or a dry-processed Brazil Santos, brought to a dark but not too dark roast. However, any moderately dark-roast coffee will make a plausible base for a New Orleans blend. Next, buy ground French chicory, sold at some specialty coffee stores and Internet sites (see Sending for It). A New Orleans blend costs a little less than coffee and goes farther, which is another reason for developing a taste for it. Now simply experiment by varying the proportions of chicory to ground, dark-roast coffee. About 10 percent chicory will barely affect flavor, but will considerably increase the body and darkness of the brew. The peppery taste clearly emerges at 20 percent, but still does not overpower the coffee flavor, and you can drink such a blend black with pleasure. Many New Orleans blends are 30 to 40 percent chicory. At these proportions the bitter chicory flavor at least equals the coffee flavor, and I think most people would have trouble drinking such a blend black.

In Great Britain a blend of coffee and roast ground fig is popular. Fig has a flavor very different from the heavy, peppery bite of chicory. Mixed in proportions of one part fig to seven parts ground coffee, fig adds considerable body and a delicate fruity sweetness to the cup. I much prefer it to chicory, but since it is unavailable commercially in the United States and most readers will hardly bother to roast and grind it themselves, I will not carry on about it.

FLAVORED COFFEES

Flavored whole-bean coffees—the hazelnut cremes, Irish cremes, and chocolate raspberries of the specialty coffee world—are neither as innovative nor as decadent as they may appear at first glance. Although this particular approach to flavoring coffee in its whole-bean form did not come on the scene until the late 1970s, the notion of adding other ingredients to coffee to complicate or enhance its natural flavor goes back to the first coffee drinkers, the Arabs of what is now Yemen, who from the very beginning added a variety of spices to coffee during brewing.

Combining chocolate with coffee was an innovation of seventeenth-century Europeans, for whom coffee and chocolate were stimulating novelties from the opposite ends of the known world. The practice of adding citrus to coffee also has a long history, as does the practice of combining spirits and coffee.

In fact, if we examine the list of best-sellers among the flavors used to enhance whole-bean coffees today, we will find very little new. The leading seller by far is hazelnut. The association of this flavor with coffee almost certainly rose from the long-standing association of Frangelico, a traditional Italian hazelnut-flavored liqueur, with coffee. With the second most popular flavor, Irish creme, the relationship may derive either from the liqueur of the same name, or, more likely, from one of the most popular American coffee drinks of all time, Irish coffee, with its combination of Irish whiskey, coffee, and lightly whipped cream. Most of the rest of the list of top-selling flavors can be similarly placed in a traditional context: chocolate with the tradition of the coffee-chocolate drink, mocha; cinnamon with the practice of combining cinnamon with coffee that began with the first coffee drinkers of the Middle East; amaretto with the traditional liqueur; and so on.

Tradition and Modern Chemistry

Thus, coffee tradition had already established the compatibility of certain flavors with coffee long before the advent of flavored whole-bean coffees. The difference, of course, is that the traditional drinks added flavoring during or after brewing the coffee, whereas the contemporary versions are flavored well before brewing.

This difference means that coffee flavorings added to the whole bean need to be considerably stronger than those added after the coffee is brewed. The whole-bean flavors need to carry through the brewing process; to assert themselves in the context of the already powerful coffee flavor; to give the sensation of sweetness without sugar, of creaminess without cream, of whiskey or liqueur with only a tiny addition of alcohol; and to maintain their freshness in a product that is largely handled in bulk and exposed to air and oxidation for weeks.

Such impressive versatility and durability can be achieved only through the wonders of modern chemistry. To my knowledge, no flavoring used in whole-bean coffees is entirely natural and many are, in the technical sense, entirely artificial. The natural flavors used in many sophisticated soft drinks and ice creams, for example, would not have the staying power to remain with the coffee during its long odyssey from roasting plant to cup.

The people who create and market flavors for the specialty-coffee trade usually provide flavors and fragrances for a variety of purposes and draw from a growing body of technical and aesthetic knowledge that includes aspects of physiology, chemistry, botany, and the long cultural traditions of flavor- and fragrance-making. Thus, the flavors added to whole-bean coffees are suggested by tradition, created by chemistry, and ultimately chosen by the roaster, who may further suggest new flavors or request custom modification of the old. Consequently, one roaster may carry a creamier version of hazelnut and another a nuttier or less assertive version, even though both purchase their flavors from the same vendor. Some roasters work closely with the flavor chemists, building a common vocabulary of reference. So even in this relatively artificially defined arena, specialty coffees still exhibit an individualism absent in most commercial products.

Flavoring Families

Flavor specialists often divide the flavors used in flavoring whole-bean coffees into four families. The vanilla-based group includes not only the various cremes and vanillas, but all the nut flavors, including the best-selling hazelnut, amaretto (almond), and macadamia. The majority of the public's favorites come from this group. Second in popularity are flavors based on chocolate. Third are flavors based on fruit (the favorite is coconut), and finally come flavors based on spice, notably cinnamon.

Marriage of Love or Convenience?

If you ask either flavor specialists or roasters what their goal is in flavoring coffee, they would unanimously declare that their hope is to enhance the coffee or achieve a balanced marriage of coffee and flavor. This may well be their goal, but if it really is a marriage, the flavoring part is definitely the spouse who does the talking. It would doubtless be possible to produce a flavored coffee in which the added flavor component is muted and understated, so evanescent that it merely whispers romantic innuendos to the unconscious; but with most flavored coffees I have tasted, the flavoring pretty much shouts, if not screams and has tantrums.

Marketing people tell me that consumers prefer it that way. Perhaps. Perhaps specialty roasters have two clienteles, a clientele that is genuinely attracted to coffee and loves its subtle range of sensual experience, and another clientele that simply likes to be surprised and entertained by interesting novelties. And perhaps marketing people listen too closely to the second group. It is interesting to note that hazelnut has come to the fore as the best-selling flavor for whole-bean coffee, despite the fact that it is not a flashy flavor like amaretto or piña colada and lacks the romantic associations of flavors like macadamia nut or passion fruit. In fact, hazelnut is a rather rich, quiet flavor that marries particularly well with coffee and allows some of the natural roast and flavor to come through. It may be that specialty-coffee consumers are ahead of the marketers, as often happens in a business that was created in part out of a rebellion against the domination of marketing over substance.

In Flavor or Against

Specialty roasters themselves divide into two camps on the issue of flavored coffees. Some, usually those who sell their coffees directly through their own stores, refuse to produce flavored coffees for a variety of reasons. The most frequently cited of these reasons: Flavored coffees do not taste good; their aggressive fragrances overpower other, more authentic aromas in a retail environment; and they contaminate the store grinders. Other roasters, usually wholesale roasters who need to please large, retail customers like supermarkets, have little choice in the matter. They produce flavored coffees because they must in order to stay competitive.

The taste issue is easily pinpointed: All flavorings added to whole-bean coffees leave a flat, metallic aftertaste. With some flavors this aftertaste is barely discernible; with others it is inescapable. And recall that the effect of a well-brewed cup of coffee does not stop at the point the cup is empty. The experience rings in the senses, humming just below the surface of consciousness for minutes, perhaps even hours, mingling agreeably with the stimulation of the caffeine. However immediate the first burst of pleasure from a good flavored coffee, its aftertaste never quite delivers the same resonance the aftertaste of an unflavored coffee does.

There are doubtless other, vaguer issues that come into play when a roaster or old-time coffee lover confronts a flavored coffee. Specialty coffee roasters and aficionados have always been the rebels and idealists of the coffee world, and I suspect that flavored coffees smack too much of commercial compromise and technological contrivance for them. There always comes a moment when dedicated coffee roasters and brokers begin talking about why they love the business, and the main point invariably seems to be there is always more to learn, more subtleties to be fathomed, more discoveries to be made. The coffee bean is an extraordinarily complex chemical system, with some five hundred chemical constituents already identified and, I am told, at least two hundred to three hundred more still not even known or named. It is this tiny but potent natural universe that draws one on and simultaneously both satisfies and tantalizes the senses and the mind.

However much intelligence and creativity goes into producing flavored coffees, they are still more cultural production than natural mystery. For many coffee lovers they are too predictable. If tasting natural coffees is rafting a wild river, then for coffee aficionados tasting flavored coffees is a little like taking the water slide in a suburban theme part.

From Coca-Cola to Coffee

There is a well-worked-out rationale among specialty roasters in regard to flavored coffees. This is the notion that they provide a comfortable transition to "real" coffees for consumers who were raised on soft drinks. The idea is that you graduate from cherry cola to hazelnut coffee to Guatemala. Supporters of this idea point out that the generation raised in the 1960s rejected coffee for several reasons: First, because coffee was seen as an establishment habit indulged in by over-the-hill fossils and warmongers; second, because coffee in the 1960s had become a lousy drink anyhow, competition and cost cutting having ruined it; and third, because bottled and canned cola drinks had become widely available as consistent and flavorful coffee substitutes. Thus, the theory runs, the continuity of the coffee-drinking tradition was broken, and subsequent generations now need to be wooed back into the coffee fold by ingratiating beverages like flavored coffees, which link high-quality coffee with more familiar and accessible flavors like chocolate, vanilla, and cinnamon.

There may be something to this theory. It would also account for the growing popularity of espresso drinks with milk, since those beverages, particularly when drunk with sugar, are much easier for the novice coffee drinker to enjoy than a cup of black, unsweetened, medium-roast coffee.

At any rate, people who do enjoy flavored coffees obviously should drink them and thumb their collective nose at the purists in the roasting room. If you are trying flavored coffee for the first time, you might want to start with one of the more popular varieties: one of the variants of hazelnut, for example; or an Irish creme, or a chocolate, macadamia nut, or amaretto; or one of the variants of coconut. An even more systematic approach might be to try one from each of the four flavor families I noted earlier: the vanilla and nut, the chocolate, the fruit, and the spice.

Flavoring Compromises and Alternatives

On the other hand, if you are already drinking flavored coffees and are interested in experimenting with the unadorned product, you might begin with one of the more distinctive single-origin coffees, particularly those that are striking in flavor yet not overpoweringly acidy: an Ethiopia Yirgacheffe, a Yemen, or a good Brazil Santos. Or try a moderately dark-roast version of one of these coffees and add a little cream or milk to your cup.

Or you might flavor that brewed coffee yourself. Rather than buy amaretto-flavored coffee, add a little actual amaretto or almond extract to your cup. Or try a drop or two of vanilla and a twist of orange peel.

In one of the companion volumes to this one, *Home Coffee Roasting: Romance & Revival,* I offer a chapter of recipes for adding completely natural flavorings to whole-bean coffee: orange zest, vanilla bean, and the like. Most people who have tried these recipes feel they produce a better-flavored cup than any of the artificially flavored coffees sold by specialty outlets.

A final note of warning to those who grind their own beans: Flavored coffees are liable to ruin grinders that use burrs rather than blades to process the coffee. The flavoring material clings to the burrs and complicates cleaning and is almost impossible to remove completely. In other words, once you grind French vanilla, you will continue to grind French vanilla for a while, whether you like it or not. And if you grind several flavored coffees in a row, you may begin to get a sort of combined, omnibus flavor out of your grinder no matter what you put into it. Even the little blade grinders need to be carefully cleaned after grinding a batch of flavored coffee so as not to contaminate the next lot.

6 HOW IT CAN MAKE THE WORLD BETTER

Coffee, people, and environment
Organic, shade-grown, fair-trade, and
sustainable coffees

Coffee ranks with oil and steel as one of the world's most intensely traded commodities. Many smaller countries depend on coffee for almost all of their foreign exchange. Millions of families worldwide depend on coffee for their livelihood. The majority are subsistence farmers who tend a few trees along with some chickens and vegetables and count on the coffee to bring them just enough cash to buy the few tools and staples they need to survive.

THE SPECIALTY-COFFEE STRATEGY

As the specialty segment of the coffee industry grows in power and sales figures, it has occurred to many people that niche marketing of specialty coffee can be a tool to help both coffee growers and coffee-growing countries lift themselves out of poverty. To put it simply, if coffee sells as a complexly marketed specialty beverage like wine rather than an anonymous, price-driven commodity like branded supermarket coffee, and if some of the premium paid for those complexly marketed specialty coffees actually makes it back to the pockets of subsistence growers rather than staying in the hands of marketers and dealers, then specialty coffee becomes part of a self-regulating, market-oriented solution to the rural poverty that haunts many parts of the tropics.

And, from an ecological point of view, coffee is a crop that is already easier on the environment than many competing crops. Most of the small subsistence farmers I described have never used agricultural chemicals, and grow their coffee mixed in with other crops and often in shade. I recall being in parts of Central America where it is difficult to pick out the coffee trees from the rest of the random tangle of fruit trees and vegetables. Even traditional larger farms with neatly tended shade trees and windbreaks tend to be far more ecologically sound in their agricultural practices than large farms that grow many other cash crops. Consequently, specialty coffee also offers the opportunity for concerned consumers to reward environmentally sound agriculture and discourage destructive practices.

In the very broadest sense, every time you buy a coffee on the basis of origin from a specialty vendor rather than on the basis of price from a supermarket you are supporting a market-based solution to tropical poverty and environmental degradation. In fact, you are helping everyone. You are helping yourself to better coffee and a more expressive choice of coffee; you are helping a college-student clerk work at something slightly more interesting than taking orders at a fast-food outlet; you are helping roasters, dealers, and exporters lead more interesting lives based more on shared passion than on pure number crunching; and you are recognizing and rewarding the hard work of mill operators and growers.

All of this for a few cents more per cup.

SPECIFIC REMEDIES: CAUSE COFFEES

However, coffee buyers can be even more specific in their support of subsistence growers and the environment. They can choose from a growing array of what, for lack of a better term, I call "cause coffees."

Subsistence farmer and his crop of coffee fruit, East Africa.

The Original Cause Coffees: Organics

The granddaddy of all cause coffees, and still the most impeccable in its credentials, is the organically grown category. Organics, as they are called in the coffee business, are coffees that are certified by third-party agencies as having been propagated, grown, processed, transported, stored, and roasted without contact with synthetic chemicals—particularly without contact with pesticides, herbicides, and various other-cides. The certification process is lengthy, thorough, rather expensive, and, so far as I am able to determine, largely reliable and free of abuse.

The organic movement is fueled in part by consumers' health concerns. People are understandably wary of consuming agricultural poisons along with their vegetables. With coffee, however, the health issue is less persuasive than it is with most other agricultural products—apples or carrots, for example, which we consume whole and often raw. We do not consume the fruit of the coffee tree. Instead, we strip the fruit off and compost it, retaining only the seed, which we then dry, roast at very high temperatures, grind, and soak in hot water. Subsequently we throw away the dried, roasted, ground seeds and drink the water. It seems unlikely that even the tiny amount of chemical residue that may or may not survive in the seed actually survives roasting and brewing to make it to the cup.

Early on, however, idealists in the coffee industry—people like Paul Katzeff of Thanksgiving Coffee; Gary Talboy, originally of Coffee Bean International; Karen Cebreros, one of the founders of Elan Organic Coffees; and David Griswold, one of the founders of Aztec Harvest—seized on the organic idea with a larger vision in mind. They saw that they could work with cooperatives of subsistence growers who had never used chemicals in their growing practices, help get these cooperatives certified as organic, and market their coffees directly to specialty roasters or consumers. By doing so they could assure the growers a premium for their coffee—organic coffee, like organic produce generally, retails for more than conventionally grown coffee—and make sure, through vertically integrated, direct marketing arrangements, that a good portion of that premium actually makes it back to the growers. Growers would make more money, take more pride in what they were doing, and the environmental advantages of organic procedures would be confirmed and institutionalized.

These early organic cooperative coffees—Aztec Harvest from Mexico, Inca Harvest from Peru, and others—were successful mainly on the basis of their stories. Their quality was often spotty, owing to the difficulty of bringing disciplined processing practices to large numbers of isolated subsistence farmers. Nevertheless, these pioneer organics were successful enough to encourage many other cooperatives, farms, mills, and, eventually, international development agencies to pursue the same strategy. Today we have large-scale, internationally supported efforts to establish organic cooperative coffees from Haiti, East Timor, Papua New Guinea, and Sumatra, joining the many similar efforts taking place in Latin American countries and elsewhere.

Joining organic coffees produced by progressive cooperatives are coffees grown on larger farms that have successfully converted to organic procedures. Although most of these farms are in Mexico, Central America, and Brazil, the idea will doubtless continue to grow and establish itself in other parts of the world.

As more organic coffees come on the market produced in a variety of contexts, the overall quality of organics improves. Today, some certified organic coffees rival the finest conventionally grown origins in quality and distinction.

Project and Donation Coffees

Another tack was also taken by early specialty-coffee idealists. A percentage of the purchase price of certain coffees was put back into development projects directly benefiting subsistence growers. Coffee Kids, founded by Bill Fishbein in 1989, was one of the earliest organizations to promote this approach. Coffee roasters and retailers either make direct contributions to Coffee Kids and its development projects or contribute a set percentage of the sales price of designated coffees or other products.

Roasting companies and retailers often make their own, direct sponsorship arrangements with coffee-growing communities. A roasting company may market a cooperative's coffee and return a percentage of the retail price directly to the community in support of various development efforts. These arrangements are typically well advertised by the companies that sponsor them, and justifiably so.

Shade-Grown and Bird-Friendly Coffees

Coffee is traditionally grown in shade in many, but certainly not all, parts of the world. In some places the arabica trees require protection from the tropical sun. In other, wetter places, shade is not practical because it encourages leggy, disease-prone trees. Shade

Members of a cooperative of peasant growers bringing in bags of freshly picked, organically grown coffee fruit, San Juan La Laguna, Guatemala.

may be provided by rows of carefully managed non-native trees that are often sterile to prevent their seeds from sprouting and competing with the coffee. In many parts of the world, however, shade is a serendipitous business, and coffee is grown by small farmers as one component in a rich jumble of native trees, fruit trees, legumes, and other vegetables. It is this kind of shade that scientists and birders discovered was providing particularly important habitat for migrating song birds, especially those that migrate through Central America.

Meanwhile, more and more shade coffee was being replaced or displaced by what environmentalists call "technified" coffees. These are coffees from recently developed hybrid varieties of arabica that grow well in full sun. These hybrid trees are disease resistant and bear more coffee faster than traditional varieties. They

also require more chemical fertilizers, pesticides, and fungicides, and may also display less quality and character in the cup.

The Smithsonian Institution has led a movement to define and certify coffees that are grown in the diverse, multispecies shade that prevails among many subsistence growers. The Smithsonian's well-organized, well-publicized effort has been met with anger and hurt among many coffee growers with larger farms who feel that they are being ecologically responsible, but who feel, for a variety of reasons ranging from economic (high labor costs) to climatic (too much rain and cloud cover), that they cannot grow their coffee in dense, multispecies shade.

As I write, the debate concerning a proper definition for "shade-grown" is working its way through E-mails and coffee conferences, hopefully toward a defintion that is both fair and environmentally sound. As it is now, the only existing certification procedure is very limited. The Smithsonian Institution licenses certified organic coffees that also meet Smithsonian criteria for growth under a biodiverse shade canopy. Such ultimately environmentally correct coffees are permitted to use the Smithsonian Migratory Bird Center's "Bird Friendly" trademark. As for other, conventionally shade-grown coffees, you will have to take the seller's word in regard to their avian congeniality.

Fair-Traded Coffees

A Fair Trade Certified seal means that growers, usually subsistence growers, have been paid a reasonable, formula-defined price for their coffee. The fair-trade movement is quite prominent in Europe, less so in the free-trading, price-busting United States.

Sustainable and ECO-O.K. Coffees

The latest and most ambitious initiative by coffee idealists is the sustainable coffee movement, a big-tent effort to bring together everyone from cranky connoisseurs to birders, health fanatics, and social progressives. The goal is to rally them in common cause against the coffee-as-faceless-commodity system that, in its anonymous emphasis on price alone, is the ultimate cause of coffee's exploitation of both human beings and environment.

One version of the sustainable vision has been implemented by the Rainforest Alliance, whose ECO-O.K. seal certifies that ECO-O.K. inspectors have found that qualifying coffee farms and mills meet a wide variety of environmental criteria, including wildlife diversity, nonpolluting practices, and responsible and limited use of agrochemicals, as well as social and economic criteria that support the welfare of farmers and workers.

Unfortunately, the current sustainable movement offends some supporters of organically grown coffees, who feel that the sustainable idea is a warm, fuzzy rip-off that dilutes everything they have worked for. It also bothers quality-oriented purists, who feel that the only criterion for selling coffee should be how good the coffee tastes in the cup. Time will tell whether the inclusive goals of the sustainable movement can be turned into a practical system with clear and verifiable criteria satisfactory to coffee's many passionate voices and communities.

99

7 ROASTING IT

How coffee is roasted
Formula vs. eye, ear, and nose
How to roast your own

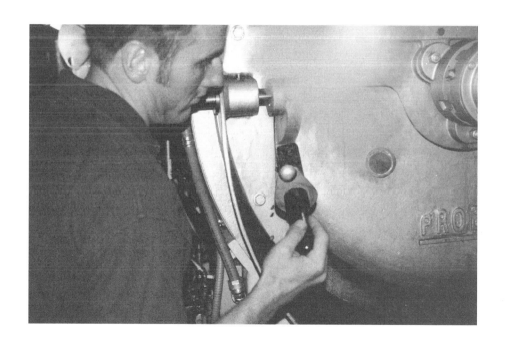

Since we have come to associate the word coffee so absolutely with a hot, aromatic brown liquid, some may find it hard to believe that human beings apparently waited for several hundred years before concluding that the most effective way to get what they wanted from the coffee tree was to roast the dried kernel of the fruit, grind it, and combine the resulting powder with hot water to make a beverage. The alternative solutions are many, and some apparently still survive as part of the cuisines of Africa and Asia. The berries can be fermented to make a wine, for example, or the leaves and flowers cured and steeped in boiling water to produce a coffee-tea. In parts of Africa, people soak the raw beans in water and spices, then chew them like candy. The raw berries are also combined with bananas, crushed, and beaten to make a sort of raw coffee and banana smoothie.

In Yemen, where coffee was first cultivated as a commercial crop, the husks of the dried coffee fruit are boiled with spices to produce a sweet, light beverage called *qishr*. It is served cool as a thirst quencher in the afternoon, much as we might serve iced tea.

The key to the success of the current mode of coffee making is the roasting process, to which we owe the delicately flavored oils that speak to the palate as eloquently as caffeine does to the nervous system. "The coffee berries are to be bought at any Druggist," says a seventeenth-century English pamphlet on coffee drinking, "about three shillings a pound; take what quantity you please and over a charcoal fire, in an old pudding pan or frying pan, keep them always stirring till they be quite black, and yet if you exceed, then do you waste the Oyl, which only makes the drink; and if less, then will it not deliver its Oyl, which must make the drink."

We may disagree with the Englishman's taste in roasting ("quite black" sounds more Neapolitan than English), but he knew what counted: the breaking down of fats and carbohydrates into an aromatic, volatile, oily substance that alone produces the essential coffee flavor and aroma. Without roasting, the bean gives up its caffeine and acids, and even its protein, but not its flavor.

THE ROAST TRANSFORMATION

The chemistry of coffee roasting is complex and still not completely understood. This is owing to the variety of beans, as well as to the complexity of the coffee essence, which still defies chemists' best efforts to duplicate it in the laboratory.

Much of what happens to the bean in roasting is interesting but irrelevant. The bean loses a good deal of its moisture, for instance, which means it weighs less after roasting than before (a fact much lamented among penny-conscious commercial roasters). It loses some protein, about 10 to 15 percent of its caffeine, and traces of other chemicals. Sugars are caramelized, which contributes color, some body, and sweetness, complexity, and flavor to the cup.

Roasting is simple in theory: The beans must be heated, kept moving so they do not burn or roast unevenly, and cooled, or quenched, when the right moment has come to stop the roasting. Coffee that is not roasted long enough or hot enough to bring out the oil has a pasty, nutty, or breadlike flavor. Coffee roasted too long or at too high a temperature is thin-bodied, burned, and industrial-flavored. Very badly burned coffee tastes like old sneakers left on the radiator. Coffee roasted too long at too low a temperature has a baked flavor.

During the early part of the roast, the bean merely loses free moisture, moisture that is not bound up in the cellular structure of the bean. Eventually, however, the deep-bound moisture is forced out, expanding the bean and incidentally producing a snapping or crackling noise. So far, the color of the bean has not changed appreciably (it should be a light brown), and the oil has not been volatilized. Then, when the interior temperature of the bean reaches about 370°F, the oil suddenly begins developing. This process is called *pyrolysis*, or volatilization, and it is marked by darkening in the color of the bean.

At some point after pyrolysis sets in, but before the bean is terminally burned, the moment of truth arrives for the roastmaster, because the pyrolysis of the coffee essence must be stopped at precisely the right moment to obtain the degree of roast and associated flavor desired. The beans cannot be allowed to cool of their own accord or they may overroast. With smaller-scale equipment the cooling may be managed by fans that pull room-temperature air through the hot beans while they are stirred, a procedure called air quenching. Larger roasting machines may permit the roastmaster to water-quench the beans, or kick off the cooling process with a brief spray of water. If the water quenching is done properly and discreetly, the water evaporates immediately from the surface of the hot beans and does not adversely affect the flavor of the coffee. In fact, coffee that has been correctly water-quenched often tastes better than air-quenched coffee because the cooling is more decisive.

ROASTING EQUIPMENT

When delivered to the roaster in burlap sacks, the coffee bean ranges in color from light brown to whitish green to a lovely bluish emerald green. The beans are always stored in their raw, or green, state. Roasted whole beans begin to deteriorate in flavor within days after roasting, and ground coffee may taste stale within an hour of grinding; whereas green coffee, stored in cool, dry, well-ventilated conditions, remains stable for years.

The exact nature of the equipment used to roast coffee depends on the ambitions of the roaster. Most large commercial roasters resemble a gigantic screw rotating inside a drum. The screw works the coffee down the drum; by the time the coffee reaches the end of the drum, it is roasted and ready to be cooled by air or water. The temperature is controlled automatically, and the roaster includes equipment that monitors both the air temperature and the temperature inside the moving mass of beans to monitor their progress. Such roasters are called continuous roasters for obvious reasons and are inappropriate for specialty coffee roasting because they cost too much, roast too much coffee at a time, and cannot be easily stopped to reload with new and different kinds of coffee.

The average specialty roaster uses a batch roaster, which simply means any machine that roasts a batch of coffee at a time rather than the same coffee for most of the day. The most common design of batch roaster consists of a rotating drum above a heat source, usually a gas flame. Operating like a Laundromat clothes drier, the rotating drum tumbles the beans, ensuring an even roast, while convection currents of heated air move through the drum. Drum roasters may be as large as five or six feet in diameter, or as small as a small waste can set on its side.

To the right is an illustration of the simplest kind of small drum roaster. The drum (A) tumbles the roasting coffee over the gas flame (B). The fan (C) sucks the smoke and chaff out of the drum. When the beans are dumped into the cooling box (D), ready to be quenched, the fan is reversed, and cool air is forced through the hot beans in the box.

More sophisticated batch roasters retain the basic structure of drum, heat, and cooling box, but may use a stronger current of hot air to heat the beans, so that the metal drum itself remains relatively cool. These are sometimes called convection roasters. Another kind of recently developed batch roaster uses radiant heat panels on either side of the drum. Some contemporary roasters, called fluidized-bed roasters, carry the hot air principle of convection roasters even further by dispensing with the drum entirely and agitating the beans with a column of hot air, much as an electric popcorn popper does with corn kernels.

In all cases, the goal of the technology is to offer the operator maximum control over the process, and to keep the beans from touching hot metal for anything longer than a split second at a time to prevent scorching or uneven roasting. Proponents of the various styles of batch roaster all make cogent arguments for their

The simplest kind of small, traditional drum coffee roaster. The drum (A) tumbles the roasting coffee over the gas flame (B). The fan (C) maintains a convection current of hot air through the drum that carries away smoke and chaff. When the roast is ready to be terminated, the hot beans are dumped into the cooling box (D) where the fan pulls room temperature air through them.

favored system and in mild deprecation of rival approaches, but to my knowledge no conclusive comparative tests have ever been conducted to validate any of these claims and counterclaims. In my observation and experience, all batch-roasting apparatus, including the oldest and crankiest, can produce outstanding coffee if used with care and knowledge.

John Weaver of Peet's Coffee & Tea watches just-roasted beans tumble out of roasting drum into cooling tray.

A battery of small drum roasters used to prepare coffee samples for cupping, Old Tavern Estate, Jamaica.

ROASTING PROCEDURE: FORMULA VS. EXPERIENCE

Roastmasters tend to fall into two schools: technical roasters, who follow a system involving precisely defined and monitored variables like time and temperature, and craft roasters, who depend mainly on eye, ear, nose, and accumulated experience.

Roasting by Instrument

The key to technical roasting is an electronic thermometer or heat probe designed to rest inside the bed of beans as they roast. Since degree or darkness of roast precisely reflects the internal temperature of the roasting beans (think of the thermometers you stick into roasting turkeys or meat), the heat probe permits the roastmaster to follow the development of the roast inside the machine with confidence. A second heat probe registers the temperature of the air inside the roasting chamber. The roastmaster, using various formulas that define the optimum relationship between these two temperatures plus information regarding air velocity inside the roasting chamber, profiles the roast, adjusting temperature ratios and air velocity to control the intensity of the pyrolysis and the length of the roast. And, I might add, profoundly influencing how the coffee eventually tastes, because two batches of the same coffee roasted to exactly the same degree of roast but using two different profiling strategies will taste dramatically different.

Roasting by Eye, Ear, and Nose

Craft roasters also profile coffees, adjusting temperature and air velocity inside the roasting chamber as the roast progresses. However, their adjustments are based not on formula but on long experience with roasting generally, with roasting specific coffees, and with the peculiarities of their machines.

Internal bean temperature is not the only way to tell what is going on inside a roasting machine. Roasting coffee signals its internal changes by a number of rather dramatic external signs. As well as changing in color, roasting coffee speaks to the roaster by emitting a crackling sound at two very predictable moments in its development—the "first crack" when pyrolysis begins, and the "second crack" when the woody matter of the bean begins to transform and the beans start to enter the pungent, bittersweet realm of darker roasts. When craft roasters speak about a specific green coffee and how to roast it, for example, they speak in terms of the crack—just before the second crack, just at the second crack, just into the second crack, well into the second crack, and so on.

The changing smell of the roasting smoke also tracks the development of the roast, starting with a bready smell before the first crack, to a fuller, sweeter, more rounded scent between the first and second cracks, to a pungent, sharper, oilier odor during the second crack. The best old-time craft roasters can control the roast quite accurately based on the smell of the roasting smoke alone.

Neither technical roasters with their thermometers and formulas nor craft roasters with their eye, ear, nose, and accumulated experience necessarily produce the best coffee. But both produce far better coffee than people who "just roast 'em till they're brown," or relative newcomers who think they are craft roasters but are not. True craft roasting demands long training and experience. The average accountant or English major with no coffee experience who decides to open a store and roast coffee is best served by taking a seminar on technical roasting and installing a heat probe in his or her new roasting machine.

A CRAFT ROASTER REMEMBERED

As for a craft roaster of the old school, I recall the old Graffeo coffee shop in San Francisco, locally famous for its rich, sturdy espresso coffee. In years past, Graffeo coffee was roasted in a small, old-fashioned batch roaster by John Repetto, the father of the present proprietor and a craft roaster if there ever was one.

Three open bags of green coffee stood next to the roasting machine. Two contained coffees from South and Central America, one with lighter and the other with heavier body. The third bag was a mix of several bright, distinctively flavored coffees: Yemen Mocha, Kenya, or Ethiopia Yirgacheffe, for instance. Repetto would nonchalantly scoop almost equal parts of each into the rotating drum of the roasting machine, close the door, and turn up the flame. He then wandered around the store, waiting on customers and following this timetable, which anyone who roasts coffee at home would be wise to follow as well:

1. Coffee smells like the sack (do something else for a while).
2. Coffee smells like bread (do something closer to the roaster).
3. The beans begin to crackle (prepare for action).

When he heard the beans crackle, Repetto would begin to check the color of the beans by collecting a few with a little spoonlike implement called a trier, which he stuck through an opening in the front of the roasting cylinder. He also sniffed the odor of the beans that wafted from the trier and kept his ear open for the second crack.

Just into the second crack, when the color was medium dark brown (the shop sold and still sells mainly dark-roast coffee), he opened a door in the cylinder and the beans tumbled out into the box in front of the roaster. The roasting continued inside the steaming, crackling beans for a moment or two while Repetto stirred them and studied them for color. When they were dark brown ("the color of a monk's tunic"), he tripped a lever on the side of the fan box, forcing cold air up through perforations at the bottom of the box to conclude the roast.

Some Years Later . . .

Much excellent specialty coffee is still roasted in similarly informal fashion in similarly charming old machines. I recall revisiting the Graffeo shop, however, and finding the old roasting machine holding up plants in the store window while John's son, Luciano, wearing a white smock, watched dials on the front of a chrome box.

I recognized this box as a Sivitz roaster, the creation of Michael Sivitz, a well-known coffee researcher and technical writer who had gone into the business of producing his own roasting equipment based on the fluidized-bed principle mentioned earlier, a principle that Sivitz pioneered. Rather than rotating the beans inside a cylinder, fluidized-bed machines use a powerful column of hot air to both roast and agitate the beans. Sivitz also was one of the pioneers of technical roasting in the United States and one of the first to install heat probes in small batch roasters.

Coffee from the Sivitz machine with its heat probe tasted good, and so did coffee from the old machine.

Roasting coffee in Ethiopia for a village coffee ceremony.

The uniting principle here is that both John and Luciano cared about what they were doing and roasted with tact and precision.

ROASTING AT HOME

Those who want to be certain their coffee is fresh—in fact, anyone who wishes to drink the best cup of coffee possible—may want to experiment with roasting coffee at home. Home roasting takes about as much time and skill as cooking spaghetti and is considerably simpler than other, more fashionable back-to-basics activities, such as baking bread or making beer. Any small mistakes in the roasting process are far offset by the advantages of freshness.

Ground, roasted coffee is actually as much a convenience food as instant coffee or frozen foods are. Americans roasted their own coffee until the late-nineteenth century, and many people all over the world still do. Jabez Burns, inventor of the continuous roaster, the first modern production roaster, insisted that some of the best coffee he ever tasted was roasted in a corn popper. On a recent visit to the Ethiopian countryside I was treated almost daily to servings of coffee that had been roasted on the spot in shallow pans over coals, and that coffee, despite what appeared to be a scattering of black, overroasted beans, invariably tasted superb.

Home-Roasting Methods

The physical requirements for roasting coffee correctly are very simple: the coffee needs to be kept moving in air temperatures of at least 400°F and must be cooled at the right moment. There are many ways to meet these requirements in home kitchens, which can be divided into four main approaches: (1) in the oven; (2) on top of the stove; (3) in a hot-air popcorn popper; and (4) in a small, commercially produced, electric home roaster. Those who wish to experiment with one of the first three methods should purchase my *Home Coffee Roasting: Romance & Revival*, also published by St. Martin's Press. I give detailed instruction for each method and advise on improvising equipment.

Here, however, are a few words of advice and instruction in regard to the fourth and easiest alternative, commercially produced, home-roasting machines. Most of these devices work on the fluidized-bed principle, meaning the beans are simultaneously heated and agitated by a column of hot air jetting up through the roasting chamber.

Three Home-Roasting Machines

At this writing three such devices are on the market, retailing from $100 to $140: the Fresh Roast Coffee Bean Roaster, Hearthware Gourmet Coffee Roaster, and Hearthware Precision Coffee Roaster. If you have difficulty finding a source for these devices, see Sending for It. All are easy to use, though they roast a relatively small volume of beans per session. All incorporate a glass roasting chamber, enabling you to observe the changing color of the beans; a chaff collector at the top or back of the roasting chamber to prevent the brown flakes that roasting removes from coffee beans from blowing around the kitchen; and an adjustable timer, which controls the length of the roast by automatically triggering a cooling cycle. The controls for the Hearthware Gourmet and Fresh Roast units allow the user to manually override the timer, an important feature.

The Tricky Part: Timing the Roast

The only trick with these devices is to learn when to stop the roast to get the darkness of roast and hence the taste you prefer. The longer the green beans roast, the darker the color and the deeper and less bright the taste. Because batches of green coffee beans differ from one another in density and moisture content, it is impossible for the manufacturers (or for me) to specify exact roasting settings or times.

The Experimental Approach

One way to approach timing the roast is to roast a batch of beans on the Medium setting, brew the result, and fine-tune the setting from there for subsequent batches, based on whether you want a sweeter, richer, more pungent taste (set the timer for a longer roast) or a brighter, drier, brisker taste (set the timer for a shorter roast).

When you arrive at a setting that produces a roast that satisfies you, make a note of it. You should be able to set the timer to the same point and obtain similar results for subsequent roast sessions. However, every time you buy a new batch of green beans you probably will need to experiment again, modifying the setting slightly to produce your preferred roast color and taste. Decaffeinated beans and aged beans,

both of which start out brown and roast either very quickly (decaffeinated beans) or very slowly (aged beans), may require particularly watchful experimentation to obtain a satisfactory roast.

The Imitate-the-Color Approach

Another, less hit-or-miss approach involves putting a handful of beans from a coffee store roasted to the degree or color you prefer on the counter next to the machine. You then start the roast at the maximum Dark setting, watch the raw beans through the glass as they roast until they are just slightly lighter than your sample beans, and at that point manually override the timer by advancing the timing dial to Cool or by pushing the appropriate roast-stopping button.

With some particularly dense or moist beans you may need to turn the timing dial back (or add time to the roast cycle with digitally controlled models) to prolong the roast long enough to achieve the darkness of roast you favor. One of the three currently available fluidized-bed devices, the Fresh Roast, has a switch that slightly increases the heat in the roasting chamber to facilitate achieving darker roasts. When using the Fresh Roast, I suggest you start your roasting experiments by placing this switch on the Dark setting and the timer on Medium. If, after tasting the resulting roast, you want a brighter, drier, brisker taste, move the switch to Light.

Again, after you have determined the right length of time to roast a given batch of beans to the style you prefer, you should be able to set the timer and walk away for subsequent roast sessions. Nevertheless, you probably still will need to hover over the roaster once again to determine the appropriate setting when you buy a new batch of beans. Again, decaffeinated beans and aged beans require particular attention.

Buying Green Coffee

All home-roasting machines come with order forms for green beans. Internet sites provide additional sources for green beans, including very exotic origins. If you need help finding an appropriate site, see Sending for It. Consult Chapter 5 for more on choosing beans by origin and blending them.

After the Roast

Always remove freshly roasted beans from the machine immediately after the cooling cycle has concluded. Leaving beans in a still-warm roasting chamber will dull taste. Freshly roasted coffee is at its best if it is allowed to rest for about twenty-four hours after roasting, permitting the recently volatilized oils to stabilize. If you are impatient or needy, however, grind immediately and enjoy.

Home-Roasting Precautions

Coffee roasting produces smoke. This smoke presents two problems: It can set off smoke alarms if not ventilated, and however pleasant it smells during roasting, it clings and becomes cloying over the long run. Always set up your home-roasting machine under the hood of your range and turn on the fan. In clement weather you can roast out-of-doors on porch or patio.

A second precaution: Always use exactly the volume of beans recommended by the manufacturer of your roasting device. Too many or too few beans may not agitate properly and may roast unevenly.

8　GRINDING IT

Keeping it fresh
Choosing the right grinder and grind

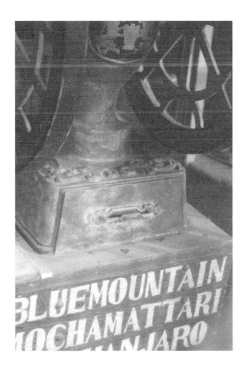

Every step of transforming green coffee into hot, brewed coffee makes the flavor essence of the bean more vulnerable to destruction. Green coffees keep for years, with only a slow, subtle change in flavor. But roasted coffees begin to lose flavor after a week, ground coffee an hour after grinding, and brewed coffee in minutes.

Traditional Arab, Ethiopian, and Eritrean cultures still have the best solution: roast, grind, brew, and drink the coffee all in the same sitting. The process takes close to an hour, however, so I do not expect it will catch on with urban professionals. Roasting your own coffee every three or four days is an excellent compromise, but most of us are too busy to take that step either and prefer to let others do the roasting for us.

KEEPING IT FRESH

Roasted whole coffee beans keep fairly well. The bean itself is a protective package, albeit a fragile one. Stored in a dry, airtight container to prevent contamination or contact with moisture, roasted whole-bean coffee holds its flavor and aroma for about a week. After two weeks, it still tastes reasonably fresh, but the aroma begins to slip; after three, the flavor starts to go as well. Whole-bean coffee kept past a month, though still drinkable, will strike the palate as lifeless and dead.

But if the natural packaging of the bean is broken—that is, if the coffee is ground—it goes stale in a few hours. The delicate oils are exposed and immediately begin evaporating. An airtight container helps, but not much. The oxygen and moisture shut inside with the broken coffee destroy the delicate oils, even if you never open the container again.

Canning coffee is one of the useless gestures typical of convenience foods. Essentially, the natural coffee package, the bean, is broken down and replaced with an inefficient, artificial package, the can. Furthermore, canned coffee is not only preground, but prestaled. Freshly roasted and ground coffee releases carbon dioxide gas. If the coffee were put in the cans fresh, the gas would swell even the strongest can and turn it into an egg-shaped time bomb. Various technological solutions have been found for this problem, but none is conducive to ensuring richly flavored coffee. When consumers break open the artificial package, they may find a coffee that is relatively fresh—but not for long. Since the small natural packages that make up a pound of ground coffee have already been broken, the oxygen that enters the can every time you peel off the plastic lid rapidly completes the job the canning process started.

So the easiest and most effective approach is to break down the beans as close as possible to the moment you want to use them—in other words, grind your coffee just before you brew it. Grinding coffee fresh takes very little time. Grinders are inexpensive and range from efficient electrics to picturesque replicas of old hand grinders. Grinding coffee fresh is the single best thing that you can do to improve the quality of your coffee.

STORING COFFEE

The ideal coffee routine for the urban home would be as follows: Buy the coffee as whole beans. Put the beans in an airtight container in a cool, dark place and take out only as much as you want to grind and brew immediately. Airtight means airtight: no recycled coffee cans or cottage cheese cartons with plastic lids. Rather, a solid glass jar with a rubber gasket inside the cap that gives a good seal.

Putting beans in the refrigerator is downright foolish, even if you use an airtight container. Moisture is the enemy of roasted coffee. The flavor "oils" in roasted coffee are not oils, but very delicate, volatile, water-soluble substances that moisture immediately dilutes and odors taint. Recall that refrigerators tend to be both moist and full of odors.

Freezing, however, is an excellent way to preserve whole-bean coffee if you do not intend to drink it within a week. Seal the beans in a freezer bag, put the bag in a part of the freezer that does not lose temperature every time you open the door, and remove only as many beans as you intend to consume in a day, returning the rest to the freezer. Thaw the liberated beans before grinding and brewing.

GRINDING YOUR OWN

Despite the pretensions of modern technology, there are still only four ways to grind coffee. The oldest is the mortar and pestle. The next oldest is the millstone, updated to steel burrs or corrugated plates. The next is the roller mill, which is used only in giant commercial grinders. The most recent is the electric blade grinder, which works on the same principle as an electric blender.

Grinders Using Steel Plates or Burrs

The earliest coffee drinkers broke up their coffee beans with a mortar and pestle, but very early in its history coffee began to be ground between the same millstones that the early peoples of the Middle East used to reduce grain to flour. Later, the Turkish-style coffee grinder evolved, a portable, specialized device similar in size and function to the contemporary pepper mill. Small, corrugated metal plates replaced the large millstones, creating a grinder technology that has never been improved upon. Many variations have been developed, including hitching the plates to an electric motor, but the principle remains the same.

The heart of the grinder consists of either two little corrugated metal disks or a corrugated metal cone that fits inside a second, hollow, corrugated cone. One element is stationary and the other is rotated by a handle or motor. The coffee is fed, a bean or two at a time, between the corrugated disks, where it is crushed until it drops out of the bottom of the grinder. This solution has never been improved upon because the grind is uniform and adjusting the space between the plates regulates the fineness of the grind accurately and consistently.

Hand Burr Grinders. The cheapest burr grinders are the wooden, hand-held models. The beans are fed through a little door in the top of the box, and the ground coffee falls into a drawer at the bottom. These grinders are adjustable for any except the finest grind. Most look like something out of a Dutch genre painting but are manufactured everywhere from Japan to New Jersey, and range in price from $10 to as much as $60. For a hand grinder that works well, however, you probably need to pay $40 to $50 for one of the Zassenhaus line of grinders. They impose a clean, northern European look on the box grinder and are technically excellent.

The box grinder presents several problems: The cheaper versions harbor small, inefficient burrs. In even the good ones, the crank may be too short for good leverage. Worst of all, the grinder tends to slide around on the table. One of the Zassenhaus designs solves this problem by introducing small indentations in opposite sides of the grinder, thus permitting you to sit and hold the grinder between your knees as you crank.

Hand grinders that can be mounted on the table or wall solve most of the problems posed by smaller, hand-held box grinders. They can be screwed down, have longer handles, and usually produce more uniform grinds because the grinding plates are larger. The best is a wonderful, early industrial-age-looking, cast-iron grinder available through Fante's in Philadelphia (around $60; see Sending for It).

Electric Burr Grinders. Here a small but noisy electric motor powers the burrs or steel plates. The big grinders in grocery and coffee stores work on this principle, as do the specialized espresso grinders in caffès.

Small household versions of these large grinders are produced by several manufacturers. The less expensive models by Braun, Capresso, Bunn, and others ($40 to $60) work well with all brewing devices except espresso brewers that use a pump or piston to push the hot water through the coffee. Pump and piston espresso machines (Categories 3 and 4, pages 180–86 require a more expensive, specialized espresso grinder ($120 to $300) that allows you to modulate the fineness of the grind to match the pressure exerted by the brewing water.

All burr grinders, regardless of size and price, work approximately the same way. A receptacle at the top of the grinder stores a supply of beans. When you activate a timer, beans feed automatically, a few at a time, through the burrs, which spray the ground coffee into a removable receptacle at the bottom front of the appliance. The timer shuts the grinder off automatically. These machines produce a more consistent grind than the cheaper electric blade grinders; they usually do not have to be fussed over while they grind, and they definitely do not need to be cranked by hand. You must be prepared, however, to clean the aperture for the ground coffee after every third or fourth use (some coffee stores sell a brush for this purpose; a small, still paintbrush works fine), and periodically to open the grinder and clean the burrs. If you grind oily, dark roasts, you may find that a brush is not enough for cleaning your grinder; you may have to literally carve the caked coffee from parts of your grinder when you carry out a major cleaning. Finally, burr grinders cannot be used successfully with flavored coffees. The flavoring liquids absorbed in the beans both gum up the burrs and taint subsequent batches of nonflavored coffees.

The warning signs that a small burr grinder needs cleaning are simple. If the coffee fails to come out or the motor seems to be working too hard, you need to clean the aperture where the ground coffee sprays out. If the coffee beans refuse to feed smoothly, you need to run the grinder empty on the coarsest setting or unscrew the top (see the instructions that come with your grinder) and do a thorough cleaning of the burrs and feed channel.

Specialized Espresso Grinders. The ultimate benefit of the electric burr grinder can be gained only by spending $100 to $300 on one of the large machines intended for use with home espresso machines. For committed espresso fanatics and owners of home pump or piston machines, these sturdy, reliable grinders are a necessity. For the general coffee enthusiast, they can grind coffee for all brewing needs. The least expensive is the Saeco MC 2002. The heavier home espresso grinders from Rancilio, Gaggia, and other Italian manufacturers all cost $200 or more. All of the machines I have tried in this class are strong, well-made appliances. I have used the same Saeco MC 2002 daily for years without problem.

Electric Blade Grinders

The third and most recent development in coffee grinding is original to the age of electricity. Two steel blades powered by a small electric motor whirl at ex-

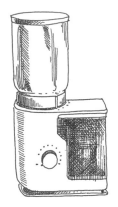

Top, electric burr grinder. Middle, hand box grinder. Bottom, electric blade grinder.

118

tremely high speed at the bottom of a cuplike receptacle and knock the coffee beans to pieces. With the burr method the fineness of the grind is controlled by the distance between the burrs, whereas with the blade method fineness is controlled by the length of time you let the blades whang away at the coffee. This makes the whole process a little hit and miss, unless you are so systematic you start timing the process.

If you aim for a fine grind with blade designs, grind in spurts of a few seconds each. It also helps to bounce the bottom of the grinder gently on the counter between spurts to tumble the partly ground coffee back down around the blades.

Blade Grinder Minuses. The disadvantages of blade grinders? Above all, they grind less consistently and predictably than do burr grinders. Even the less expensive burr grinders hold their setting well and give you the same grind day after day. Only the most attentive and compulsive among us are capable of achieving the same consistency with a blade grinder. For brewing methods using paper filters, minor inconsistencies in grind do not matter much. For plunger-style brewing, drip-brewing without filters, open-pot brewing, and espresso, all of which demand a more consistent grind for success, anyone who has taken the trouble to read this far will probably want the more predictable results obtainable either from the best hand grinders, like the Zassenhaus coffee grinders, or from a good electric burr mill, like the Capresso, Braun, Bunn, or Pavoni. Committed enthusiasts will want to go a step further and purchase one of the specialized $100 to $300 espresso grinders extolled earlier.

Blade grinders also cannot produce the extremely fine, powdery grind required for Turkish- or Middle Eastern-style coffee, for which, again, you need either a good hand grinder, such as the Zassenhaus, or one of the specialized "Turkish" hand grinders that look like large pepper mills. The best electric espresso grinders usually work for Middle Eastern coffee as well.

Another minor drawback to the blade grinder is the difficulty presented in getting the coffee out from under the little blades and into a brewer. You face the same problem when you clean the grinder.

Blade Grinder Pluses. The advantages of blade grinders are more succinctly stated: they are cheap, grind quickly, and don't take up much space in the kitchen. You also can use them to pulverize nuts and similar cooking ingredients, and, unlike burr grinders, they can be used with flavored coffees. Blade grinder features: replaceable blades (worthwhile), and a transparent top with a magnifying feature to help you see the grind (in my experience, useless).

HOW FINE THE GRIND

In general, grind coffee as fine as you can without clogging the holes of the brewer or turning the coffee to mud. The finer the grind, the more contact there will be between coffee and hot water, and the faster and more thoroughly the essential oils will be released, without activating harsher, less-soluble chemicals.

On the other hand, you do not want to grind your coffee to a powder because completely pulverizing it destroys the essential oil, which is partially vaporized by the heat and friction of the grinding process. Nor do you want to clog the holes in a coffee maker or filter, or fill your cup with sediment.

Some brewing methods have special requirements. Both Middle Eastern coffee (powdery grind) and espresso (extra fine grind) are special cases, as are open-pot (medium grind) and French press or plunger-pot coffee (coarse to medium grind). See the sections on these brewing methods in Chapters 9 and 11.

9   BREWING IT

Choosing a method and a machine
Brewing it right

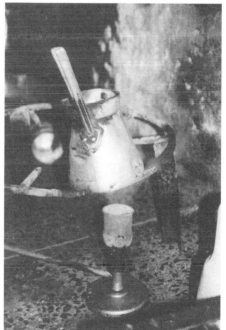

No matter what we call them, all ways of brewing coffee are basically the same: the ground coffee is soaked in the water until the water tastes good. Nobody, to my knowledge, has figured out a different way to make coffee. The only equipment you really need to make great coffee is an open pot, a flame, and possibly a strainer.

THREE VARIABLES, THOUSANDS OF IDEAS

It is a tribute to human imagination and lust for perfection, however, that the simple act of combining hot water and ground coffee has produced so many ingenious variations and occupied so many brilliant people for uncounted hours over the past three centuries. Thousands of coffeemakers have been patented in the United States and Europe, but of this multitude only a handful have had any lasting impact or embodied any genuine innovation. The few ideas to achieve greatness can be divided according to three variables: how hot you make the water, how you get the water to the coffee, and how you separate the spent grounds from the brewed coffee.

Brewing Temperature

Until the eighteenth century, coffee was almost always prepared by boiling the water and grounds. Boiling, however, damages coffee flavor because it vaporizes much of the coffee essence while it continues to extract other bitter-tasting chemicals. The French began steeping, as opposed to boiling, coffee in the early eighteenth century, but this innovation did not penetrate the coffee-drinking mainstream until the nineteenth century and had to wait until the twentieth to triumph. Today, all American and European methods favor hot water (around 200°F), as opposed to boiling.

If boiling water has been universally rejected, cold water has not. You can steep coffee in cold water and get substantially the same results as with hot water. The only differences are that the process takes longer (several hours longer) and makes an extremely mild brew. Cold-water coffee is made concentrated and, like instant, is mixed with hot water.

Getting the Water to the Coffee

The second variable—how you get the water to the coffee—is a question of convenience. If you are not in a hurry, you might just as well heat the water and pour it over the coffee yourself. But if you want to do something else while the coffee is brewing, you might prefer the hot water to deliver itself to the coffee automatically. Furthermore, coffee making requires consistent and precise timing, a virtue difficult to maintain in this age of distractions. The advantage to machines is their single-mindedness; they make coffee the same way every time, even if the cell phone rings.

The Bubble Power of Boiling Water. One of the earliest efforts at automation was the pumping percolator, patented in 1827 by Frenchman Nicholas Felix Durant. The French ignored it, but the United States, the cradle of convenience, adopted it enthusiastically. The pumping percolator uses the bubble power of boiling water to force little spurts of hot water up a tube and over the top of the coffee. The hot water, having seeped back through the coffee, returns to the reservoir to mix with the slowly bubbling water at the bottom of the pot. The process continues until the coffee is brewed.

Ironically, the principle of the automatic filter drip, which was destined to supplant the pumping percolator in the United States starting in the 1970s, was patented a few months earlier than the percolator. Jacques-Augustin Gandais, a Parisian jewelry manufacturer, patented a device that sent the boiling water up a tube in the handle of the brewer and, from there, over the ground coffee. Gandais's device even looks a bit like the first automatic, filter-drip brewers of the 1970s. It apparently was ignored for the same reason it was later enthusiastically adopted: It sent the water through the coffee only once, rather than repeatedly, as the pumping percolator did.

The Vacuum Principle. Around 1840, the vacuum principle in coffee brewing was simultaneously discovered by several tinkerers, including a Scottish marine engineer, Robert Napier. Napier's original device looks more like a steam engine than a coffeemaker, but, as it has evolved today, the vacuum pot consists of two glasses globes that fit tightly together, one above the other, with a cloth or metal filter between them. The ground coffee is placed in the upper globe, and water is brought to a boil in the lower. The two globes are fitted together and the heat is lowered. Pressure develops as water vapor expands in the lower globe, forcing the water into the upper globe, where it mixes with the ground coffee. After one to three minutes, the pot is removed from the heat, and the vacuum formed in the lower globe pulls the brewed coffee back down through the filter.

Twentieth-Century Refinements. The twentieth century has brought us both the automatic electric percolator and the automatic, filter-drip coffeemaker, an improved electric version of Gandais's 1827 device. In the automatic, filter-drip coffeemaker, the water is held in a reservoir above or next to the coffee, heated, and measured automatically over the ground coffee by the same bubble power that drives the percolator. The latest challenge to innovation in automated brewing is the microwave oven. The various (largely commercially unsuccessful) attempts at taking advantage of its unique technology have not broken new ground, however. The solutions proposed by appliance companies are all interesting variations on time-honored technologies, ranging from microwave oven pot to microwave vacuum and filter drip.

Separating Brewed Coffee from Grounds

Now we reach the brewing operation that has stimulated coffeepot tinkerers to their most extravagant efforts: the separation of brewed coffee from spent grounds. Again, original ideas are few, refinements endless. People in many places in the world—the Middle East, Eastern Europe, Indonesia—have the most direct solution: They simply let most of the grounds settle to the bottom of the cup or pot and drink whatever remains along with the brew.

The original coffee drinkers, the Arabs of what is now Saudi Arabia and Yemen, apparently ground their beans coarsely and strained the coffee into the cup. Ethiopians and Eritreans still use simple strainers, often little wads of horsehair stuck into the narrow opening of the coffeepot.

Europeans Rediscover Strained Coffee. By the time Europeans discovered coffee via the Turks, the settling-to-the-bottom-of-the-cup approach to separating grounds and brew was near universal. Filtering was not reintroduced into the mainstream of coffee culture until 1684, after the lifting of the siege of Vienna, when Franz George Kolschitzky opened central Europe's first café using coffee left behind by the routed Turks. Kolschitzky first tried to serve his booty Turkish style, but, according to legend, the Viennese resisted. They called it "stewed soot" and continued to drink white wine and lager with breakfast. But when Kolschitzky started straining the coffee and serving it with milk and honey, his success was assured. Within a few years the great café tradition of Vienna was well established. Strained or separated coffee has dominated European and American taste ever since.

The Ubiquitous Drip Method. A Frenchman named Jean-Baptiste de Belloy is credited with inventing the world's favorite technology for separating coffee from grounds, the drip pot, in 1800. Hot water is poured into an upper compartment containing the coffee and is allowed to drip through a strainer or filter into a lower compartment, leaving the coffee grounds behind. An impressive variety of refinements has been developed since, including the Neapolitan flip pot, cloth filters, and disposable paper filters.

The Plunger Method. One other method of separation deserves mention. After the coffee is steeped, a metal filter or strainer is forced down through the coffee like a plunger, pressing the coffee grounds to the bottom of the pot and leaving the clarified coffee above. There is no accepted generic name for this sort of brewer. Some call it a plunger pot, others French press, after the country in which it first became popular.

GENERAL CONSIDERATIONS FOR BREWING APPARATUS

Ideally, coffee brewers should be made of glass or porcelain. Stainless steel will do. If you have a choice in the matter, avoid aluminum. Food cooked in aluminum absorbs minute traces of the metal; coffee held in aluminum develops a metallic flatness. Add aluminum's tendency to pit and corrode, and I think there is ample reason to avoid this metal in a coffeemaker. Tin plate may also faintly taint the flavor of coffee.

A pot should be easy to clean. Coffee is oily, and accumulated oil eventually contributes a stale taste to fresh coffee. Stubborn brown stains in the corners can be soaked out with a strong solution of baking soda or one of the commercial urn cleaners on the market. Glass and porcelain are the easiest to clean; aluminum and tin-coated metal the hardest. It is wise to avoid pots with seams or cracks, especially in the parts that come in direct contact with the brewed coffee. Check to make sure you can take the whole apparatus apart easily for an occasional thorough cleaning. In areas with alkaline, or hard, water, a lime deposit builds up even in the parts of the maker that are untouched by coffee. The universal remedy is a strong solution of vinegar. Run it through the works of the brewer, then rinse thoroughly.

BREWING INJUNCTIONS

Now for the inevitable list of brewing rules and precepts.

- Grind the coffee as fine as you can make it without losing any through the holes in the filter of the coffeemaker. Never grind it to a powder. French press and conventional (nonfilter) drip require a medium to coarse grind.
- Use plenty of coffee: at least 2 level tablespoons or 1 standard coffee measure per 5- to 6-ounce cup. You may want to use more, but I strongly suggest you never use less unless your coffeemaker explicitly instructs you to. Most mugs hold closer to 8 ounces than 6, so if you measure by the mug use 2½ to 3 level tablespoons for every mug of water. Coffee brewed strong tastes better, and you can enjoy the distinctive flavor in your favorite coffee more clearly. If you brew with hard water or if you drink your coffee with milk, you should be especially careful to brew strong. If you feel that you are sensitive to caffeine, adjust the caffeine content of your coffee by adding some caffeine-free beans.

- Keep the coffeemaker clean and rinse it with hot water before you brew.
- Use fresh water, as free of impurities and alkalines as possible.
- Brew with hot water, as opposed to lukewarm or boiling water (Middle Eastern and cold-water coffees are exceptions). A temperature of 200°F is ideal, which means bringing the water to a boil and then waiting a minute or two before brewing. If you have done everything else right and you are in a rush, however, water that has just stopped boiling will not seriously damage a good, freshly ground coffee.
- In filter and drip systems, avoid brewing less than the brewer's full capacity whenever you can. If the pot is made to brew six cups, the coffee will taste better if you brew the full six.
- Some don'ts: Do not boil coffee; it cooks off all the delicate flavoring essence and leaves the bitter chemicals. Do not percolate or reheat coffee; it has the same effect as boiling, only less so. Do not hold coffee on heat for more than a few minutes for the same reason. Do not mix old coffee with new, which is like using rotten wood to prop up a new building.

Water Quality and Coffee Quality

Ninety-nine percent of a cup of coffee is water, and if you use bad, really bad, water, you might just as well throw away this book and buy a jar of instant. If the water is not pleasant to drink, do not make coffee with it. Use bottled water or a filter system. Hard, or alkaline, water does not directly harm flavor and aroma but does mute some of the natural acids in coffee and produces a blander cup with less dry brightness. Water that has been treated with softeners makes even worse coffee, however, so if you do live in an area with hard water, you might compensate by buying more acidy coffees (African, Arabian, and the best Central American origins) or by brewing with bottled or filtered water. Some automatic, drip coffeemakers come equipped with built-in filters. Although these integral filters are effective, they seem fussy and overspecialized to me. It might be better to buy a filtration system that can be used for all of your water needs, rather than one that is irrecovably stuck inside the coffee brewer.

BREWING METHODS AND MACHINERY

About 70 percent of the coffee consumed in the United States is brewed with paper filters, a method that produces coffee in the classic American style: clear, light-bodied, with little sediment or oil. Any other brewing method (except cold-water concentrate) produces a coffee richer in oils and sediments and heavier in flavor than the typical American cup of filter coffee. Those adventurers who experiment with other brewing methods should keep this difference in mind.

Open-Pot Brewing

The simplest brewing method is as good as any. You place the ground coffee in a pot of hot (just short of boiling) water, stir to break up lumps and saturate the coffee, strain or otherwise separate the grounds from the brewed coffee, and serve. Open-pot coffee is a favorite of individualists and light travelers. I had a sculptor friend who insisted on making his coffee in a pot improvised from a coffee can and a coat hanger. For such nonconformists, the challenge is separating the grounds from the coffee without stooping to the aid of decadent bourgeois inventions like strainers.

Bring the cold water to a boil and let it cool for a minute or so. Toss in the coffee. Use a moderately fine grind, about what stores call drip. Stir gently to break up the lumps and let the mixture steep, covered, for 2 to 4 minutes. If you are willing to compromise, obtain a very-fine-mesh strainer; the best are made of nylon cloth. Strain the coffee and serve. If you consider yourself too authentic for a strainer, pour a couple of spoons of cold water over the surface of the coffee to sink whatever grounds have not already settled. In theory, at least, the cold water, which is heavier than the hot, will carry these stubbornly buoyant pieces to the bottom.

For the lazy or less committed, some specialty stores sell a little nylon bag (about $5) that sits inside the traditional, straight-sided coffeepot, supported on the outside by a plastic ring. This simple device is a modern version of the Biggin pot, a device named after its early nineteenth-century English inventor. The Biggin pot was popular in England in the late-nineteenth and early twentieth centuries. It has the added advantage of permitting a much finer grind of coffee than traditional open-pot methods. You put the ground coffee in the nylon bag, pour hot water over it, and stir lightly to break up the lumps. In 2 to 4 minutes, you simply lift the bag and grounds out of the brewed coffee.

French press or plunger brewer.

French Press or Plunger Brewing

French press is essentially open-pot coffee with a sophisticated method for separating the grounds from the brew. The pot is a narrow glass or metal cylinder. A fine-mesh-screen plunger fits tightly inside the cylinder. You put coarse-to-medium-ground coffee in the cylinder, pour water just short of boiling over it, and insert the plunger in the top of the cylinder without pushing it down. After about 4 minutes, when the coffee is thoroughly steeped, you push the plunger through the coffee, clarifying it and forcing the grounds to the bottom of the pot.

The plunger pot was apparently developed in Italy during the 1930s, but found its true home in France after World War II, when it surged to prominence as a favored home-brewing method.

The growing popularity of this method in the United States has unleashed a flood of French-press brewers, most of them manufactured everywhere except France. A consumer's first decision in purchasing such a brewer is whether to spend a little money on a version that supports the glass, brewing receptacle in a plastic frame ($15 to $30), or to spend considerably more on a brewer with a metal frame ($40 to the totally unreasonable). A third alternative, and a good one, are designs that insulate the brewing receptacle to keep the coffee hot after brewing.

Complicating the decision is the enthusiasm with which the design community has embraced the French press. Its technical simplicity and potential as an after-dinner conversation piece has provoked an orgy of visual invention almost equaling the similar attention lavished on the designer teapot. Designer French presses range from inexpensive, urban-chic, plastic-framed units to understated, metal-sheathed designs that murmur money.

The plunger pot is an enthusiast's brewer. It appeals to those who like to dramatize their coffee making. With the plunger brewer, coffee is not an after-dinner option that emerges routinely from the kitchen. It is the product of a small but satisfying ceremonial event that unfolds at the table.

The coffee the plunger brewer produces is heavy and densely flavored. The subtle, aromatic notes present in fresh, well-made filter coffee are overwhelmed by a deep, gritty punch. Many coffee drinkers prefer such coffee; others may find it muddy and flat-tasting. Those who take their coffee with milk or cream may prefer it; those who drink their coffee black may not. Some may like it after dinner but not before. It is neither better nor worse than coffee made with filter paper, just different. Its heavyish flavor and dense body are owing to the presence of sediment, oils, and minute gelatinous material that chemists call colloids, all of which are largely eliminated by paper filters.

Style of coffee aside, the advantages of the plunger brewer are its drama, its portability, and its elegance, all of which make it an ideal after-dinner brewer. It is more difficult to clean than most drip or filter pots, and, unless you buy a design with an insulated decanter, the coffee must be drunk immediately, which is just as well, since coffee ought to be drunk immediately.

Another virtue of the plunger pot emerged with the development of the travel press, a one-serving French-press brewer the size of a tall travel mug. A good version is distributed by Bodum. With this commuter-friendly device, it is possible to pour the hot water over the coffee on your way out the door, depress the plunger in the car while waiting for the first traffic light, and drink the fresh coffee directly out of the mug/pot while you maneuver down the freeway.

When you brew with your plunger pot, take care to preheat it with hot water, and take care to use a medium-to-coarse grind. With a fine grind the plunger will become almost impossible to push down. Also be careful to press the plunger straight down. If you try to push from an angle, you are likely to break the glass decanter.

Drip Brewing Without Filters

Invented by a Frenchman, the drip pot was popularized by Benjamin Thompson, an eccentric American who became Count von Rumford of the Holy Roman Empire, married two rich widows, and spent much of his leisure time making enemies and coffee. The drip maker typically consists of two compartments, an upper and a lower, divided by a metal or ceramic filter or strainer. The ground coffee is placed in the upper compartment and hot water is poured over it. The brewed coffee trickles through the strainer into the lower compartment.

The traditional American, straight-sided, metal drip pot has gone out of fashion, but an attractive, French-silhouette, porcelain version can be bought through some specialty stores and catalogs.

Gold-plated mesh filter units that turn any appropriately sized receptacle into a drip brewer are available for about $10 to $20, depending on size. Some can be purchased with a matching insulated serving carafe. You drip the coffee through the gold mesh filter into the carafe. From a technical point of view, such filter-insulated carafe sets are superior to the traditional drip pot, since keeping the coffee hot during brewing is one of the challenges of drip brewing. Make sure you preheat the carafe, however.

Use a medium grind of coffee in a drip brewer. If the coffee drips through painfully slowly or not at all, or if you find more sediment in your cup than you prefer, try a coarser grind. Even with the correct grind, you may find that you occasionally need to tap or jostle the pot to keep the coffee dripping. When you pour the hot water over the ground coffee, make certain that you mix it lightly to saturate all of the coffee. Cover to preserve heat. Mix the coffee lightly again after it has brewed, since the first coffee to drip through is stronger and heavier than the last.

Traditional ceramic drip brewer.

Both drip and filter coffees often cool excessively during the brewing process. If you are not brewing into an insulated carafe, preheat the bottom half of the pot with hot tap water before brewing. If that is not enough, buy a heat-diffusing pad and keep the pot on the stove while brewing.

Flip-Drip or Neapolitan *Macchinetta* Brewing

A popular variation of the drip pot was invented in 1819 by Morize, a French tinsmith. This is the reversible, double, or flip-drip pot, which has since been adopted by the Italians as the Neapolitan *macchinetta*. Rather than being laid loosely on top of the strainer, as in the regular drip pot, the ground coffee is secured in a two-sided strainer at the waist of the pot. The water is heated in one part of the pot, then the whole thing is flipped over, and the hot water drips through the coffee into the other, empty (and

nicely warm) side. These devices make excellent drip-style coffee.

Several versions of the flip-drip pot are manufactured, but can be difficult to turn up. See Sending for It. An aluminum version is the cheapest (around $10). Since aluminum is an undesirable material for coffee brewers, I recommend instead a traditional-look copper version (around $40) or a contemporary-look stainless ($40 and up).

Pumping Percolator Brewing

Until about thirty years ago, the pop of a pumping percolator–producing coffee ranked with the acceleration of a well-tuned car as one of North America's best-loved sounds. Now the pumping percolator has gone the way of tail fins and bologna sandwiches. However reassuring the sensuous gurgle of a percolator is psychologically, chemically it means only one thing: the percolator is boiling the coffee and prematurely vaporizing the delicate flavoring oils. Every pop of the percolator means another bubble of aroma and flavor is bursting at the top of the pot, bestowing its gift on your kitchen rather than on your palate.

Opinions differ as to the extent of the damage that the percolator inflicts on coffee flavor. In 1974, when the pumping percolator was still holding off the automatic, filter-drip brewer, *Consumer Reports* served coded cups of drip and percolator coffee both to experts and to its staff. The experts unanimously and consistently preferred the drip coffee to the perked coffee, but the staff's reaction was mixed. I find I can invariably pick out perked coffee in a similar test by the slightness of its aroma and the flat, slightly bitter edge of its flavor. However, there are more ways to ruin coffee than to put it in a good pumping percolator; stale coffee, for instance, tastes bad no matter how you brew it. Freshly opened canned coffee brewed with care in a good pumping percolator tastes better than mishandled, three-month-old Jamaica Blue Mountain put through a filter.

If you must have a pumping percolator, a good electric is probably the best choice, since the heat is automatically controlled to produce perked rather than boiled coffee, and most electrics incorporate a thermostat intended to reduce the heat at the optimum moment to prevent overextraction.

Recall that in the vaccum filter method heat forces water from one sealed chamber into a second, where it mixes with the ground coffee. The vacuum created by the departure of the water from the first chamber then draws the now-brewed coffee back through a filter into the chamber. Because the manipulations involved in the vacuum brewing are a bit more complex than those demanded by the filter method, the vacuum pot has lost considerable popularity since its heyday in the 1920s and 1930s. But, for some, the leisurely and alchemical shifting of liquids in the two chambers has a continuing appeal.

Cultures that value ceremony are particularly fond of the vacuum filter. In Japan, for example, one-cup vacuum brewers are widely used in coffeehouses to custom-brew specialty "call" coffees. The heat is provided either by torchlike gas flames that shoot dramatically straight out of metal counters or by halogen

Vacuum brewer.

lamps that cast a mesmerizing glow up through the brewing coffee.

Furthermore, coffee brewed by the vacuum method often tastes fuller and richer than coffee brewed through paper filters, while remaining free of the grit that often mars the taste of French-press-brewed coffee. Perhaps for this reason, the vacuum pot is undergoing a bit of a renaissance among specialty coffee insiders.

Unfortunately, that renewal of interest is only marginally reflected in the range of vacuum pots currently available in the retail marketplace. As I write, the only vacuum brewers generally available in the United States are the simple, attractive, but rather flimsy six-cup Bodum (around $30) and large, relatively expensive ($170) Starbucks Barista Utopia. The Starbucks device represents a freshly imagined and engineered version of the vacuum brewer, with a programmable

Top, manual, pour-over, filter-drip cone and decanter. Bottom, automatic, filter-drip brewer.

heat source that automates the brewing procedure and turns the fussy old vacuum pot into a contemporary automated program-it-and-forget-it machine. Unfortunately, this admirably intentioned effort may

be too expensive to succeed in the contemporary marketplace. I hope that by the time you read these pages, someone will have supplied the market with the inexpensive, streamlined version of the vacuum pot that will succed in reviving this effective and charming brewing method.

FILTER-DRIP BREWING, AUTOMATIC AND OTHERWISE

Coffeepot tinkerers started using cloth filters around 1800; disposable paper filters came later and were never really popular until after World War II. The main objection to paper filters then and now is that they must continually be replaced. The main objection to cloth filters is that they get dirty and are difficult to clean. In this age of disposables, the paper filter has triumphed, but permanent filters, in nylon mesh or gold-plated metal, are currently making inroads. The use of permanent metal filters blurs the distinction between ordinary drip brewing and filter brewing since they essentially turn a filter-drip brewer into a nonfilter-drip brewer. The description and admonitions that follow refer to coffee brewed with paper filters, not with metal or nylon mesh filters.

Filter coffeemakers come in two basic versions: inexpensive (or nostalgic) manual designs in which you pour the water over the ground coffee yourself, and the ubiquitous automatic, filter-drip machines, which do the water pouring for you. Both fundamentally work the same way. A paper filter is placed in a plastic, glass, or ceramic holder; fine-ground coffee goes in the filter, and hot water, poured by you or the machine, goes into the filter. The coffee exits the filter into a carafe.

The advantages of filter brewing: It permits you to use a very fine grind of coffee and effect a quick, thorough extraction. The paper filters make the grounds easy to dispose of and the coffeemaker easy to keep clean. Because of their simplicity and popularity, both pour-over, manual filter devices and their automatic brethren are among the cheapest coffee-brewing devices on the market. Those who like a light-bodied, clear coffee free of oils, colloids, and sediment will enjoy a good filter coffee; those who like a heavier, richer brew will prefer other methods.

A Note on Filter Papers

Virtually all white filter papers manufactured today are whitened without use of dioxin, a carcinogen that was used in bleaching paper through the late 1980s. For this reason, I feel confident in recommending white filter papers in preference to brown, which impart a cardboardy taste to the brewing water and which may harbor some dubious chemicals of their own, including tars.

Permanent, Nonpaper Filters

A note on permanent filters: I do not recommend cloth filters, since they are difficult to keep clean. Gold-plated permanent filters, in both standard Melitta wedge and basket styles, are excellent products, but, if you like filter coffee, you may not like coffee made with these filters as much as you like coffee brewed with paper filters. The mesh allows a good deal of sediment and colloids to enter the brewed coffee, which gives it a heavy, often gritty taste, closer in style to French-press coffee. Permanent filters also require a coarser and more uniform grind to work correctly.

Manual, Pour-Over Filter Brewing

Fewer and fewer people choose to pour the water over the coffee themselves when automatic, filter-drip brewers sell for as little as $15 or $20. Reasons to pour yourself: The basic plastic cone-and-glass decanter set is still the cheapest brewing device on the market, short of a tin can and coat hanger; pour-over units do not require counter space, you can be absolutely sure all the ground coffee is saturated because you are doing the pouring yourself; and you can congratulate yourself on being a coffee purist.

Most important, however, you can stir the water and grounds in the cone as they steep. This last possibility is of great importance to some aficionados. I live in an area dominated by the cult of Peet's Coffee, and friends often ask me why, when they get their pound of Major Dickason's Blend home, they cannot get it to taste like the extraordinarily deep-bodied but clear-tasting drip coffee they drink at Peet's stores. For two reasons, I tell them. First, they need to brew extremely strong (about 3 tablespoons of ground coffee to every 5- or 6-ounce cup); and second, they need to stir the grounds as they steep, an impossible action with automatic, filter-drip brewers. So if you do prefer a coffee almost as full-bodied as French press but without the French-press grit, you may need to experiment with a manual, pour-over brewer. After you saturate the grounds, stir them with a long-handled spoon until most of the coffee has exited the filter.

The disadvantages to manual, pour-over, filter-drip brewers? In addition to the obvious inconvenience of heating and pouring the water yourself, it is also very difficult to keep the coffee hot. You need to either preheat the decanter and drink the coffee immediately, keep the decanter atop an electric warmer or other heating device, or brew directly into a preheated, insulated decanter, probably the best approach.

At the most democratic end of the price-design spectrum for manual, pour-over brewers are simple plastic filter holders, sold either with matching decanter or without. More costly and more idiosyncratic are various models of the nostalgic, defiantly impractical Chemex, the ancestor of all American filter-drip brewers. The Chemex was developed from, and still resembles, a well-made piece of laboratory equipment. Many find its austere design (honored by the Museum of Modern Art in New York) and authentic materials (glass and wood in the traditional models) attractive, but the single-piece hourglass shape makes cleaning difficult. Another classic option is a matching porcelain cone and decanter from Melitta with classic, rounded lines reminiscent of traditional French-drip pots. Fante's in Philadelphia (see Sending for It) is a good last-resort source for exotic filter-drip models like both the Chemex and the Melitta porcelain design.

Suggestions for Manual, Pour-Over Filter Brewing. Careful brewing can make a considerable difference in the quality of filter coffee. Bring cold water to just short of boiling and pour a little over the grounds, making sure to wet all the coffee. Pour the rest of the water through. If you want a particularly strong, rich cup, stir the water and grounds as they steep and drip. Stir the coffee in the decanter lightly after brewing. If you make a small quantity, less than four cups, use slightly more ground coffee to compensate for the flavor lost to the filter, and wet the filter before you put in the ground coffee. Always preheat decanter and cups by rinsing them in hot water. If possible, brew into a preheated, insulated carafe.

Automatic, Filter-Drip Brewing

Convenience and a clear, transparent cup seem to have driven the success of the automatic, filter-drip brewer, which in the years since its introduction in the early 1970s has become America's favorite brewing device. The heart of the system is the familiar paper filter, filter holder, and decanter. The machine simply heats water to the optimum temperature for coffee brewing and automatically releases it into the ground coffee in the filter. The brewed coffee drips into the decanter, while an element under the decanter keeps the coffee hot once it is brewed. You measure cold water into the top of the maker, measure coffee into the filter, press a switch, and, in from 4 to 8 minutes, obtain 2 to 12 cups of coffee.

Furthermore, the manufacturers of these brewers have considerably improved their performance over the past fifteen years. Most of the leading makers have resolved such problems as ground coffee floating or forming a doughnut around the edge of the filter basket, variations in water temperature, and excessively slow or fast filtering.

Some years ago I was certain that I could make better filter coffee than any of these machines could simply by pouring the water over the coffee myself by hand. Now I am not so sure. Even the cheapest, mass-marketed machines have improved, with most of the egregious performers of yesteryear eliminated from the shelves. A rather rigorous 1999 test in which I took part turned up no bad performers whatsoever among the models tested. Furthermore, the low-end, mass-marketed brewers performed almost as well as a selection of more expensive, high-end models. It appears that the main criteria for choice in these brewers are appearance, the prestige of the manufacturer's name, and, above all, an impressive and often baffling array of special features.

Automatic, Filter-Drip Special Features. Following is a list of special features that attempt to lure buyers to spend more than $15 or $20 on a basic automatic, filter-drip coffee brewer. Some features are very useful; others seem like marginal marketing gimmicks.

- A pause feature enables you to temporarily interrupt the brewing cycle to pour a cup of coffee. This is a very useful feature, given that coffee drinkers are not known for their patience.
- An under-the-cabinet design saves space by allowing you to mount the machine beneath a kitchen cabinet, suspended over the counter. Obviously, only you can decide on the usefulness of this feature.
- A thermos carafe, designed to keep the coffee hot without the usual warming plate, is extremely helpful for those who want to hold coffee for any length of time. The sealed thermos retains flavor and some aroma, both of which deteriorate rapidly when the coffee is subjected to an external heat source such as a hot plate. Of course, the absolutely best solution is to buy a smaller-capacity brewer and brew more frequently.
- A closed system, designed to retain heat and aroma during the brewing process, accounts for the reticent look of many brewers. If all else is equal, a closed system undoubtedly improves flavor and aroma. However, if you let coffee sit on the hot plate of the brewer for longer than 3 to 4 minutes before you drink it, a feature like this is rendered utterly irrelevant.
- Timing devices enable you to set the brewer to wake up with freshly brewed coffee. The night before, you fill the water and coffee receptacles and set the timer. The disadvantage is that the ground coffee stales all night long. Still, I would not hold it against any coffee lover who bought one. The most exotic designs attempt to eliminate staling by incorporating a grinder into the brewer; at the appointed time these devices not only brew coffee but grind it as well. All of the grinder-brewer combinations that I have tried have proven to be technically flawed, but someone may get it right.
- Permanent filters of nylon or metal mesh. If you like the clarity and brightness of filtered coffee, you do not want this feature. Avoid buying a maker that permits you to use only the permanent filter and does not give you the option of using paper.
- The coffee-strength controls on some brewers seem to be of dubious value. With some, the strong set-

ting may even cause the coffee to be overbrewed and harsh. If you want stronger brewed coffee, simply use more ground coffee.

- A provision for brewing a smaller amount of coffee on some machines appears to mildly improve brewing quality for small batches.

- Built-in water filters have cartridges that must be replaced periodically. They correct for both impurities and extremely hard water. I give the manufacturers who feature these filters a high grade for effort but suggest that if your water is bad you may have a general problem that transcends coffee brewing and needs to be resolved with either bottled water or a filtration system.

- Various technical strategies for ensuring that all of the ground coffee is thoroughly saturated and involved in the infusion process are often touted in promotional materials. I am not certain that these strategies should be called features because all automatic filter brewers aim for thorough infusion of the coffee through one technical means or another. Publicists carry on about sprinklers, pulses, surges, and gushes. Soon I expect built-in leprechauns with spoons. The objective is to agitate the coffee, break up lumps or doughnuts of dry coffee, and ensure a thorough infusion. At this writing the only brewer with a genuinely different approach to the infusion-saturation process is the Amway Kahve Coffee Maker, which gently spins the filter basket, forcing water through the ground coffee with centrifugal action and, in effect, wringing the coffee out like washing machines wring out clothes.

- Hot plates that turn off automatically to prevent fires and fouled carafes could be extremely useful to coffee drinkers with bad memories.

- Various means have been developed to modulate the temperature of the warming plate so as to keep coffee hot with less loss of flavor. The loss of flavor through holding coffee on the warming plate is one of the great drawbacks to automatic filter machines. The best solution is to brew smaller amounts of coffee more frequently; the second best approach is to buy a machine that brews directly into an insulated carafe. Anything else, no matter how innovative, is simply another desperate expedient.

Filter Brewers with Built-in Grinders

Now and then, manufacturers bring out automatic brewers with built-in, coffee-grinding apparatus. The idea sounds like a splendid one for the time-crunched, morning-challenged gourmet: you load with whole-bean coffee the night before, set a timer, and wake up to the sound and aroma of coffee being both ground and brewed for you by your countertop robot.

So far, however, none of these attempts has met with much market success. With the earliest designs, the grinding and brewing took place in the same receptacle. After a pair of blades knocked the coffee to pieces, hot water bubbled directly over it and the brewed coffee dripped through a mesh filter into the decanter below.

These devices produced a rather heavy, silty cup for two reasons. First, the position of the grinder blades in the middle of the brewing compartment prevented the use of paper filters. Second, blade grinders tend to produce a dusty, uneven grind when they are not manipulated to keep the coffee circulated around the blades.

At least one later design attempted to solve the silt problem by separating the grinding and brewing processes into adjacent compartments, making it possible to use paper filters. But technical problems combined with high prices have prevented these later efforts from achieving succcss as well.

If any of these innovative designs could improve quality and reduce price, they might find a market in the United States. As it is, I suspect that their appeal will continue to be limited to gadget enthusiasts looking for bragging rights.

BREWING FOR ONE OR TWO

With the exception of espresso, most brewing systems produce their best coffee in larger-than-one-cup quantities. The flavor loss is particularly acute with filter coffee, since in a one cup brewer thc papcr filtcr overpowers the coffee. So, if you prefer filtered coffee and are looking for quality, you might consider buying a two- to four-cup brewer and brewing a bit more than you ncced. I use a four-cup, automatic, filter-drip brewer charged with about three (5-ounce) cups of water and three heaping measures of coffee. That formula nets a tall mug of strong, hearty coffee.

If you use a one-cup, manual, pour-over filter-drip cone, make certain you preheat the cone and cup before you brew. It also helps to wet the filter paper at the same time that you preheat the cone, to mute the impact of the filter on the coffee. The little electric cup warmers sold as desktop accessories are useful for keeping your cup hot while you brew.

If you enjoy denser, punchier coffee of the kind made without a paper filter, you have more options. One-cup, gold-plated metal mesh filters (around $10 to $15) make a good cup, providing you use a bit more ground coffee than usual and preheat the filter and cup.

Two-cup plunger or French-press brewers also make excellent coffee in the heavier style. You can get a plastic-framed version for as little as $12. Perhaps the best solution for coffee drinkers on the run is the travel press (distributed by Bodum), a one-serving press-pot that doubles as a travel mug. It allows you to press the coffee and drink it out of the same mug-sized receptacle.

CONCENTRATE BREWING

In Latin America, as well as in many other parts of the world, a very strong, concentrated coffee is brewed, stored, and added in small amounts to hot water or milk to make a sort of preindustrial-age instant coffee. It is very easy to make your own concentrate, but premade liquid concentrates are beginning to appear in supermarkets and fancy food stores. The most authentic of those I have seen, Victorian House Concentrated Coffee, is a genuine, natural concentrate produced from good coffee with no additives, but like all concentrates, it produces a light-bodied cup with little aroma. And priced by the cup, it is not cheap.

You can obtain a strong concentrate with almost

any brewing method, although only one, the cold-water method, has gained much popularity in the United States.

Hot-Water Concentrate Brewing

To make a hot-water concentrate, use 8 cups of water to 1 pound of finely ground coffee and brew in your customary fashion. If the coffeemaker is unable to handle a pound at a time, halve the recipe or brew twice. Store the resulting concentrate in a stoppered bottle in the refrigerator. To a preheated cup, add about 1 ounce for every 5 ounces of hot water. A bartender's shot glass makes a convenient measure.

Cold-Water Concentrate Brewing

The cold-water concentrate method has been adopted by the Toddy coffeemaker (around $30). You steep 1 pound of regular-grind coffee in 8 cups of cold water for 10 to 20 hours, filter the resulting concentrate into a separate container, store it in the refrigerator, and add it to hot water in proportions of 1 ounce to 1 cup.

The result is a very mild, delicate brew, with little acidity (of either the good or bad variety), light body, a natural sweetness, and an evanescent, muted flavor. Those who take coffee weak and black and who like a delicate flavor free of acidy highlights and complex idiosyncrasies may well like the cold-water method. Those who for medical reasons require a milder brew also might find it suitable. And it is convenient.

However, anyone who likes strong coffee, distinctive coffee, or coffee with milk would be better off brewing another way. Another problem: If you combine 1 or more ounces of refrigerated concentrate with 5 ounces of hot water, you produce a mixture considerably less than scalding hot. Add milk and your cup will be lukewarm.

Some people like to use cold-water concentrate in cooking, but I prefer hot-water concentrate because the coffee flavor is stronger and more distinctive. Cold-water concentrate makes everything taste like commercial coffee ice cream. The same can be said for using cold-water concentrate in cold coffee drinks: It is true you need a concentrate to compensate for dilution by ice, but some (like me) prefer the more distinctive punch of hot-brewed concentrate.

Improvised Cold-Water Brewing. You do not have to buy a cold-water brewer to enjoy cold-water coffee, although the Toddy device is more convenient than any expedient. To improvise, you need a glass bowl, a large coffee cone, filters to fit, and a bottle with an airtight (not a snap-on plastic) closure in which to refrigerate the finished concentrate. Take 1 pound of your favorite coffee, regular grind. You can use any coffee, any roast. Put it in the bowl, and add 8 cups of cold water. Poke the floating coffee down into the water so all the grounds are wet, then let the bowl stand in a cool, dark place for 10 to 20 hours, depending on how strong you want the concentrate. When the brewing period is over, use the cone to filter the concentrate into the second, airtight container and store in the refrigerator. For hot coffee, use 1 to 2 ounces per cup.

Concentrate keeps its flavor for months if the bottle is tightly capped, but it is best to make only as much as you will drink in a week or two. Some people freeze the concentrate, but I have found it loses some much-needed flavor, and I suggest you simply halve the recipe if you cannot drink 8 cups of concentrate in two weeks.

MIDDLE EASTERN
OR TURKISH BREWING

Middle Eastern coffee is most often called Turkish coffee in this country, but this is a misnomer. For one thing, it is drunk all over the Middle East, the Balkans and Hungary, not only in Turkey. Second, according to all accounts, the method was invented in Cairo and later spread from there to Turkey. Middle Eastern coffee is unique, first, because some of the coffee grounds are deliberately drunk along with the coffee, and second, because the coffee is usually brewed with sugar, rather than sweetened after brewing. Much of the coffee settles to the bottom of the cup, but some tiny grains of coffee are suspended in the sweetened liquid, imparting a heavy, almost syrupy weight to the beverage.

Equipment and Coffee for Middle Eastern Brewing

It is possible to produce good, flavorful Middle Eastern–style coffee in any pot. The investment you make in brewing equipment is more important to ritual and esthetics than to flavor. Nevertheless, ritual seems to be as significant as flavor is in the enjoyment of coffee, and you may want to be authentic. If so, you will need a small, conical pot that looks a little like an inverted megaphone, called an *ibrik* (Turkish) or *briki* (Greek). The best and most authentic are made of copper or brass, are tinned inside, and cost about $20. You should also have either demitasse cups and saucers or tiny cups with metal holders especially made to serve Middle Eastern coffee. The best place to buy such gear is in stores in Middle Eastern neighborhoods, the kind that sell spices and other foods.

The most important piece of functional equipment in making Middle Eastern–style coffee is the grinder. Since you in part drink some of the grounds along with the coffee, you do not want to be picking grains of coffee from between your teeth. Conse-

Middle Eastern– or "Turkish"-style coffee implements. Left and right, ibriks. Center, grinder.

139

Clay pot of the kind used in Ethiopia and Eritrea to brew coffee.

quently you need a very fine, uniform grind, a dusty powder in fact. Few home mills can produce such a grind. The Zassenhaus box mills described in Chapter 8 do a decent job. Countries that take this kind of coffee drinking seriously produce attractive brass hand mills especially for this brewing method. If you purchase this style of grinder, I suggest that you buy the largest and sturdiest one you can find. The cheaper ones appear to be more tourist trinkets than true grinders. Fante's in Philadelphia (see Sending for

It) carries a good selection. The only electric machines that I know for certain produce a consistently good Middle Eastern–style coffee are specialized, home espresso grinders produced by companies like Saeco and Rancilio.

Most store grinders kept in proper adjustment will produce a superfine grind appropriate for Middle Eastern brewing. The joker is the adjustment. Many supermarket grinders are perpetually out of adjustment. Try the "Turkish" setting and see whether the coffee that spews out is ground literally to a powder. If it is not—in other words, if what comes out is a fine grit rather than a powder—try another store and another grinder.

The coffee roast you choose is a matter of taste, as is the provenance of the coffee. Most "Turkish"- or Middle Eastern–style coffee sold in the United States is a fairly dark roast, the sort most stores sell as Italian. The finest and most authentic Middle Eastern coffee is a Yemen Mocha or good Ethiopia Harrar brought to a dark brown roast. A blend of any winy coffee, such as Kenya or Yemen Mocha, some Sumatra, and a good dark French roast also makes an excellent Middle Eastern coffee.

Brewing Technique for Middle Eastern Coffee

Authentic Middle Eastern coffee should have a thin head of brown froth completely covering the surface of the coffee. In Greece, this is called the *kaimaki*, and to serve coffee without it is an insult to the guest and a disgrace to the host. A Greek friend of mine tells about her mother secretly struggling in the kitchen to produce a good head of kaimaki, while the rest of the family nervously diverted the guests with small talk in the parlor. In the United States the kaimaki may be dispensed with for the simple reason that it is very difficult to produce. The Middle Eastern coffee that you make should taste good the first time you make it, and the froth can wait until you are an expert.

Never plan to fill the ibrik to more than one-half its capacity. You need the other half to accommodate the froth that boils up from the coffee. Start by measuring 2 level-to-rounded teaspoons of freshly ground coffee per demitasse into the ibrik. Add about 1 level teaspoon of sugar for every teaspoon of coffee. This makes a coffee a Greek would call sweet. Add 1½ teaspoons of sugar per 1 teaspoon of coffee and you get heavy sweet; ½ teaspoon is light sweet. Omit sugar and you are serving the coffee plain, or *sketo.*

Now measure the water into the ibrik. Stir to dissolve the sugar, then turn on the heat medium to high. After a while the coffee will begin to boil gently. Let it boil, but watch it closely. Eventually the froth, which should have a darkish crust on top, starts to climb the narrow part of the ibrik. When it fills the flare at the top of the pot and is at the point of boiling over, turn off the flame. Immediately and carefully, to avoid settling the froth, pour the coffee into the cups. Fill each cup halfway first, then return to add some froth. Again, even though you may fail with the froth, the coffee is always delicious.

Middle Easterners like to add spices to their coffee. The preferred spice, and the one I suggest you try, is cardamom. Grind the cardamom seeds as finely as you grind the coffee and add them to the water with the coffee and sugar. There are usually three seeds in a cardamom pod; start by using the equivalent of one seed (not pod) per demitasse of water, or a pinch if the cardamom is preground.

SOLUBLE OR INSTANT COFFEE

Making instant coffee is hardly brewing, but I do not have a chapter on mixing and stirring, so I will have to include my discussion of instant or soluble coffees here as an exemplary afterthought.

I would not insinuate that soluble-coffee producers are terrible people who sneak around in dark clothing and limousines, stealing the public's right to a rich, fragrant cup of real coffee. Instant-coffee technologists seem passionately involved in their quest for a better coffee. At first glance (not taste), instant coffee does seem to offer many advantages: It stays fresh longer than ordinary roasted coffee; it eliminates the mistakes that can occur when brewing ordinary roasted coffee; it can be made quickly; it can be mixed by the cup to individual taste; and it contains somewhat less caffeine than regularly brewed coffee. Furthermore, because the process of producing instant coffee neutralizes strong or unusual flavors, the manufacturer can use cheaper beans and pass the savings on to the consumer.

Dismissing Advantages

Yet few of instant coffee's apparent advantages prove out. Instant does stay fresher, but grinding your own makes an even fresher cup. Instant is cleaner, but so are frozen dinners. True, it is hard to ruin a cup of instant, but if you have read this far, you are an expert anyhow. And if it is convenience you are looking for, the one-cup drip or plunger pot will give you much better coffee and just as quickly. So I cannot see any reasons except tidy countertops and a slight edge in price to recommend instant.

And you do not need instant coffee on backpacking or canoeing trips either. Open-pot coffee works fine in the wilds and adds no more weight than instant. At five in the morning, after brushing the earwigs out of your sleeping bag and cleaning up the mess the raccoons made, you need a cup of real coffee. About the only advantage to instant is that it does not attract bears.

Finally, for those who like to experiment with authentic and unusual coffees, the instant-coffee world offers no true alternatives. The "exotic," instant-coffee mixes currently in the supermarkets are insipid fabrications. By comparison, freeze-dried Colombia is a far superior beverage. If you crave variety, you must go back to basics.

Once we dismiss the advantages of instant, the advantages of brewed-from-scratch stand out in fragrant relief. Why does instant often taste more like liquid taffy than coffee? The key, again, is the extremely volatile coffee essence, which provides the aroma and most of the flavor of fresh coffee. Remember that this oil is developed by roasting and remains sealed in little packets in the bean until liberated by grinding and brewing. Once the coffee essence hits the water, it does not last long, which is the reason coffee that sits for a while tastes so flat.

Putting the Flavor Back In

Instant coffee is brewed much the way a gourmet would brew coffee from beans at home: The beans are roasted, immediately ground, and brewed in gigantic percolators, filter urns really. But when that fresh, hot brew is dehydrated, what happens? Remember, to dehydrate means to remove the water, and with the water goes—yes, the coffee essence, the minute droplets of flavor and aroma that mean the difference between tasteless, bitter brown water and real coffee.

But here technology comes clattering over the hill to save the day. If the flavor is lost, well then, put it back in again. Coffee technologists have long known that much of the essential oil literally goes up in smoke and out the chimneys of their roasters. So—you guessed it. The instant-coffee people condense some of the essential oil lost in roasting and put it back in the coffee just before the coffee is packed. Clever? Also tricky—so much so that even according to industry admissions, the sharp corners of coffee flavor are neutralized. The instant process makes bad coffee beans taste better and good coffee beans taste bad.

Soluble Coffee and the Soul

So far in my attempts to discredit instant coffees I have stuck to concrete factors such as efficiency and price and fairly clear subjective factors such as flavor and aroma. But I must add that the ritual of making a true cup of coffee the right way every morning is good for the soul. It cuts down on heedless coffee-holism and helps to steady the heart for the more complex activities to come. It gets you started with the confidence that you can at least make a good cup of coffee, and it is always best to start out winning.

THE METHOD FOR YOU

Which brewing method is best? is a naïve question. Which brewing method is best for you is a question to which it is possible for you to approximate an answer. Take just two variables, body and convenience. Coffee made by the "Turkish" or Middle Eastern method is the heaviest in body, espresso the next heaviest, and cold-water coffee the lightest, with coffee brewed through paper filters a close second. Between them are the coffees produced by all the other methods: open pot, plunger pot, drip, and so on. Who is to say which is best?

Even the question of convenience is relative. The cold-water method is clearly the most convenient, automatic filter drip is a close second, and Middle Eastern and open pot are last. Still, no one could tell my sculptor friend that making coffee without a strainer in a coffee can is bad because it is clumsy and inconvenient. He appreciated the inconvenience; it added to his satisfaction and took his mind off the obscure anxieties of his work. One of the principal reasons for drinking coffee is the aesthetic satisfaction of ritual. You ought to love not only the coffee your pot makes but the pot itself and all the little things you do with it.

10 THE ESPRESSO SIDE OF IT

What makes espresso espresso
Espresso history
Classic, beatnik, and mall espresso

Espresso is several things at once. It is a unique method of brewing in which hot water is forced under pressure through tightly packed coffee, one or two servings at a time. It is a roast of coffee, darker brown than the traditional American roast but not extremely dark. In a larger sense, it is an entire approach to coffee cuisine, involving not only roast and brewing method, but grind and grinder, a technique of heating and frothing milk, and a traditional menu of drinks. In the largest sense of all, it is an atmosphere or mystique: The espresso brewing machine is the spiritual heart and aesthetic centerpiece of the great coffee places, the cafès, caffès, and coffeehouses of the world.

WHAT MAKES ESPRESSO ESPRESSO

The espresso system was developed in and for cafès and caffès. Despite advances in inexpensive home espresso systems, it is still difficult to duplicate the finest caffè espresso or cappuccino in your kitchen or dining room without spending several hundred dollars on equipment. Even those on a budget can come close, however, and I outline the strategy for that effort in Chapter 11. For now, I want to discuss the big, shiny, caffè machines.

Fundamentally, they make coffee as any other brewer does: by steeping ground coffee in hot water. The difference is the pressure applied to the hot water. In normal drip-brewing processes, the water seeps by gravity down through ground coffee, loosely spooned into a filter. In the espresso process, the water is forced under pressure through very finely ground coffee packed tightly over the filter.

A fast, yet thorough brewing makes the best coffee. If hot water and ground coffee stay in contact too long, the more unpleasant chemicals in the coffee are extracted and the more delicate, pleasant aroma and flavor components evaporate. Hence the superiority of the espresso system: the pressurized water makes almost instant contact with every grain of ground coffee and rapidly begins dribbling out into the cup. Another advantage of the espresso system is freshness. Every serving is brewed in front of you, a moment before you drink it; in most cases the coffee beans are also ground immediately before brewing. Other restaurant brewing methods make anywhere from a pot to an urn at a time from preground coffee, then let it sit, where it loses flavor and aroma to the detriment of the coffee and the advantage of the ambience.

EVOLUTION OF THE CAFFÈ MACHINE

The oldest caffè espresso machines and the smaller home espresso machines work on a simple principle. Water is heated to boiling inside a closed tank; a space is left at the top of the tank where steam gathers. When a valve is opened below the water line, the pressure of the steam trapped at the top of the tank forces hot water out of the valve and down through the coffee. The first European patents for the idea were filed between 1821 and 1824, and a variation of the method was first applied to a large caffè machine by

Eduard Loysel de Santais in 1843. Santais's machine wowed visitors to the Paris Exposition of 1855 by producing "two thousand cups of coffee an hour." Santais's machine brewed coffee a pot at a time, however, and used steam pressure, not to force the brewing water directly through the coffee, but instead to raise the water to a considerable height above the coffee, whence it descended through an elaborate system of tubes to the coffee bed. The weight of the hot water, not the trapped steam, applied the brewing pressure.

New Century, First Espresso Machine

It was not until the dawn of the twentieth century that the Milanese Luigi Bezzera patented a restaurant machine that used the pressure of trapped steam to directly force water through ground coffee. The Bezzera machine also innovated by distributing the freshly brewed coffee through one or more "water and steam groups" directly into the cup.

In many respects the Bezzara machine established the basic configuration that espresso machines would maintain throughout the twentieth century. See the illustration to the right. These machines decreased the size of the strainer that held the coffee, but increased the number of valves, enabling them to produce several single cups of coffee simultaneously, rather than a single big pot at a time. Then as now, the espresso operator packed a few teaspoons of very finely ground, dark-roasted coffee into a little metal filter. The filter was clamped into a receptacle called the group, which protruded from the side of the machine. When the

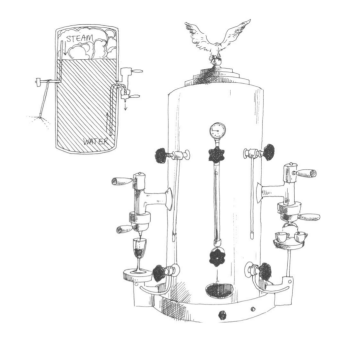

An early caffè machine of the type that helped create the culture of espresso during the first half of the twentieth century. It uses the simple pressure of steam trapped at the top of the boiler to force water through the bed of ground coffee at the right of the cross-section diagram and into the cup. A second outlet, at the top left in the diagram, taps the steam at the top of the boiler and directs it out a steam valve and wand for use in heating and frothing milk.

operator opened the valve (or, in more modern machines, pulls a handle or pushes a button), hot water was forced through the coffee and into the cup.

The early espresso machines look like shiny steam engines pointed at the ceiling. The round water tank is set on end and bristles with picturesque spouts, valves, and pressure gauges. These shiny towers topped with an ornamental eagle dominated the European caffè scene until World War II. After the war, Italians wanted an even stronger cup of coffee to go with their Vespas, and they wanted it faster.

The Gaggia Mid-Century Breakthrough

In 1948, Achille Gaggia obliged them with the first truly modern espresso machine. As Gaggia's design eventually evolved, the water tank was laid on its side and concealed inside a streamlined metal cabinet with lines like a Danish-modern jukebox. The simple valve of the old days was replaced with a spring-powered piston that pushed the water through the coffee harder and faster. The operator depressed a long, metal handle. The handle in turn compressed a spring-loaded piston that forced a dose of hot water slowly through the coffee as the handle majestically returned to its original erect position. The new spring-loaded machines pushed the water through the coffee at a pressure that is now accepted as ideal for espresso brewing: a minimum of 9 atmospheres, or nine times the ordinary pressure exerted by the earth's atmosphere. By comparison, the prewar, steam-pressure machines exerted a feeble 1.5 atmospheres of pressure.

Computer Age Espresso

In the 1960s, just when pumping the handle became the signature performance piece of espresso caffès, less dramatic and more automated means for forcing the hot water through the coffee began to evolve. The earliest of these no-hands machines were built around simple hydraulic pumps. Today's versions heat water separately from the main reservoir, control water temperature and pressure with precision, and flatter the hi-tech pretensions of the late twentieth century with digital readouts.

These push-button machines tend to carry the streamlined look to an extreme. Everything is concealed inside a single, sleek, enamel-and-chrome housing. All have one feature in common: The operator pushes a button or trips a switch rather than pumping a long handle. Since so much of the process is automated, the push-button machines are easier for the novice to master, but do not necessarily make better espresso. Proprietors of some of the better caffès in the San Francisco Bay Area, at any rate, still prefer the pump-piston machines because they give the sophisticated operator maximum control over the brewing process.

Enter Frothed Milk

With the long, gleaming handle going the way of the running board, the best routine left to the espresso operator is heating and frothing the milk used in drinks like cappuccino and caffè latte. Espresso is a strong, concentrated coffee, and, in accordance with European tradition, many of the drinks in espresso cuisine combine it with milk. If the milk were unheated, it would instantly cool the coffee. Early in the history of the espresso machine, someone, probably Luigi Bezzara in 1901, realized that the steam collected in the top of the tank could be used to heat milk as well as provide pressure for making coffee. A valve with a long nozzle was fed into the upper part of the tank where the steam gathers. When the valve is opened by unscrewing a knob, the compressed steam hisses out of the nozzle. The operator pours cold milk into a pitcher, inserts the nozzle into the milk, and opens the valve. The compressed steam shoots through the milk, heating it and raising an attractive head of froth or form.

Caffè patrons soon discovered that steamed, frothed milk both tastes and looks better than milk heated in the ordinary way, and it became an important part of espresso cuisine, particularly in the United Sates of the 1990s. The white head of foam is decorative, can be garnished with a dash of cocoa or other garnish, prevents a skin from forming on the surface of the milk, and insulates the hot coffee.

A REMARKABLE CUP OF COFFEE

It is difficult to say how much of the success of the espresso machine is due to its scientifically impeccable approach to coffee making and how much to its drama and novelty, but, given European tastes, it certainly does produce a remarkable cup of coffee: freshly ground, and brewed so quickly that, as an Italian friend of mine says, you get only the absolute heart of the coffee.

Nevertheless, many a mainstream American coffee lover facing a straight espresso for the first time may take one swallow and either finish it stoically or hide the little cup behind a napkin. The distaste is understandable. This impeccable brewing system is designed to make a cup of coffee in the southern European or Latin American tradition rather than in the northern European or North American. Good espresso is rich, heavy-bodied, and almost syrupy; furthermore, it has the characteristic bittersweet bite of dark-roast coffee.

But the sharp flavor and heavy body make it an ideal coffee to be drunk with milk and sugar, and it is this virtue that has made espresso cuisine the latest coffee rage in North America. The "latte," a drink that does not even appear on espresso menus in Italy, combines espresso with gigantic quantities of hot milk (or milk substitutes) and endlessly customized syrups and garnishes. This now ubiquitous drink seems on its way to replacing the bottomless cup of tradition in the morning hearts and bellies of America.

ESPRESSO CUISINES, CLASSIC TO POSTMODERN

There are many espresso cuisines, not just one. Every culture adopts the potential of the machine and the espresso system to its own tradition, from the sugar-heavy *tintos* of Cuba to the ultra-tiny *cafezinhos* of Brazil.

In North America at least three espresso cuisines overlap to confuse the novice. The first is the classic Italian cuisine as practiced in the best bars of Italy. The second is the Italian-American beatnik espresso of the 1950s through '80s, which still dominates in college towns and the bohemias of large cities. The third is what we might term "mall" or perhaps postmodern espresso, the thoroughly Americanized, constantly morphing, many-flavored cuisine that brought us the gigantic caffè latte and its ever-proliferating progeny.

Classic Italian Espresso Cuisine

Southern Europeans have drunk strong, sharply flavored coffee in tiny cups or mixed with hot milk for generations. Consequently, most of the drinks in espresso cuisine are not original with the machine; rather, the machine brought them from promise to perfection. Here are some of the most popular drinks from the classic Italian cuisine.

Espresso. About 1 to 1½ ounces of espresso coffee, black, usually drunk with sugar. Fills about ⅓ to ⅔ of a demitasse, no more.

Espresso Ristretto. "Restricted" or short espresso. Carries the "small is beautiful" espresso philosophy to its ul-

timate: The flow of espresso is cut short at less than 1 ounce, producing an even denser, more perfumy cup of espresso than the norm.

Espresso Lungo. Long espresso; about 2 ounces or ⅔ of a demitasse.

Double or Doppio. Double serving, or about 2½ to 3 ounces of straight espresso, made with twice the amount of ground coffee, served in a 6-ounce cup.

Cappuccino. In Italy, a single serving (about 1¼ ounces) of espresso, topped by a dense, soupy froth, served in a 6-ounce cup. The espresso goes into the cup first, then the froth, which picks up the coffee as it is poured, lifting and combining with it. The result is a delectable fusion of espresso and heavy froth. Usually the completed drink is lightly dusted with a garnish of intense, unsweetened cocoa, which further and subtly complicates the aromatics of this splendid beverage.

Unfortunately, the cappuccino is North America's most misunderstood and abused espresso drink, with versions ranging from miniature caffè lattes with virtually no froth to the Seattle "dry" cappuccino, in which the froth is stiff and meringuelike, floating like an afterthought atop an often bitter, overextracted shot of espresso.

Espresso Macchiato. A single serving (1 to 1½ ounces) of espresso "stained" with a small quantity of hot, frothed milk. Served in the usual espresso demitasse.

Latte Macchiato. An 8-ounce glass filled with hot, frothed milk, into which a serving of espresso is slowly dribbled. The coffee "stains" the milk in faint, graduated layers, darker at the top shading to light at the bottom, all contrasting with the layer of pure white foam at the top. This is the drink Italians take when they want a tall, milky morning coffee.

Classic Espresso Cuisine at Home. Detailed instructions and suggestions for brewing espresso and frothing milk with home machines are given in Chapter 11, together with recipes from all of the espresso cuisines.

Beatnik or Italian-American Espresso Cuisine

Compared to the chaste, elegantly restrained espresso cuisine of contemporary Italy, the menu of drinks that evolved from the interaction of Italian immigrant caffè owners and their youthful American counterculture customers in the 1950s through '80s moves us a bit closer to the unbridled espresso exuberance of 1990s.

Here are some variations and drinks that evolved in the heyday of navy turtlenecks and madras miniskirts. In addition to differences in how the various drinks are constructed, the coffee itself in the beatnik cuisine is sharper, more darkly roasted, and more bitter than the round, sweet, espresso blends used in Italy.

Espresso Romano. A single serving of espresso served in a demitasse with a twist or thin slice of lemon on the side. The lemon is wiped around the lip of the cup leaving a faint trace of lemon oil. The scent of the lemon subtly (and exquisitely) combines with the aromatics of the coffee as you sip it.

Beatnik or Italian-American Cappuccino. About one-third espresso, one-third milk, and one-third froth, served in a heavy 6-ounce cup, garnished with unsweetened cocoa. Not quite as elegant as the true Italian cappuccino with its enveloping, soupy froth (page 151), but Allen Ginsberg liked it this way.

Caffè Mocha. As served in the Italian-American caffès of the 1950s onward, about one-third espresso, one-third strong hot chocolate, and one-third hot, frothed milk. The milk is added last, and the whole thing usually is served in an 8-ounce mug, sometimes topped with whipped cream. With the classic mocha the hot chocolate is made very strong, so it holds its own against the espresso, and is at most lightly sweetened. The customer adds sugar to taste. Most contemporary caffès add chocolate fountain syrup to a caffè latte and call it a mocha. So be it.

Caffè Latte. At least until recently, ordering a "latte" in Italy got you a puzzled look and a glass of cold milk. The American-style caffè latte does not exist on the menus of Italian caffès, except perhaps in a few places dominated by American tourists.

Exactly who in America started the practice of serving a little espresso with a lot of hot milk in a very large bowl or glass and calling it a caffè latte is open

to question. Obviously breakfast drinks of this kind have existed in Europe for generations, but the contemporary caffè version of the drink is an American invention. I was told by Leno Meiorin, proprietor of the original Caffè Mediterraneum in Berkeley, that he invented it in 1959 when customers complained that the latte macchiati and cappuccini he was serving were too stingy in size. Certainly the Mediterraneum was the first place I saw caffè latte listed on a menu. For the first year or two Leno served his caffè lattes in lovely fluted glass bowls but switched to the now-classic, 16-ounce beer glasses when too many of the bowls walked out the door with his customers. Some upscale caffès have returned to serving their caffè lattes in bowls.

Espresso con Panna. In its original Italian-American configuration, the con panna consists of a big dollop

of very lightly sweetened, heavy whipped cream laid atop a single long serving of espresso in a 6-ounce cup, garnished with unsweetened cocoa.

Café au Lait. In some American caffès, a drink made with about half filter coffee and about half hot milk and froth, served in a 10-, 12-, or 16-ounce glass or bowl. The proportion of coffee to milk has to be larger than with the espresso-based caffè latte, because American filter coffee is so delicate in flavor and light in body compared to espresso.

The Italian-American or Beatnik Cuisine at Home. Detailed instructions and suggestions for brewing espresso and frothing milk with home machines are given in Chapter 11, together with recipes from all of the espresso cuisines.

Postmodern or Mall Espresso Cuisine

Americans have subjected the classic espresso cuisines to their own brand of cultural innovation. In general, it would seem that we are frustrated by the brevity and precision of the classic cuisines, and want bigger drinks with more in them. Perhaps an ounce of coffee in a tiny cup does lack comfort in the middle of the Great Plains or atop the World Trade towers. Still, I think it would be better if Americans understood and experienced the intensity and perfection of the classic espresso cuisine before immediately expanding it, watering it down, or adding ice to it. But, for better or worse, the latte cuisine is here to stay. Here are some of the more honorable results of American espresso cuisine tinkering.

Caffè Latte by the Ounce. A Brazilian friend of mine always expresses amazement at what she sees as evidence of American practicality and directness. Somewhere along the line in the 1980s, American espresso operators dispensed with all of the fancy names and cups of the classic Italian and beatnik cuisines and simply started asking customers how much espresso they wanted, how much milk, and put the two together in a series of ever larger cardboard or Styrofoam® plastic cups. The result is certainly practical, though hardly elegant. Furthermore, to satisfy the precise and conflicting needs of dieters, the milk part of the menu was expanded to include everything from skim milk to soy milk.

Thus, rather than a cappuccino, latte macchiato, or caffè latte, American espresso drinkers simply specify the number of servings of espresso they prefer (single, double, triple, or the murderous quad), the volume of milk (small or short, or enough milk to fill an 8-ounce container; tall, enough to fill a 14-ounce container, or various pop terms like grande, 16 ounces, or venti or mondo, enough to fill 20 to 24 ounces) and kind of milk (non-fat, 1 percent, 2 percent, 3 percent, or 4 percent butterfat, soy, or rice). Example: "Triple soy grande," which translates as three shots of espresso in hot soy milk with a light head of froth to fill a 16-ounce cup.

Flavored Caffè Latte by the Ounce. During the heyday of Italian-American or beatnik espresso, every big-city caffè sported a lineup of colorful Italian-style syrup bottles on the back bar put out by the family-owned Torani company of San Francisco. These syrups were added to seltzer or sparkling water to make various soft drinks. In the late 1970s, L. C. "Brandy" Brandenburger, an entrepreneur from Portland, Oregon, thought to begin adding these syrups to milk-based espresso drinks like cappuccino and caffè latte. The idea caught on, and was elaborated with particular enthusiasm in Seattle in the early 1990s, where experimentation with syrups reached truly baroque dimensions. One kind of syrup might be added to the espresso, a couple of others to the frothed milk, and the whole concoction might be topped with whipped cream blended with still a fourth flavoring.

Meanwhile, the discreet garnish of unsweetened cocoa added to a classic cappuccino became similarly elaborated. I recall visiting an espresso cart in Seattle in the mid-1990s that offered customers the option of at least a dozen different garnishes for the froth on their espresso drinks, ranging from fresh-grated nutmeg through orange-flavored sugar and powdered vanilla. Thus, our hypothetical latte—one flavor in the coffee, two more in the milk, and a fourth in the whipped cream—might be further elaborated with the addition of a fifth flavor of garnish on the whipped cream.

The human nervous system, not to mention the memories of baristas and the budgets of caffès, could hardly sustain such extravagance. Today the flavoring craze seems to be abating. The flavored caffè latte may be here to stay, but the Cherry Cheesecake Latte and Raspberry Truffle Latte appear to be on their way out. Caffès increasingly follow the lead of Starbucks, which limits its syrups to a few popular favorites with proven affinity with coffee (hazelnut, chocolate, vanilla, raspberry, Irish creme, almond, mint) and its garnishes to chocolate, cinnamon, and nutmeg.

Double Cappuccino. (Or double cap, as in baseball cap.) If this innovation is made correctly, you should get about 3 ounces of uncompromised espresso, brewed with double the usual amount of ground coffee, topped with 3 to 5 ounces of hot milk and soupy froth. Usually served in an 8-ounce cup or mug. If the ground coffee is not doubled, and the operator simply forces twice as much water through one serving's worth of ground coffee, you are getting a bitter, watery perversion, rather than a taller, stronger version of a good drink.

Mocha Latte, Moccaccino. The rugged, rich, original mochas of the old-time caffès (see page 152) have been replaced by a more ingratiating drink. When made properly, this mall version of the mocha consists of a serving of espresso pulled directly into an ounce or so of good chocolate fountain syrup, after which the two are mixed and frothed milk is added to make a mocha with caffè latte proportions. Caffè Strada, in Berkeley, is reputed to be the original of the White Chocolate or Bianca Mocha, which replaces the usual chocolate syrup with either white chocolate melted in a double boiler or a special white chocolate syrup.

Iced Espresso. This is usually a double espresso poured over plenty of crushed, not cubed, ice, in a smallish, fancy glass. Some caffès top the iced coffee with whipped cream. Caffès that brew and refrigerate a pitcher of espresso in advance when they feel a hot morning on the way fail to deliver the brewed-fresh perfume of true espresso, but the practice still makes a fine drink and one that does not need to be iced and diluted as much as the version made with fresh espresso.

Iced Cappuccino. Best made with a single or double serving of freshly brewed espresso poured over crushed ice, topped with an ounce or two of cold milk, then some froth (not hot milk) from the machine to top it off. This drink should always be served in a glass. The triple contrast of coffee, milk, and froth, all bubbling around the ice, makes a pleasant sight on a hot day.

Granitas, Latte and Otherwise. Espresso granita is an Italian-American specialty that has morphed into a popular mall espresso drink that is usually called latte granita or, in Starbucks-speak, frappuccino.

Traditional Italian-American granitas usually involved freezing strong, unsweetened espresso, crushing it, and serving it in a parfait glass or sundae dish topped with lightly sweetened whipped cream.

The latte granita is a tall, smoothly icy drink that blends espresso, milk, ice, ample sugar, and (usually) vanilla. In the best caffès and bars the mixture is made with freshly brewed espresso and combined in powerful bar blenders. Less authentically, the ingredients are mixed in special dispensing machines. Made with fresh espresso the latte granita can be a very agreeable summer drink. If chocolate syrup is added to the mix it is called a mocha granita. Like the original caffè latte the latte granita can be endlessly elaborated with flavorings.

Chai, Chai Latte. Chai traditionally is a mixture of spices and black tea drunk with hot milk and honey in the Middle East, India, and Central Asia. The spice mix is usually boiled for 15 or 20 minutes and combined with black tea brewed in the usual way. This liquid concentrate is then strained and mixed with hot milk and honey. Some innovator in the American Northwest came up with the notion of making the hot milk component of traditional chai, hot, frothed milk. Chai is now part of the repertoire of American espresso cuisine, usually as a tall, hot milk drink called a chai latte. The tingly, lively spice mix carries the tea taste through the milk and allows tea drinkers to enjoy a milky morning beverage analogous to the caffè latte.

The traditional black tea chai has been joined by various noncaffeinated herbal tea chais, usually mint-based. The spices in traditional chai always include ginger, cinnamon, and cardamom, but may include smaller amounts of coriander, nutmeg, cloves, star anise, fennel, black pepper, and orange zest. Americans are wont to add vanilla to sweeten and mellow the mix, but vanilla is not a typical component in authentic chais. Lately instant chai mixes have appeared that are as stupid, cloying, and insipid as Middle Eastern Kool-Aid. If the idea of chai appeals to you, try to find a caffè that uses a chai mix brewed in the traditional way, with real spice and real black tea.

ESPRESSO MISUNDERSTANDINGS AND MISREPRESENTATIONS

Unfortunately, America has contributed more than innovation to the classic espresso cuisine. It has also watered it down, misunderstood it, and misrepresented it.

The art of espresso cuisine, as practiced in the best bars of Italy, is a masterpiece of coffee making, once tasted, seldom forgotten. Unfortunately, few American coffee drinkers have an opportunity to experience the aromatic perfection of a perfectly brewed single espresso or classic cappuccino. There are a growing number of American places where you can experience precise, knowledgeable espresso making, but even in these places, production is uneven, and you are as likely to encounter overextracted coffee drowned in scalded milk as you are a good cappuccino. Of the ninety or so caffès in the city I live in—Oakland, California—only two consistently produce genuine, authentic espresso. Good espresso cuisine demands not only a technically complete system and good intentions on the part of the caffè owner but a skilled and attentive operator, or barista. And the barista, as any conscientious caffè owner will tell you, is the most difficult part of the equation.

The Sin of Overextraction

The most prevalent and destructive mistake of novice espresso operators is running too much water through the coffee, often in a generous effort to provide customers with something more substantial than a little black stuff at the bottom of a demitasse. Instead of substance, of course, the customers are rewarded with a thin, bitter, watery drink that will make them wish they had ordered filter coffee or mint tea. Such overextracted coffee destroys all beverages in which it appears, including cappuccino and caffè latte.

The espresso system is so efficient that the goodness is extracted from the ground coffee almost immediately, making a small amount of intense brew, usually no more than 1¼ ounces per serving. Any water run through the coffee after that moment of truth contributes only bitter, flavorless chemicals to the cup. Those who want greater quantity should drink another style of coffee or order a double, which doubles both the amount of ground coffee and the amount of hot water run through it. As for cappuccino, the most egregious error is drowning the coffee in hot milk, which produces a weak, milky drink closer to a caffè latte than an intense, perfumy cappuccino.

AUTOMATED ESPRESSO

To compensate for untrained or careless baristas, the espresso industry in both Italy and the United States has been busily producing innovations essentially designed to automate the espresso brewing process to the point that the operator is reduced to irrelevant schlep or predictable button pusher. The most distressing result, which fortunately has not found much foothold in the United States, is machines that mix cappuccino and caffè latte in a device that works much like a commercial hot chocolate dispenser. The result is little more than instant coffee mixed with hot milk.

Other innovations are more positive. There are machines that grind the coffee, load it, and brew the espresso, all at the push of a single button, for example. The operator still has to heat and froth the milk, however. Even here help is on its way. The American Acorto company produces machines that do everything at the touch of a button, including frothing the milk and combining it with appropriate amounts of freshly brewed espresso. Kept properly tuned, the very expensive Acorto machines produce excellent beverages.

The simplest of these new, easy espresso expedients are pods of preground, prepackaged espresso coffee. The pod looks like a disk-shaped tea bag filled with ground coffee. The operator simply pops one (or two for a double) of these pods into a specially designed espresso filter, clamps the filter onto the machine, pushes the button or depresses the lever, and the brewing proceeds as usual. The operator still needs to know when to stop the brewing process, but the grind and measurement of coffee remain consistent.

Pod espresso is now available in home machines, and provides a helpful introduction for espresso beginners. See pages 182–83.

11 ESPRESSO AT HOME

How to brew the coffee, froth
the milk, assemble the drinks,
and find the right equipment

If you have enjoyed authentic espresso or cappuccino and you want more, you may prefer to produce your own. In this case, the first step should be deciding what you like about the encounter.

If you enjoy the pungent flavor of the espresso and are indifferent to the rich texture of the coffee itself or the effect of frothed milk, then you may be just as happy with a moderately dark-roast coffee brewed as you would any other coffee. Start with a half pound of coffee roasted dark brown but not black (variously called espresso, French, or Italian), ground for your regular coffeemaker. Experiment with different styles or colors of roast until you hit on one that satisfies. If you want to add frothed milk to your cup, there are several stand-alone devices that produce respectable froth. See page 168.

But if you like the rich, syrupy body of true espresso and the way it carries through hot milk, you will need to purchase specialized espresso brewing apparatus. If your espresso desires are limited to drinks that combine the espresso with hot milk, like cappuccino or caffè latte, you can get away with one of the modest steam-pressure devices with milk frothing wand described in Category 2, pages 179–80. But if you enjoy the smooth, heavy perfume of straight espresso without milk, you will need to buy a more expensive pump or piston machine of the kind described in Categories 3, 4, and 5, pages 180–88 plus (in the case of Categories 3 and 4) a specialized coffee grinder specifically designed for espresso brewing.

Detailed advice on choosing a home machine that fits your espresso preferences and budget appears in the last section of this chapter on pages 177–90.

Pages 164–67 describe brewing and milk-frothing procedures, and 169–76 detail how to produce the growing menu of espresso drinks.

HOME ESPRESSO BREWING

Producing good espresso drinks at home is one of those activities that require some practice and attention, but not a lot. Certainly nothing that even a distracted, overworked, overcommuted contemporary coffee lover cannot learn in a few sporadic five-minute experiments over the course of a week or so. But you will be frustrated if you simply muddle directly into espresso brewing and milk-frothing without at least skimming through the following pages.

And try not to be afraid of the espresso brewing machine because it exudes steam and hisses like a bomb about to go off. It is not a bomb; it is your friend, and it will not go off. Even cheap espresso machines have well-tried safety mechanisms to prevent explosive escapes of steam.

Espresso Coffee and Roast

Espresso typically is brewed using a coffee roasted dark brown, but not black. This roast is called espresso or Italian in stores. Remember, however, that you can use any coffee in your espresso brewer as long as the beans are properly ground. You may prefer a coffee darker than espresso roast with a slightly burned taste (often called dark French or dark Italian) or lighter with a brighter, drier taste. Some coffee companies, like Peet's Coffee & Tea, may roast all of their coffees dark and bittersweet, making all of them appropriate for espresso.

The espresso method will produce a rich-textured and heavy-bodied beverage, no matter what coffee you choose. But only with the classic espresso roast will you achieve the sweet, rich, smooth tang of caffè espresso. Always use at least as much coffee as is recommended by the manufacturer of your machine. Never use less. If in doubt, use a minimum of 2 level tablespoons of finely ground coffee for every demitasse of espresso. If you are using a pump or piston machine (Categories 3 or 4, pages 181–86), you may find that, to get good results, you need to use the double filter basket rather than the shallower single filter basket, regardless of whether you are brewing one serving of espresso or two.

Espresso Brewing Principles

There are two requirements for making good espresso. First, you need to grind the coffee just fine enough, and tamp it down in the filter basket just hard enough, so that the barrier of ground coffee resists the pressure of the hot water sufficiently to produce a slow dribble of dark, rich liquid. Second, you need to stop the dribble at just the right moment, before the oils in the coffee are exhausted and the dark, rich dribble turns into a tasteless brown torrent.

The Key to Espresso Brewing: The Proper Grind

The proper grind texture for espresso is very fine and gritty, but not a dusty powder. If you do not have an appropriately fine grind, your espresso will taste thin and watery. If it is too fine, your espresso will taste bitter and burned.

If you look at the ground coffee from a foot away, you should barely be able to distinguish the particles. If you rub some between your fingers, it should feel gritty. Most canned espresso coffees, such as Medaglia d'Oro, are ground much too coarsely.

Store Grinding for Espresso Brewing. If you have whole beans ground at a specialty coffee store, ask for an extrafine grind for an espresso machine. If you use a grinder in a grocery story, set the dial to the Espresso setting. If the grinder has two settings for espresso, use the finer one if you have a pump or piston machine (Categories 3 and 4, pages 181–86), or the coarser of the two espresso settings if you have a steam pressure brewer (Categories 1 and 2, pages 178–80).

Grocery store grinders are often out of adjustment. Consequently, it is a good idea to test the setting before grinding your coffee. Set the dial to the setting recommended in the previous paragraph, drop a few beans into the hopper, and turn on the machine with your hand under the spout so that it touches and depresses the little lever behind the spout. If the coffee that dribbles onto your hand looks too coarse, move the setting to Turkish and try that. If it still looks too coarse, go to a different store with a better maintained grinder.

Home Grinding for Espresso Brewing. The best way to grind coffee for espresso brewing is to grind it yourself at home.

For steam-pressure brewers you can determine the right grind by sight and feel alone. (Try for a fine grit but not a powder). For pump or piston machines you can approximate the correct grind by sight and feel, but ultimately you can only evaluate grind setting by brewing ("pulling" in espresso-speak) a serving of coffee. A single or double serving or pull of espresso should dribble out in a steady, pointed, golden stream, shaped, as Italians say, like the tail of a mouse. A 1-plus-ounce, single serving or 2-plus-ounce, double serving should issue out of the filter holder in about 17 to 22 seconds after the first dribble appears. If the coffee gushes out in less than 17 seconds, make the grind finer by slightly tightening the wheel or dial that controls fineness of grind. If it drips out slowly and blackly in more than 22 seconds, loosen the setting slightly.

Typically you will find that every time you change to a different coffee or the humidity changes, you will need to make slight changes in the grind adjustment. This procedure may sound cumbersome and fussy, but once gotten used to it becomes almost automatic. On a morning when your shot issues out slightly too quickly, you will find yourself reflexively adjusting the grinder so that the following morning it will be just right.

Filling the Filter Basket and Tamping

Fill the filter basket of your machine with coffee to the indicated point (or to just below the brim if there is no indication), spread it evenly, then lightly tamp it down. Do not hammer on it. Either use the little round, flat-bottomed device called a tamper that may have come with your machine or lightly press the coffee down across its entire surface with your fingertips. If you fear the grind is too coarse, press a little more heavily; if too fine, press lightly or not at all. Never use

Steps in espresso brewing
1. *Fill filter basket with coffee ground to a fine grit.*
2. *Tamp (press down) ground coffee firmly and evenly.*
3. *Clamp portafilter in place.*
4. *Force hot water through coffee by opening coffee valve, activating pump, or depressing lever.*

less than the minimum volume of ground coffee recommended for the machine, even if you are brewing a single cup. If the coffee gushes out rather than dribbling, compensate by using a finer grind or by tamping harder. If it oozes out rather than dribbling steadily, use a coarser grind or go easier on the tamping.

Brewing the Espresso

Timing is everything in espresso brewing. The richest and most flavorful coffee issues out right at the beginning. As brewing continues, the coffee becomes progressively thinner and more bitter. Consequently, collect only as much coffee as you will actually serve. If you are brewing one serving, cut off the flow of coffee after one serving has dribbled out, even if you have two servings' worth of ground coffee in the filter. If you are brewing two servings, cut off the flow after two. And no matter how many servings you are trying

Diagnosing espresso brewing
1. *Coffee ground too finely and/or packed too tightly— espresso leaks out in dark little droplets.*
2. *Coffee ground too coarsely and/or packed too loosely— espresso gushes out.*
3. *Coffee ground to a perfect grit and gently but firmly tamped—espresso dribbles out in a deliberate, thin stream.*

to make, never allow the coffee to bubble and gush into your serving carafe or cup. Such thin, overextracted coffee will taste so bad that it is better to start over than to insult your guests or palate by serving it.

Gauge when to cut off the flow of coffee by sight. The fineness of the grind may vary, as will the pressure you apply when tamping. Consequently, the speed with which the hot water dribbles through the coffee will also vary from serving to serving. If in doubt, cut off the flow of coffee sooner rather than later. Better to experience a perfectly flavored small drink than an obnoxiously bitter large one.

With pump or piston machines, a common practice is to pull the coffee into shot glasses, one for a single serving and two next to one another for a double serving. The line on a shot glass measures 1¼ ounces, the perfect length for a properly pulled espresso shot.

If you are using a steam-pressure brewer and if it does not incorporate a mechanism for cutting off the flow of the coffee, and if the design of the machine permits, use two separate coffee-collecting receptacles, one to catch the first rich coffee dribbles, which you will drink, and a second to catch the pale remainder, which you will throw away. Whatever you do, do not spoil the first bloom of coffee by mixing it with the pale, bitter dregs.

FROTHING THE MILK

Most Americans prefer espresso blended with hot, frothed milk as cappuccino or caffè latte. Fortunately, most espresso-brewing appliances now sold in the United States have built-in steam valves and wands suitable for frothing milk. If you like espresso drinks with milk, make certain that the machine you purchase has such a mechanism.

Heating milk with an espresso machine is easy; producing a head of froth or foam is a little trickier, but, like riding a bicycle or centering clay on a potter's wheel, exquisitely simple once you have broken through and gotten the feel of it.

Steps in Making Drinks with Frothed Milk

There are three stages to making an espresso drink with frothed milk. The first is brewing the coffee; the second is frothing and heating the milk; the third is combining the two. Never froth the coffee and milk together, which would stale the fresh coffee and ruin the eye-pleasing contrast between white foam and dark coffee. Nor is it a good idea, even if your machine permits it, to simultaneously brew espresso and froth the milk. Concentrate on the brewing operation first, taking care to produce only as much coffee as you need. Then stop the brewing and turn to the frothing operation.

The Frothing Apparatus

The steam wand, also called steam stylus, pipe, or nozzle, is a little tube that protrudes from the top or side of the machine. At the tip of the wand are one to four little holes that project jets of steam downward or diagonally when the steam function is activated. Nearby you will find the knob that controls the flow of steam. It may be conveniently located next to the steam wand, or it may be a foot or so away at the side or top of the machine. While you are brewing coffee, this knob and the valve it controls are kept screwed shut.

Some machines do not have a screw knob to control the flow of steam for frothing. Instead, you simply activate the steam function with a switch and take what you get. In general, it is better to purchase a machine in which the steam pressure for frothing is adjustable.

The transition between brewing and frothing in inexpensive, steam-pressure machines and in piston machines is usually accomplished simply by closing the coffee-brewing valve and opening the steam valve. In button-operated pump machines, there may be a more complex transitional procedure, which will be described in the instructions accompanying your machine.

A Dry Run Before Frothing

Before attempting to froth milk for the first time, practice opening and closing the steam valve with the machine on, the brewing function off or closed, and the steam function activated. Get a general sense of how many turns of the knob it takes to create an explosive jet of steam and how many to permit a steady, powerful jet. It is the latter intensity that you will use to froth milk: not so powerful that the jet produces an overpowering roar, but powerful enough to produce a strong, steady hiss.

Note that steam cools rapidly as it exits the nozzle of the wand. Even four inches from the nozzle the steam is merely wet to the touch (try it) and presents no danger of injury. Hot milk churning or spattering out of the pitcher during incorrect frothing can cause at least mild burns, however. Follow the instructions below carefully.

If you are using one of the rare stovetop steam-pressure brewers with a steam wand, and if the steam does not produce a sturdy hiss when you open the valve, raise the heat under the brewer slightly, and make certain that pressure is not escaping through the coffee valve of the brewing device. If steam explodes out of the wand at the first half turn of the knob, reduce the heat. You should be able to open the knob at least a half turn before the full force of the steam is heard and felt.

Raising the Froth

You can froth the milk in a separate pitcher, or in each cup before you add the coffee. In either case, fill the container or cup about halfway with cold milk (the colder the better; hot milk will not produce froth). Open the steam valve for a few seconds to bleed any hot water from inside the wand. Then close the valve until just a wisp of steam appears from the tip of the wand. This is to prevent milk from being

Steps in frothing milk

1. Insert steam wand and open valve

2. Raise wand tip to just below surface of milk. Follow the developing froth upward with wand tip.

3. When froth has developed drop wand tip deeply into milk to heat it.

sucked back up into the wand as you immerse it into the milk.

Immerse the tip deeply into the milk. Slowly open the valve, then gradually close it until you get a strong, but not explosive, release of steam that moves the surface of the milk, but does not wildly churn it. Now slowly lower the milk container, thus bringing the tip of the wand closer to the surface of the milk. When the wand tip is just below the surface of the milk you will hear a hissing sound, the surface will begin to seethe, and frothy bubbles will begin to form. If the wand tip is too deep in the milk, there will be no hiss and the surface will not seethe; if it is too shallow, you will spray milk all over your counter. If it is just right, a gratifying head of froth will begin to rise from the surface of the milk. You need to follow the froth upward as it develops. Listen for the hiss; if you do not hear it, or if it turns to a dull rumble, the wand is too deep in the milk.

The first swelling of froth will be made up of largish, unstable bubbles. Periodically drop the tip of the steam wand back into the milk and hold it there for a moment, to let some of these bubbles pop and settle. Then bring the tip of the wand back to just below the surface of the milk again to rebuild the head of froth. Repeat this process until you have a creamy, dense head of froth made up of a stable matrix of tiny bubbles.

Heating the Milk

At this point, feel the sides of the milk container to see if the milk is hot. If it is not, lower the wand tip completely into the milk and keep it there until the container's sides heat up. Never heat the milk to boiling, and again, always froth the milk first, before you heat it, since cold milk froths best. If you are frothing milk for the first time and you end up with hot milk and not much froth, enjoy what you have and try again later with cold milk.

After Frothing

Always end the frothing operation by opening the steam valve for a few seconds to clear milk residues from the holes at the tip of the wand. If you are using an inexpensive machine that utilizes steam pressure to brew the coffee, it is a good idea to let the steam valve remain open when you turn off the machine, so as to bleed the remaining steam from the boiler and relieve pressure on the valves and gaskets.

If you do not immediately raise an impressive head of froth, be patient. You may have to suffer through a few naked cappuccini at first, but inside a week you will be frothing like a Milanese master.

MILK-FROTHING GADGETS

Most manufacturers of espresso machines have attempted to simplify the milk-frothing operation by adding little gadgets to the steam wand. A couple of these devices work very well; most simply complicate cleanup.

Of the devices currently marketed, the two most effective are the Krups Perfect Froth and a can-shaped, plastic gadget called Cappuccino Magic (Faema) or whatever other names machine distributors assign to it.

The Cappuccino Magic device literally sucks cold milk out of a container, heats and froths it, and spews it back out again. It requires no skill to operate, but it does require attention—a good deal of attention. To continue to work properly it needs to be taken apart and cleaned virtually after every milk-frothing session. Furthermore, some machines are permanently equipped with these milk-sucking, froth-spewing devices, giving users no option of frothing milk in the conventional way. Most people I know who have purchased machines with permanently installed versions of these little plastic froth robots have regretted the decision.

On the other hand, the Krups Perfect Froth is a simple attachment that fits onto a conventional frothing wand. It still requires you to pour cold milk into a container and stick the wand into the milk. However, rather than holding the tip of the wand at the surface of the milk, you immerse it completely. The Perfect Froth introduces a jet of room-temperature air into the milk again with the steam and froths the milk from the inside, as it were, rather than from the surface. The Perfect Froth can be removed, enabling you to froth milk in the usual way, it is relatively easy to keep clean, and it is virtually foolproof.

All of the competing milk-frothing gadgets I have tried still require you to froth milk in the conventional way. Some make this process a bit easier for beginners; some do not.

The Braun turbo cappuccino is a tiny plastic turbine at the end of the steam wand. The steam passes through the turbine, spinning it, which beats the milk and supposedly helps froth it. The device produces a wonderfully gratifying, jet-engine whine when it is fully revved up, but it does not help the frothing operation much and complicates cleanup.

Other frothing aids are essentially aerating devices that introduce additional room-temperature air into the milk along with the steam. Why they fail to perform as dramatically as Perfect Froth does, I can't say, but all require good traditional frothing technique to work.

Recommendation:
Do It the Traditional Way

I suggest that those who enjoy espresso drinks with frothed milk buy a machine without fussy attachments and learn to froth in the traditional way. As I indicated earlier, anyone with the smallest amount of patience can master the normal frothing operation and in the process gain considerably more control over the texture and dimension of the froth than is possible even with the best of these attachments. And even if in the future someone does invent the perfect, no-miss, totally controllable milk-frothing nozzle, frothing milk the old-fashioned way may still turn out to be one of those noble, Zen-like rituals that stubbornly resist progress, like manual shifting in sports cars, wooden bats in baseball, and catching fish with dry flies.

STAND-ALONE, MILK-FROTHING DEVICES

With the popularity of caffè latte and other big-milk drinks, an array of inexpensive, stand-alone devices have appeared on appliance shelves that are designed simply to froth milk. You can use them to add frothed milk to drip or French-press coffee, for example, as well as to espresso.

Some stand-alone, milk-frothing devices are simply stove-top steam boilers with valve and wand. They sell for around $30. You use them to heat and froth milk just as you would any of the espresso brewers in Categories 2 through 5 and as outlined on pages 179–88.

Other frothing devices take a very different approach. With the most popular design, you pour milk into a glass or metal decanter and pump a sort of perforated piston through it until it is frothed. These $15 to $40 devices have no generic name. Asking the clerk for a "pumping milk frother" will probably get you to the right shelf in the store.

These gadgets are reassuring to milk-frothing novices because all they ask of the user is enough energy to pump a piston vigorously for thirty seconds. The froth produced is rather heavy and inert, however, satisfactory for a caffè latte but not for a classic cappuccino. Furthermore, heating the milk is a separate operation from frothing. The most convenient designs have no metal parts connected to the decanter, which permits you to place the decanter and milk directly into a microwave oven. Designs with metal decanters require you to heat the milk on the stove or transfer it to a metal-free container for heating in the microwave. Some designs recommend that you heat the milk before frothing, others after.

I certainly would not blame a beginner for buying one of these devices, but if you brew espresso and if your espresso brewer incorporates a steam wand, you will find it easier and simpler over the long haul to learn to froth milk in the conventional way.

ASSEMBLING THE DRINKS

Straight Espresso

If you are after the perfection of the classic, tiny cup of straight espresso at home, you need to purchase a pump or manual-lever machine (Categories 3, 4, and 5, pages 180–88). Brewing devices that work by steam pressure alone, like those in Category 2, pages 179–80, will make authentic espresso drinks with milk, but at best produce a flavorful but thin-bodied imitation of an unadorned straight espresso. A perfectly pressed espresso exits the filter holder in majestic deliberation, all heavy golden froth that only gradually condenses into a dark, rich liquid as it gathers in the cup. Such results can only be gotten with good technique on machines that exert more than the relatively feeble pressure generated by the steam-only devices in Categories 1 and 2.

Once you have mastered the brewing routine (see pages 161–64), the next step in making straight espresso the way you like it is to experiment with blend and roast (see Chapters 3 and 5). If your espresso tastes too sharp, try lighter-roasted blends of sweeter coffees until you find one that suits you. If your espresso lacks punch, try a darker-roasted blend. If you crave still more sharpness, try a dark-roasted blend of higher-grown coffees like Guatemalas, Costa Ricas, or Kenyas.

Do not feel reluctant to add sugar to straight espresso for reasons of sophistication, by the way. Italians almost universally sweeten espresso, and the prejudice against adding sugar to coffee is one of those Puritan tics peculiar to some North Americans. In terms of taste, the best sweetener for straight espresso is probably raw or demerara sugars. Honey tends to die when added to espresso.

Crema. The golden froth that mists over the surface of a well-made, straight espresso is the subject of mystical rhapsodies by Italian espresso lovers and can present a problem for those who brew espresso at home. You can consistently achieve it only with the pump or piston machines in Categories 3, 4, and 5. If you own such a machine, and brew carefully, following the given prescriptions, your espresso should display the rich flavor and heavy body of the true product, together with at least some crema. If your espresso tastes good but you are not getting enough crema to make you happy, make certain you are dribbling the espresso directly into a small, straight-sided, narrow demitasse cup that has been preheated by running steam from the steam wand into it.

Receptacles for Straight Espresso. Unadorned espresso is traditionally served in a 3-ounce cup (demitasse, French; tazzina, Italian), with appropriately proportioned spoon and saucer. To serve a single shot of espresso in anything except a small porcelain cup is like serving a fine wine in a jelly glass.

Straight Espresso Variations

The normal serving size for a true, aficionado's espresso is about ⅓ to ½ the volume of a 3-ounce demitasse, or about 1¼ ounces. *Corto,* short or short pull, means an espresso cut short at less than 1 ounce. *Lungo,* long or long pull, refers to an espresso that fills about ⅔ of a demitasse. In both cases, the amount of ground coffee filling the filter basket should be the same, about 1 heaping or 2 level tablespoons. The difference is the amount of water you allow to run through the coffee.

Espresso Romano. This Italian-American innovation adds a twist of lemon peel on the saucer next to a normal serving of espresso. You rub the outer surface of the lemon peel around the edge of the tiny cup so as to lightly and exquisitely scent the espresso as you drink it.

Doppio or Double Espresso. Simply two servings of espresso, brewed with two servings' worth of ground coffee. The doppio, properly made, should fill only ⅓ to ½ of a 6-ounce cup with rich, creamy espresso.

Hybrid Drinks: Caffè Americano and Depth Charge

Americano. This innovation permits you to produce something resembling North American–style filter coffee on an espresso machine. The trick is to make a single, one-to-two-ounce serving of espresso, then add hot water to taste. If you simply run several ounces of hot water through a single dose of ground coffee, you will end up destroying the subtle aromatics of the espresso with the harsh-tasting chemicals that continue to be extracted from the coffee after it has given up its flavor oils. If, on the other hand, you make a 6-ounce cup of coffee with three doses of coffee you are simply delivering a triple espresso, rather than an Americano, which tried to keep the perfumes of the original espresso while extending them into a longer drink with hot water. You can brew medium-roast varietal coffees as well as dark-roast coffees using the Americano method—an Ethiopia Harrar Americano, a Sumatra Americano, etc.

Depth Charge. This caffeine-underground invention drops a serving of espresso (tastes best made short, about 1 ounce) into a cup of regular-drip coffee. Caffeine overload aside, this can be a very pleasant and complex drink, particularly when the coffee is freshly brewed. (Try a brightly floral coffee like an Ethopia Yirgacheffe.)

Basic Drinks with Frothed Milk

The distinctions among the various classic caffè drinks involving coffee and hot milk described below—cappuccino, latte macchiato, caffè latte, etc.—may seem a bit arbitrary. After all, the only actual differences are simple: the proportion of espresso to milk, the texture of the froth, how the milk and coffee are combined, and the kind of receptacle used.

However, I can vouch for the fact that these seemingly insignificant differences in procedure and presentation make for rather dramatic differences in taste among the various traditional drinks. So even though the distinctions among the various espresso-milk drinks may blur when you are making them at home, it is well to understand the gustatory goals behind these differences.

Here is advice for assembling the traditional coffee-milk drinks at home, starting with drinks that add the least milk to the espresso to those that add the most.

Espresso Macchiato. This drink (espresso "marked" with frothed milk) is simply a demitasse of straight espresso topped with a tiny dollop of hot, frothed milk. The milk barely mellows the bite of the coffee, and the espresso comes through in its full-bodied, sweetly pungent completeness. An excellent way to take espresso for those who avoid sugar but want the power of unadorned espresso. Good also after dinner, when a milkier drink like a cappuccino tastes too diffused and looks unsophisticated. Like straight espresso, served in a preheated 3-ounce demitasse.

Cappuccino. This prince (or princess) of espresso drinks is traditionally served in a 6-ounce cup. A dense, soupily frothed milk is added to the coffee in the cup. If a cappuccino is made correctly, the perfume and body of the espresso completely permeate the froth and milk, extending throughout the drink without losing a molecule of power, while the sharpness of the coffee is softened without being subdued.

Here is how to assemble an authentic cappuccino at home. Make a perfectly pressed, very rich, small quantity of espresso, 1 to 1½ ounces, no more. Follow the instructions for brewing espresso on page 164 as precisely as possible. Pour the freshly brewed espresso into a warm 6-ounce cup.

Froth the milk to the point that it is still dense and a bit soupy, full of many tiny bubbles rather than a relatively few large ones. It should barely peak if you move a spoon through it. It should not stand up puffily. It should be hot, but not scalding. See pages 164–67 for instructions on frothing milk.

Pour the frothed milk into the cup. If you have frothed the milk correctly, and if you are using a thin-edged metal pitcher, the milk and froth should move together into the cup. You may need to encourage the froth with a spoon, however. The milk should not (cannot if it is frothed correctly) stand up like meringue above the top edge of the cup. A visual mark that you have done everything correctly is a brilliant white oval or heart shape on the surface of the drink, surrounded on all sides by a ring of dark brown, created by the espresso crema that has been carried to the surface of the milk.

Obviously, such precision does not come with your first home cappuccino. But, if you have some idea what you are trying to achieve, your very first attempts should taste better than the clumsy, uninformed production of most North American caffès.

Latte Macchiato. Milk "marked" with espresso. The complement to espresso macchiato, in which the milk marks the espresso rather than espresso the milk. There is not a great difference between espresso macchiato and caffè latte. Certainly made at home the two drinks will tend to overlap. With the latte macchiato the espresso is poured into a medium-size glass of hot milk. The emphasis is on the milk, not the froth, and the coffee, then dribbled into the glass, tends to stain the milk in gradations, all contrasting prettily with the modest white head of froth.

Caffè Latte. The caffè latte dilutes the espresso in even more milk, in a taller glass or a bowl. Traditionally the espresso and milk are poured simultaneously into the glass or bowl. The "latte" is definitely a breakfast drink. The essential idea is to provide something to dip your breakfast roll into and enough liquid to wash the roll down afterward. As with the latte macchiato, the head of froth is usually modest, so as not to interfere with the roll-dipping operation and not to distract from the psychological sensation of virtually bathing in hot, milky liquid.

The North American "latte" usually combines one longish serving (about 1½ ounces) of espresso with enough milk to fill a 12- to 16-ounce glass. This recipe produces a weak, milk drink and has encouraged various customizations involving less milk and more espresso. Obviously, at home you are free to experiment with the proportions of milk to coffee until you arrive at a balance that is particularly satisfying to your palate and nervous system. Most people customize the proportions to suit the moment: They may crave a stronger or a weaker drink depending on the time of day and the current state of their nervous systems and work schedule.

The standard receptacle in the United States for the caffè latte is the plain, 16-ounce tapered restaurant glass used in the other contexts for serving everything from milk shakes to beer. A more interesting, and arguably more authentic, serving receptacle for the caffè latte is a relatively deep, 12- to 16-ounce ceramic or glass bowl.

Caffè Mocha

Next to the cappuccino, the caffè mocha is probably the most abused drink in the traditional espresso cuisine. The classic Italian-American caffè mocha combines an American-size serving (1 to 2 ounces) of espresso and perhaps 2 ounces of strong, usually unsweetened hot chocolate in a tallish, 8-ounce ceramic mug, topped with hot milk and froth. The drink is sweetened to taste after it has been assembled and served, just as with any other espresso beverage.

This drink, smoothly perfumy and powerful, has been turned into a sort of hot milk shake by most North American caffès, where operators essentially make a caffè latte with a dollop of chocolate fountain syrup in it.

The only trick to making such counterfeit caffè mochas at home is mixing the chocolate syrup with the espresso before you pour in the milk. Use any good chocolate fountain syrup and adjust the volume of syrup and milk to taste.

Those interested in experimenting with the classic caffè mocha will need to make a chocolate concentrate. One part unsweetened, dark chocolate powder mixed with two parts hot water makes an authentic version of this concentrate. The powder and water can be combined while heating them with the steam wand of the espresso machine. As you direct the steam into the water and chocolate, stir with a spoon or small whisk, working the floating gobs of dry chocolate down into the gradually heating water. Either sweeten the mixture to taste when you mix (try brown or demerara sugar) or leave it unsweetened, giving you and your guests an opportunity to sweeten the assembled drink after it has been served. If you prefer a lighter-tasting concentrate, add a few drops of vanilla extract to the mix while you are heating it.

Try about ¼ teaspoon to every cup of chocolate powder, adjusting to taste.

To assemble the classic caffè mocha, combine about 2 ounces of this concentrate with one serving 1¼ ounces) of espresso and enough hot, frothed milk to fill an 8- to 10-ounce mug. Vary the proportions of chocolate, espresso, milk, and froth to taste.

Once mixed, by the way, the chocolate concentrate can be stored in a capped jar in the refrigerator for up to three weeks. The mixture may separate; when you are ready to use the concentrate, invert and shake the jar, then pour out into a frothing pitcher or mug as much concentrate as you want, and reheat it, using the steam wand.

White-Chocolate Mocha, Mocha Bianca. For this sweet, delicate version of the mocha, melt in a double boiler approximately 2 ounces sweetened, white baking chocolate in ½ cup boiling water. Bring the mixture to a boil, then reduce heat to a low bubbling boil for about 3 minutes, stirring regularly. This concentrate also can be refrigerated for up to three weeks. Substitute it for the chocolate concentrate in caffè mocha and other chocolate-espresso-frothed milk drinks. It contributes a sweet, delicately flavored chocolate flavor. The Torani and DaVinci syrup lines both offer a premade white chocolate syrup that can be ordered through their respective web sites (see Sending for It). Both of the made-from-scratch chocolate concentrates can be used to make hot chocolate drinks with espresso. Simply combine the concentrate to taste with hot, frothed milk.

Adding Flavors to Espresso Drinks

Flavoring Frothed Milk Drinks. Simply add Italian-style fountain syrup to taste or as indicated below. Several brands of flavored syrup, made in both the United States and Europe, now compete with the widely distributed Torani line. The Monin and Stirling lines have a reputation for subtlety, the Torani for energetic directness. If you try one of these syrups at home, keep in mind that they sweeten as well as flavor. If you are a sweet-loving sugar avoider, try one of the sugar-free syrups put out by DaVinci, Torani, and others, or the Stirling line of "light" syrups, which sweeten with a combination of diabetic-friendly fructose and small amounts of aspartame, or the Capriccio line, which is intensely flavored but low on sugar. DaVinci offers all-natural-ingredients syrups. If you have trouble finding syrups retail, consult Sending for It. Here are some suggestions for specific drinks.

Flavored Caffè Latte. If you make your caffè latte in a 12-ounce glass, start with ½ to 1 ounce of syrup to one serving (1¼ ounces) of espresso and about 8 ounces of hot, frothed milk. Put the syrup in the glass, add the freshly pulled espresso, mix the espresso and syrup lightly, then add the frothed milk. Adding the syrup last, after the milk, tends to dull the drink. Nut flavors (amaretto, orgeat/almond, hazelnut) and spice (vanilla, anisette, crème de menthe, chocolate mint) are good places to start with your syrup experiments. Berry flavors are attractive, but most tropical fruit and soda fountain (root beer, etc.) flavors seem not to resonate well with coffee.

Flavored Cappuccino. Go very lightly with the syrup here, ¼ to ½ ounce at the most, or you may ruin the balance of the drink. Add the syrup to a classic cappuccino, mix lightly, and add the milk. If you enjoy visual drama, try applying a thin, moving dribble of syrup across the surface of the froth.

Flavored Caffè Mocha. Make a mocha, adding a dash of hazelnut, almond, orange, or mint syrup mixed in with the chocolate syrup.

Flavored Garnishes. Garnishes sprinkled over the head of frothed milk that covers the surfaces of drinks like cappuccino and caffè latte have become a ubiquitous part of North American espresso cuisine. The original unsweetened chocolate of the Italian cuisine is often replaced by a sweetened chocolate, for example, and some use Mexican chocolate, a sweetened, spiced chocolate sold in cake form that must be grated over the frothed milk. Still others prefer to grate or shave baking chocolate—unsweetened, semisweet, or white—over their frothed milk drinks. A good cheese grater works well.

The traditional garnishes (unsweetened chocolate, cinnamon, grated nutmeg, and grated orange peel) are now augmented by an array of specialized sweetened and unsweetened garnishing powders. If you combine one flavor of syrup and another of garnish you have an opportunity to either subtly delight the palate or grossly confuse it. Flavor combinations that seem to marry well with espresso are orange and chocolate, almond and chocolate, hazelnut and chocolate, mint and chocolate, and orange and vanilla. Make the syrup one choice and the garnish the other. Specialty coffee stores usually sell the classic garnishes, and others can be found in the spice section of large supermarkets.

Adding Whipped Cream

Once you have mastered the basic vocabulary of espresso, syrups, frothed milk, and garnishes, you may want to add whipped cream to your repertoire. Add moderately stiff whipped cream (sweetened or unsweetened) to any espresso drink in place of a roughly similar volume of frothed milk. In other words, if you make a caffè mocha, omit about 2 ounces of frothed milk and replace it with a healthy dollop of whipped cream to fill the mug. Garnish the whipped cream as you would the frothed milk.

The Torani syrups company suggests flavored whipped cream. Blend 1 pint whipping cream with 3 to 4 ounces syrup. Store this sweetened, flavored whipped cream and use it as suggested above. Thus, if you are careful and avoid getting too dizzy with our choice of flavors, you can serve a caffè latte with milk and coffee augmented by one flavor and whipped cream by a second. And, of course, a dash of garnish to the whipped cream will complicate the business still further.

Try, for example, orange-flavored whipped cream on a classic caffè mocha; or simply vanilla-flavored whipped cream on straight espresso, with a garnish of chocolate powder. I will not tempt the ghost of espresso purists past with anything more complex than those rather modest suggestions—experiment. Maraschino whipped cream on a passion fruit–flavored cappuccino, garnished with orange peel?

Coffeeless Espresso Cuisine

As long as you have the machine, the garnishes, the milk, and the syrups, you might consider some espresso cuisine without the espresso.

Flavored Frothed Milk. This drink appears in caffès under a variety of names, from the no-nonsense "Steamer" to the fanciful "Moo." Add frothed milk to syrup (start with ½ to 1 ounce syrup per 8 ounces milk) and mix.

Hot Chocolate, Cioccolata. Make a chocolate concentrate (see pages 172–73), and top 3 to 4 ounces of hot concentrate with 4 to 5 ounces of hot, frothed milk to fill an 8-ounce mug. Garnish with either chocolate powder, vanilla powder, grated orange peel, or shaved white chocolate. Or simply stir chocolate fountain syrup to taste into milk while frothing it.

Hot Chocolate with Whipped Cream, Cioccolata con Panna. Halve the milk in the previous recipe and top with whipped cream, either unsweetened, sweetened, or flavored (for flavoring whipped cream see page 174).

Cold Espresso Drinks

The Traditional Cuisine Iced. You can make almost any espresso drink iced. Use cold milk rather than hot milk in iced cappuccino, caffè latte, etc., so as not to melt the ice prematurely, thus overly diluting the coffee. If you wish to provide a decorative head of froth to dress up the drink and provide a setting for gar-nishes, add a modest topping of hot froth (not milk) after you have combined the ice, coffee, and cold milk. Espresso that has been brewed and then refrigerated will not make as flavorful a drink as freshly brewed hot espresso but holds its strength better when poured over the ice. Take your choice.

Latte Granita, Granita Latte, Frappuccino (Starbucks). Unlike straightforward iced espresso drinks, which are cold versions of the classic cuisine and sweetened to taste after serving, these are the slushy, sweet, partly frozen drinks served in caffès and espresso bars.

It is difficult to make a drink with quite the heavy, smooth-yet-grainy texture of the commercial latte granita using a home blender, but you can produce a very attractive drink, better flavored than most caffè productions, and tailored to suit your own tastes.

For each serving brew one serving (1¼ ounces) of full-strength espresso. While the espresso is still hot, dissolve in it 1 to 3 rounded teaspoons of sugar. One teaspoon produces an austere if seductive drink; three will probably satisfy those with a sweet tooth. Combine the sweetened espresso in a blender with about 2 ounces of cold milk and 3 ice cubes per serving (partly crushed), plus a few drops of vanilla extract. Blend until the ice is barely pulverized and still grainy; serve immediately. You can brew and sweeten the espresso in advance and store it in a stoppered jar in the refrigerator for convenience, although the longer you refrigerate it the slightly less flavorful your latte granita will be.

For a mocha granita dissolve ½ to 1 fluid ounce of

chocolate fountain syrup in the freshly brewed espresso along with the sugar. Proceed as above. For every ½ ounce of chocolate syrup, reduce the sugar by 1 teaspoon.

Soda Fountain Espresso

Espresso, cold milk, ice, flavored syrups, garnishes, ice cream, and whipped cream can be combined in an endless number of ways. Here are just a few suggestions.

Affogato. Pour 1 to 2 servings (the shorter the better) of espresso over vanilla ice cream. Either stop there and start eating, or top with whipped cream, flavored or unflavored, and garnish with grated chocolate, white or dark, chocolate powder, or grated orange peel.

Cappuccino and Ice Cream. Combine one serving (1¼ ounces) espresso with 4 ounces cold milk; lay on a scoop of vanilla, chocolate, or coffee ice cream. If you prefer, top with a dollop of whipped cream and a dash of garnish.

Espresso Fizz. Pour one serving (1¼ ounces) freshly brewed espresso in a tall 12-ounce glass; mix in sugar to taste (try 1 teaspoon); fill glass with ice and soda water. Serve without mixing so that the drama of the sugared espresso lurking at the bottom of the drink can be appreciated. Before drinking, mix with an iced tea or soda spoon.

Espresso Egg Cream. Pour one serving (1¼ ounces) freshly brewed espresso in a tall 12-ounce glass; mix in sugar to taste (try 1 teaspoon). Add 1 ounce whole milk or half-and-half and fill glass with ice and soda water. Serve as in the previous recipe.

Mocha Egg Creme. Pour one serving (1¼ ounces) freshly brewed espresso in a tall, 12-ounce glass; mix in ½ to 1 ounce commercial chocolate syrup. Add 1 ounce whole milk or half-and-half and fill glass with ice and soda water. Serve as in the previous recipes.

Italian Sodas. The syrups used in the contemporary American espresso cuisine were originally intended as soft drink syrups. Combine 1 to 1½ ounces of one of these Italian-style syrups with ice and soda water to fill a tall 12-ounce glass. If you have not already, try orgeat (almond) or tamarindo (tamarind). Garnish the tamarindo with a slice of lemon.

Italian Egg Creme. Pour 1 ounce whole milk or half-and-half and 1 to 1½ ounces syrup in the bottom of a tall 12-ounce glass. Fill with ice and soda water.

Espresso Float. Make an espresso fizz or espresso egg creme with chilled soda water but without the ice; leave space at the top of a 12- or 16-ounce glass; add 1 or 2 scoops of any flavor ice cream.

Espresso Ice Cream Soda. Make an espresso float in a 16-ounce glass, leaving room at the top for whipped cream, flavored or unflavored, garnished with grated chocolate or orange peel.

Chai and Chai Latte

Chai, the strong, spicy black tea served mixed with frothed milk in espresso caffès is made with a concentrate of tea and spices. It is quite possible to grind and blend the spices for a chai mix yourself, but most people find the mixes sold at large, natural food stores more convenient.

The least convenient but most authentic chai mixes come in the form of separate packets of spice mix and black tea. You boil the spices for about 20 minutes, allow the black tea to steep in the hot spice mixture for about 4 minutes longer, then strain the resulting concentrate and store it in a stoppered bottle in the refrigerator. When you are ready to enjoy a chai latte, you simply combine the concentrate with hot milk in equal parts, heat with the steam wand, and add honey to taste.

Other chai mixes are prebrewed and sold in bottles in the refrigerated sections of natural foods stores and upscale supermarkets. The most authentic are unsweetened, which permits you to add honey to taste, and do not contain vanilla, which tends to blunt the intensity of the spice.

Still other liquid mixes contain preservatives and are sold in cartons that do not require refrigeration. Those that I have tried have not impressed me. The spicy intensity of true chai has been lost in vanilla and sweetener.

CHOOSING A HOME ESPRESSO MACHINE

If you are still tempted to acquire a home espresso machine after my detailed directions and admonitions, begin by studying the charts on pages 178–87.

The machines represented range from those that are virtually impossible to use to make true espresso (Category 1), through moderately priced machines that will make decent espresso drinks with milk if used with care and intelligence (Category 2), to expensive machines that will make near-restaurant quality and quantities of espresso (Categories 3, 4, and 5). Note, however, that the relatively expensive machines that make up the last three categories still require knowledge and attention. Espresso is an area of human endeavor, however modest, in which excellence still needs to be learned rather than purchased.

The key technical difference between the Categories 1 and 2 machines and the more expensive machines in Categories 3, 4, and 5 is the degree of pressure applied to the hot water during the brewing operation. Recall that the creamy heaviness and rich flavor of espresso result from a rapid and thorough extraction of the flavor components from the coffee, achieved by forcing hot water under pressure through compacted, finely ground coffee. The espresso brewers in Categories 1 and 2 generate the requisite water pressure by the simple means of trapped steam. The expanding steam needs to get out, the water is in the way, so the steam pushes the water out through the ground coffee, transforming it into espresso. A cutaway diagram of the simplest style of steam-pressure machine appears on page 148.

The brewers in Categories 3, 4, and 5 exert considerably greater pressure on the water by means of

a pump (Categories 3 and 5) or a lever-controlled piston (Category 4). This more intense, better-controlled pressure produces a richer, fuller-bodied espresso with a superior head of the attractive brown foam Italians call crema. But again, the espresso from these more sophisticated machines will be better only if the operator manages the process correctly. I can make better espresso with a $40 countertop steam-pressure brewer than half of the espresso operators in the country can make with their $7,000 caffè machines.

INEXPENSIVE MACHINES

Brewers in Category 2 are reasonable, inexpensive choices for home espresso brewing. Those in Category 1 are problematic in a variety of ways, but I have included them because they are part of the array of choices the consumer encounters in stores and advertisements.

BUYING ESPRESSO-BREWING APPARATUS

Category 1. Stove-top Espresso Brewers
- without wand for frothing and heating milk
- without mechanism for controlling coffee output
- brewing pressure supplied by natural buildup of steam trapped in boiler

Advantages. Some models are very inexpensive; others are very attractive. Require no counter space.

Disadvantages. Cannot produce espresso drinks using frothed milk. Require great care to produce even passable espresso. Can only brew multiple servings.

Aluminum models:	$15–$25
Stainless steel models:	$25–$50
Designer models:	$50–$250

Buying Strategies. Models that use glass or ceramic for the part of the pot that receives the freshly brewed coffee, or which dispense the coffee directly into the cup, are technically superior to designs that dispense coffee into metal receptacles. The metal tends to burn the first, flavorful dribbles of coffee. Also see page 179. Specialty coffee or cooking ware stores, catalogs, or web sites are the best places to shop for these devices, particularly for high-end designer models.

Category 1 Brewers

The brewers in Category 1 are the simple little stovetop apparatuses Italians call *caffettiere*, or coffeepots. They are so limited that they barely qualify as espresso makers. Since they lack the means to cut off the flow of coffee, you must load them with precisely the right amount of brewing water to prevent an excessive flow of water through the coffee and the production of a thin, bitter, overextracted brew. More important for the cappuccino or caffè latte drinker, these machines do not have a valve and wand for frothing and heating milk. The only reason I can think of to buy one is aesthetic: some are among the most lovely of coffee makers. The Alessi device is rightly enshrined in the design collection of the Museum of Modern Art in New York, and others ought to be, including the technically superior Bodum Verona, which brews into a glass receptacle.

Category 2 Brewers

As I indicated earlier, machines in Categories 1 and 2 work essentially in the same way. Simple expanding steam pressure in a boiler forces hot water out through the ground espresso. In the Category 2 machines, however, steam from the boiler is also tapped by a steam wand for use in frothing milk, a feature that distinguishes the units from the simpler brewers in Category 1.

Most Category 2 brewers sold today are small countertop devices with built-in electric heating elements. See opposite page for an illustration of a typical Category 2 countertop brewer.

Occasionally you may see stovetop versions for sale, made of metal, that look a little like small pressure cookers with a spout and a steam wand protruding from the top or side. These stovetop designs hold

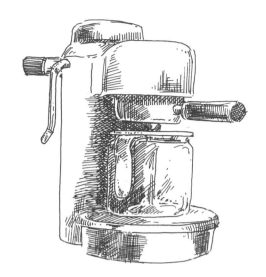

the ground coffee in a sort of largish sleeve hidden inside the brewer, whereas the electric countertop designs contain the coffee in a detachable, caffè-style filter holder protruding from the front of the machine. If you buy a Category 2 brewer, I strongly recommend purchasing one of the countertop electric designs. The internal heating element provides consistent, predictable steam pressure, and the external filter holder makes loading and cleanup easier and permits brewing smaller servings.

Category 2. Small, Countertop Steam-Pressure Espresso Brewers

- with wand for frothing and heating milk
- brewing pressure supplied by natural buildup of steam trapped in boiler

Advantages. Relatively inexpensive. Do not require purchase of a specialized espresso grinder. Operated carefully, can produce acceptable espresso drinks with frothed milk.

Disadvantages. Require close attention to make acceptable espresso. Occupy some counter space. Some models (not recommended) do not have a means for ending the brewing operation short of turning off the machine or allowing it to run out of water.

Models without switch or valve to control
coffee output: $40–$70
Models with switch or valve to control
coffee output: $50–$100

Buying Strategies. Avoid units that lack a switch or valve for cutting off coffee flow. Such inferior designs seldom mention this crucial omission on the box. Consequently, it is best to shop for these devices in the more informed context of a coffee store or web site, even though they can be purchased at almost any department store, discount or otherwise. If in doubt, purchase the Braun Espresso Master. See above.

Category 2: Recommendations

All of the Category 2 brewers, used following the instructions on pages 162–67, will make excellent espresso-and-frothed-milk drinks. However, avoid buying any brewer that does not allow you to cut off the flow of water through the coffee. This deficiency has two consequences: First, it makes controlling the brewing operation difficult, and second, the continually running coffee dissipates the steam pressure available to froth milk. If in doubt on this very important point, ask. If you are lost in the wilds of a discount department store and there is no one to ask, hold off and buy a Braun Espresso Master, a proven design.

MORE EXPENSIVE MACHINES

With Categories 3, 4, and 5, we enter the world of the true espresso machine. These miniature versions of the caffè giants generate higher water pressure and hence richer espresso than the smaller machines, give the skillful operator even more control over the brewing process, and permit the making of a rapid-fire succession of drinks without interrupting the process for cool-down and refill, thus making them appropriate for entertaining or small offices.

Category 3. Larger Countertop Pump Espresso Machines
- with wand for frothing and heating milk
- switch-activated pump system controls coffee output
- brewing pressure supplied by electric pump

Advantages. Make near caffè-quality espresso and espresso drinks with frothed milk if used correctly. Refillable reservoirs make it possible to produce any number of espresso drinks without interruption or cooldown. Achieve brewing temperature relatively rapidly. Some machines give the espresso beginner the attractive option of using preground, premeasured espresso "pods" that simplify the brewing operation.

Disadvantages. Take up counter space. Relatively expensive. Intense brewing pressure requires a fine, precise grind that can only be gotten consistently from a specialized espresso grinder or from expensive pods. Most reticent and less romantic in appearance and operation than Category 4 machines. Cheaper models ($150–$250) tend to be flimsy and subject to breakdown.

Cheaper, less sturdy models with plastic housings:	$150–$250
Sturdier models with metal housings:	$350–$800

Buying Strategies. If you brew espresso on a daily basis, buy only a sturdy, mid-to-high-priced, time-tested model ($350–$800) from a reputable manufacturer. Cheaper, flimsier machines may be satisfactory for those who brew espresso only occasionally. If you are an espresso novice, buy a machine that gives you the option to use (but does not require you to use) ESE-standard pods of preground, premeasured coffee. If you do not buy a machine that gives you the option of using pods, make certain to buy a specialized espresso grinder ($120–$300) at the same time that you buy your machine, because pump machines will only brew satisfactory espresso with fine, precisely ground coffee. Also see pages 187–88. Low-end machines in this category can be purchased at upscale department stores, but it is best to buy from a specialized coffee or cookware store, catalog, or web site.

Category 3: Pump Machines

The machines in Category 3 retailed for anywhere from $150 to $500 in early 2000. The price range is significant. The machines on the lower end of the price spectrum (say $200 and under) are flimsy and prone to breakdown, but those near the upper end are sturdy, serviceable, and good choices for the espresso afficionado.

General Features. All models, regardless of price, use pumps to pressure the hot water through the coffee. All employ the familiar, caffè-style, detachable filter and filter holder, which clamp onto the front of the machine, and brew multiple single or double servings of espresso. All have a largish water reservoir separate from the heating unit. Most heat the water to brewing and frothing temperature in a small boiler; some machines use a thermal block system—a long stretch of coiled pipe encased in a heating element. All can be refilled while in use. Most of the reservoirs are removable to facilitate the refilling procedure. The listed reservoir capacity (which is always more than the actual, functional capacity) ranges from 12 to as many as 40 cups, with the average around 25. Remember, however, that because these machines separate the water reservoir and the heating function, they can be refilled at any time, making a small reservoir less of an inconvenience than it would be in a machine that needs to be cooled down to be refilled.

All require you to follow a transitional procedure in changing from brewing espresso to producing steam for frothing milk. This transition is necessary because the optimum water temperature for brewing is lower than the optimum temperature for steam production. The transition tends to be simplest and fastest in thermal block machines. The time required for the transition can be an important decision point in deciding which machine to purchase; it can range from a few seconds to as high as one minute, which is a lot of dead kitchen time for a type-A espresso drinker.

Weight and Materials. The less expensive Category 3 machines have plastic housings, aluminum boilers, and plated brass fittings. The better and more expensive models have metal housings, brass boilers, and heavier forged-brass components.

Filter Basket Catch. Most machines have a catch that holds the filter basket inside the filter holder, enabling you to turn the filter holder upside down and knock the spent grounds into the trash without losing the filter basket in the process. Until you own an espresso machine without this feature, it is difficult to imagine how much time you can spend digging compacted grounds out of a filter basket with a spoon or digging the filter basket itself out of the garbage, where it landed after you catapulted it there by digging, banging, or spitting on it. Some kinds of catches are more effective than others. Spring-loaded rings inside the filter holder are probably the best; little plastic flaps that you need to keep a thumb on are virtually useless.

Frothing Mechanism Design. There are several design issues related to the frothing apparatus that may influence your choice of machine. Observe the positioning of the steam wand, for example. Remember that you have to manipulate a small pitcher under it.

Does it give you enough room? Or is it stumpy and half hidden under another part of the machine? Many machines have wands that are adjustable and that swing out of the way when not in use. Also, look at the knob that controls the output of steam. Is it convenient to reach and adjust while you are holding a pitcher under the steam wand? Designers have become cute about where they put the knob on some machines, apparently opting for looks rather than convenience. In some machines there is no knob; you simply activate the steam function and it takes care of itself. Adjustable controls clearly are better.

Indicator Lights and Gauges. Some machines do not provide a light or other indication that the machine has reached brewing temperature, a troublesome omission. Most machines have a simple window that permits you to check the water level in the reservoir without opening the lid.

Category 3 Pump Machines: Special Features

Pump machines in Category 3 set out to seduce the buyer with a potentially bewildering array of special features. Here are some of the more important.

Espresso Pods, ESE and Otherwise. Pods are one-serving, teabag size pouches of espresso coffee, preground and ready to use in the special pod-compatible filters that come with some Category 3 machines. Pods eliminate the most troublesome aspect of espresso brewing, which is grinding, dosing, and tamping the coffee. Unfortunately, pods are expensive, deliver somewhat less-than-fresh coffee, and require a machine with pod-compatible filters.

Pod-capable machines roughly break into two subcategories: those that can be used only with proprietary format pods specific to that single brand of machine, and those that accept standardized, generic pods and permit you to switch between conventional brewing and pod brewing. Machines that take the standardized format pods usually carry the ESE (Easy Serving Espresso) trademark.

If you are interested in the option of using pods, I strongly recommend that you buy a machine that allows you to switch between conventional load-and-tamp brewing and pod brewing using the ESE standard. Pods are wonderful for beginners and occasional espresso drinkers, but anyone who uses their machine regularly eventually will want to switch to whole-bean coffees for reasons of price and variety.

Crema-Enhancing and Other Special Portafilters. Portafilters are the smallish objects with plastic handles that hold the filter and coffee and clamp into the front of espresso brewers.

Some machines incorporate special portafilters that churn the espresso before releasing it into the cup, promoting formation of crema, the golden froth so important to a proper-looking demitasse of straight espresso. These crema-enhancing devices work, although a reasonably careful operator using the right grind of fresh coffee should have no problem producing crema with any Category 3 machine, regardless of attachment.

At least one currently available machine, the Pro-teo Barista sold by Starbucks, incorporates a portafilter that permits you to slow down or speed up the brewing process by moving the handle of the portafilter to left or right. Recall that good espresso brewing requires a balance between pressure of the brewing water and resistance from the bed of ground coffee, a balance that results in a slow but steady dribble of coffee into the cup at the rate of about 20 seconds per pull or brewing episode. Normally the resistance to the brewing pressure is regulated by the fineness of the grind and the firmness with which the ground coffee is tamped, or pressed, into the filter. The Pro-teo Barista and similar machines allow you to compensate for a less-than-optimum grind and tamp by artificially closing or opening the bottom of the portafilter, allowing more or less coffee to escape the filter.

Like pods, this feature is a reassuring expedient for beginners but not particularly useful for those who have learned how to brew in the conventional way.

Built-in Water-Softening Filters. Calcium build-up from tap water is one of the main causes of malfunction in the Category 3 pump machines. The calcium clogs the pump and valves, often rendering a new machine inoperable after only a few months of use. Some machine owners (including me) brew with distilled water; others regularly decalcify their machines with special compounds. A third alternative is provided by machines that come with built-in water-softening filters. The filters typically must be replaced every six months or so.

Waste Trays. Some machines have little built-in drawers called waste trays, meant to facilitate knocking spent grounds out of the filter when you are making multiple servings of espresso. These are handy little conveniences, but most are far too flimsy to let you nonchalantly knock the grounds out of the filter and into the drawer as caffè operators do. If you use your little plastic drawer to dispose of grounds, you probably will need to dig them out of the filter with a nonnonchalant spoon.

Milk-Frothing Aids. Almost all machines sold in milk-happy America incorporate devices intended to simplify milk-frothing. Many of these special nozzles are close to useless. Others work well but have their drawbacks. See pages 149–56.

Category 3 Pump Machines: Recommendations

To my knowledge, all Category 3 pump machines currently on the market produce satisfactory espresso, although many are flimsy and will not produce satisfactory espresso for very long. Others, like those that offer the option of using espresso pods, are easier to use for beginners. There are far too many trade-offs among price, features, and quality of materials for me to make any clear-cut, overall recommendation. I would advise against flimsy machines that cost less than, say, $250 to $300 and in favor of machines that give novices the option of using (but do not require using) ESE pods. If you have problems finding a good selection of pump machines, see Sending for It.

Category 4. Larger Countertop Piston Espresso Machines

- with wand for frothing and heating milk
- hand-operated piston controls coffee output
- brewing pressure supplied by manual or spring-powered piston

Advantages. Make near caffè-quality espresso and espresso drinks with frothed milk if used correctly. Sturdier in construction and more conversation-provoking in appearance and operation than Category 3 machines. Offer more finely tuned control of brewing pressure than Category 3 machines.

Disadvantages. Take up counter space. Expensive. Slower to warm up than Category 3 machines. Must be turned off and bled of steam pressure before refilling. Boiler is exposed in most machines and hot to the touch. At this writing no machine in this class offers the possibility of using pods of preground, premeasured espresso.

Models with manual, lever-piston
arrangements: $450–$750
Models with spring-loaded pistons
(Riviera Bristol and Electra): $700–$800

Buying Strategies. These machines fall into two categories: first, those in which the user provides the brewing pressure by leaning on a lever and, second, those in which a manually operated lever compresses a spring that drives the piston. The direct-piston

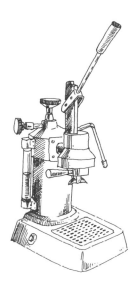

models without spring are much easier to use than the spring-driven models. In fact, they are among the most user friendly of espresso-brewing apparatus. Make certain to buy a specialized espresso grinder ($120–$300) at the same time you buy your machine, however, because piston machines will only brew satisfactory espresso with finely, precisely ground coffee. See below. The Pavoni Europiccola is the only widely distributed model in this category. For sources for other models, including the Pavoni Professional and spring-driven piston models, see Sending for It.

Category 4: Piston Machines

These shiny, old-fashioned little machines bristle with picturesque dials and knobs and supply brewing pressure via a piston operated by a long handle that protrudes from the front of the machine. They look a bit like traditional pump-piston caffè machines but most work differently. The caffè machines push water through the coffee with a spring-loaded piston. When you pull down the handle you compress a spring, and the spring propels the water through the coffee while the handle rises. With most of these smaller, home machines, there is a direct relationship between handle and piston. As you pull down on the handle, it directly propels the piston downward, forcing the hot water through the coffee. You supply the power, not a spring. Only the top-of-the-class Electra and Riviera Bristol offer a true, spring-loaded, caffè-style piston.

Regardless of how the piston works, the machines in this category all are heavy, extremely well made, and redolent with caffè nostalgia. But since they heat up an entire reservoir of water at a time, they are much slower to achieve brewing temperature than the Category 3 pump machines; most average around five minutes. And because the entire tank of water is heated, these machines much be turned off and the steam pressure relieved before being refilled.

I suppose that, from a get-on-with-it, turn-of-the-millennium point of view, a quick-to-warm-up, cheaper pump machine is preferable to these relics of an earlier era. But from the point of view of romance, durability, and maximum control over the brewing process, you cannot do better. All have been imported for years without significant change in design or construction. Most have elegant pre–World War II silhouettes, often complete with eagle atop the boiler. And this is honest romance, based on genuine relationship of form to function.

At this writing machines in this category retail for

about $450 to $800, depending on the following points of comparison.

Boiler Capacity. Since these devices need to be cooled down before being refilled, and once refilled take ten minutes or more to achieve brewing temperature, a large-capacity boiler is a distinct advantage for those who entertain.

Piston Mechanism. At this writing two machines in this category, the Riviera Bristol and the Electra, offer a true, spring-loaded, piston mechanism, whereas others simply use the muscle power of the operator to force the brewing water through the coffee. The spring-loaded design exerts considerably more pressure on the brewing water than the muscle-only models but demands a skillful operator and a precise grind to take advantage of that pressure. For espresso beginners I would recommend the much more forgiving manual piston designs.

Appearance. The romantic appearance of these devices, with their pipes, valves, and levers, is one of the main reasons many people prefer them to the more reticient-looking pump machines. Manufacturers cater to this appeal by adding fancy finishes and exotic ornament to some models, including gold plate, brass eagles, etc.

Category 4 Piston Machines: Recommendations

By far the most widely distributed and easiest-to-find machine in this category is the Pavoni Europiccola, which retails for $450 and up, depending on discount and finish. Some users complain that the Europiccola's steam production is too limited for large, frothed-milk drinks. Consequently, I recommend the Pavoni Professional or the Baby Lusso ($700 to $750), both of which incorporate larger boilers and more substantial heating elements than the Europiccola. As I indicated earlier, the spring-powered Electra and Riviera Bristol models are best purchased by experienced aficionados who know how to take advantage of their intense, unmodulated brewing pressure. If you have trouble locating a source for piston machines, consult Sending for It.

Category 5. Large, Automatic, Countertop Pump Espresso Machines
- with wand for frothing and heating milk
- grinds, loads, and brews coffee automatically
- brewing pressure supplied by electric pump

Advantages. Make near caffè-quality espresso and espresso drinks with frothed milk if used correctly. Refillable reservoirs make it possible to produce any number of espresso drinks without interruption or cooldown. Achieve brewing temperature relatively rapidly. Grinding, loading, tamping, and brewing procedures are automatic, but the operator still is required to adjust grind and froth milk. Automated grinding means no additional purchase of a specialized espresso grinder is necessary.

Disadvantages. Take up considerable counter space. Expensive. Complex mechanism means more possibility of breakdown. More reticent and less romantic in appearance and operation than Category 4 machines.

Saeco models with fewer features: $650–$800
Full-featured Saeco, Capresso, and
Gaggia models: $900–$1,200

Buying Strategies. Machines in this class may show up in upscale department stores but are easiest to find in specialized coffee or cookware stores, catalogs, or web sites. See pages 257–63.

Category 5: Automatic Pump Machines

To call these machines automatic is a bit of a stretch, since only the coffee part of the operation—grinding, loading, tamping, and brewing—is automated. You still must froth the milk and assemble the drink yourself, which is just as well, given how much people's preferences differ relative to proportion of milk to coffee. These machines also require the user to occasionally adjust the fineness of the grind so as to produce a properly slow, steady dribble of brewing coffee.

I admit that I am not much impressed by the purported advantages offered by automatic home machines. They are big, they are expensive, and they incorporate a lot of fussy, breakdown-vulnerable apparatus. Category 3 machines that accept the ESE-standard pods option are actually easier to use for beginners than these automated machines.

At this writing there are only three manufacturers

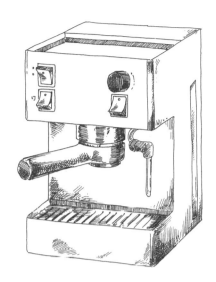

offering automatic machines. The Gaggia Automatica (around $1,200) and Capresso ($900) are better looking than the boxy-looking models in the Saeco line ($650–$1,000), but the Saecos have been around much longer and are proven performers.

(Somewhat) Beyond the Home Machine

The ultimate espresso fanatic can opt for the ultimate solution. For about the cost of a desktop computer system ($1,000 to $2,500), you can set up a small, commercial pump espresso maker in your kitchen, the kind used in smaller restaurants. Make certain that any such machine you buy has a refillable reservoir and does not require plumbing. I am particularly taken by the $1,700 ECM Giotto (See Sending for It), a very handsome, solidly built object with a gleaming chrome brewing mechanism nostalgically reminiscent of the famous FAEMA E61, the first caffè pump machine.

Final Pump or Piston Brewing Admonitions

Even with the sophisticated pump or piston machines of Categories 3 and 4, you must be sure to follow correct espresso brewing procedure: Obtain the correct grind of coffee, fill the receptacle to the point indicated, spread and tamp the coffee consistently, and stop the brewing process at the correct moment. See pages 162–63. Since these machines are rather large, complex appliances, they do not automatically transfer heat to the components that hold the coffee: the filter, the filter holder, and the group. Consequently, these components should be preheated by running hot, brewing water through them at the start of a brewing session. In addition, every machine has its own, often idiosyncratic, procedures, all of which need to be known and followed.

With the automatic pump machines in Category 5, the main trick is adjusting the grind (in small, cautious increments) to obtain the proper steady but slow 20-second extraction. See pages 187–88.

ESPRESSO GRINDERS

As you may have gathered by my obsessive carrying on about the importance of the correct grind of coffee in brewing espresso, the coffee mill or grinder is as important a piece of equipment as the brewer itself. And the more sophisticated and expensive your espresso brewer, the more expensive and sophisticated your grinder should be.

Most of the simple, inexpensive blade grinders like those described on page 119 produce an acceptable espresso grind for Categories 1 and 2 steam-pressure machines. That is, if you use them properly—if you do not load them with too many beans, if you grind in short spurts, and if you stop grinding when you have a grit just short of powder. Beware, however, of a couple of blade-style models that will not grind fine enough for any mode of espresso brewing. These espresso losers typically have "cool" in their model names.

At the other extreme, the $120-and-up specialized espresso grinders described on pages 117–18 maintain the setting for the correct grind session after session and can be adjusted in the subtle increments necessary to provide just the right fineness of grind to resist the pressure provided by Categories 3 and 4 pump or piston machines. These grinders also often include dosing mechanisms that measure portions of coffee suitable for one serving at the flick of a lever. I particularly recommend the $120 Saeco MC 2002, which is a sound, durable machine at an excellent price.

Between these extremes are the less expensive, general purpose, burr-style mills that retail between $25 and $100. The very best of these grinders, like the Capresso burr grinder and the Pavoni model PA, can be used with the finicky Categories 3 and 4 pump or piston machines. Most other burr grinders are only suitable for use with Categories 1 and 2 steam-pressure brewers, however. See pages 178–80.

ESPRESSO BAR SYSTEMS

Espresso is a complete system of coffee making, involving both grinding and brewing equipment. Several manufacturers provide the espresso fanatic the opportunity of owning a complete home espresso bar system, including matched, scaled-down versions of all of the components of a caffè setup: machine, grinder with doser, waste tray, and accessories. You can choose a modular system, with separate but complementary machine, grinder, and base or integral systems, in which everything is built into a single unit. These systems range from around $600 to $1,300. I recommend the modular systems for the obvious reason that you can repair or replace machine or grinder separately.

A GLOSSARY FOR BUYERS OF HOME ESPRESSO MACHINES

Bar System. A complete home espresso system, including brewing and milk-frothing apparatus, specialized grinder and doser, accessories, and waste tray.

Boiler. The tank in which water is heated for brewing and steam production in most espresso brewing apparatus.

Crema. The pale brown froth covering the surface of a well-brewed cup of espresso. Italians tend to diagnose espresso by the look of the crema; if the crema is too brown, the espresso has been packed too finely in the filter basket; if too pale, the espresso has been ground too coarsely or packed too loosely, and so on. This preoccupation with crema can become obsessive; sometimes Italians spend more time examining the crema than tasting the espresso. If your espresso

has thin crema but still tastes good, enjoy the flavor and forget the crema.

Doser. A spring-loaded device on some specialized espresso grinders that dispenses one serving of ground coffee per pull. These devices are mainly useful for those who entertain a good deal or those who wish to master the full espresso procedure with caffè-quality flair.

Drip Tray. A tray under the group designed to catch the overflow from the brewing process.

Filter Holder or Portafilter. The metal device with plastic handle that holds the coffee filter and clamps onto the group.

Filter or Filter Basket. The perforated, stainless-steel receptacle that holds the ground coffee during the brewing operation. It fits inside the filter holder or portafilter, which in turn clamps onto the group. Larger machines usually provide two filter baskets, one for brewing a single serving and one for brewing a double serving.

Group or Delivery Group. From Italian *gruppo,* or unit. The fixture protruding from the front of most espresso machines into which the filter holder clamps.

Piston Machine. Espresso brewing apparatus in which the intense water pressure required for espresso brewing is provided by a piston rising and falling in a cylinder, with the cylinder propelled either by the user leaning on a lever or by a lever-compressed spring.

Pull. With a pump or piston espresso machine, a single brewing episode. One pull may produce either a single serving of espresso if the single filter is used or a double serving if the double filter is used.

Pump Machine. Espresso brewing apparatus in which the intense water pressure required for espresso brewing is provided by an electric pump, rather than by trapped steam or a manually operated piston.

Reservoir. In larger, pump-activated brewing machines, the (usually removable) tank that holds the water at room temperature before it is distributed to the boiler or thermal-block unit for heating.

Shot. A serving of espresso, typically 1 to no more than 2 ounces.

Steam Wand, Nozzle, Pipe, or Stylus. All names for the little pipe that protrudes from the side of most espresso machines and provides live steam for the milk-frothing operation. Wand seems to be the currently prevailing designation.

Tamper. A little device, usually made of black plastic, that is used to distribute and compress the coffee inside the filter basket before beginning the brewing operation. Some tampers are little, hand-held accessories that you lose in drawers just when you need them and others are attached permanently to the front of larger espresso grinders or to the machine itself. These attached tampers enable you to handle the tamping operation with one-handed flair. A tamper is not a necessity, by the way. You can carry out this operation with your fingertips.

Thermal Block. A system that heats water for espresso brewing in batches by running it through loops of pipe enclosed in a boiler or heating element.

Waste Tray. A small drawer in the base of the espresso machine or bar unit designed to facilitate the disposal of spent grounds during the brewing of multiple cups of espresso.

12 SERVING IT

The social sacrament
From coffee ceremony to travel mug

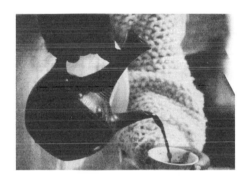

Ritual often chooses for its vehicle consciousness-altering substances such as wine, peyote, or coffee. People may assume a bit of God resides in these substances, because through using them they are separated for a moment from the ordinariness of things and can seize their reality more clearly. This is why a ritual is not only a gesture of hospitality and reassurance but a celebration of a break in routine, a moment when the human drive for survival lets up and people can simply be together. This last aspect is to me the fundamental meaning of the coffee break, the coffee klatsch, the happy hour, and the after-dinner coffee. These are secular rituals that, in unobtrusive but essential ways, help maintain humanness in ourselves and with one another.

In many cultures, the ritual aspects of drinking tea or coffee are given semireligous status. The most famous of such rituals is the Japanese tea ceremony, in which powdered green tea is whipped in a traditional bowl to form a rich frothy drink, then is ceremonially passed, in complete silence, from one participant to the next. The tea ceremony is consciously structured as a communal meditation devoted to contemplating the presence of eternity in the moment. Doubtless the caffeine in the tea aids in such psychic enterprise.

Allowed to degenerate, however, such rituals simply become excuses to display our ancient tea bowls, deco martini pitchers, or ingenious new espresso machines. The whiff of the eternal in the present, appreciated alone or shared with others, is what ultimately justifies all this fancy gear.

COFFEE AS SACRAMENT

Coffee has a long history as spiritual substance. Frederick Wellman, in *Coffee: Botany, Cultivation, and Utilization,* describes an African blood-brother ceremony in which "blood of the two pledging parties is mixed and put between the twin seeds of a coffee fruit and then the whole swallowed."

Coffee in its modern form, as a hot, black beverage, was first used as a medicine, next as an aid to prayer and meditation by Arabian monastics, much as green tea is used by Zen monks in Japan to celebrate and fortify. Pilgrims to Mecca carried coffee all over the Muslim world. It became secularized, but the religious association remained. Some Christians at first were wont to brand coffee as "that blacke bitter invention of Satan," as opposed to good Christian wine, but in the sixteenth century Pope Clement VIII is said to have sampled coffee and given it his official blessing.

The Coffee Ceremony

For people in the horn of Africa and parts of the Middle East, coffee has maintained its religious connotations, and the ritual aspects remain conscious and refined. Ethiopians and Eritreans brought their coffee ceremonies with them as they immigrated to the United States. My first experience with a formal coffee ceremony was in the apartment of an Eritrean friend in a thoroughly urban part of Oakland, California. His wife carefully roasted the green coffee beans in a shallow pan, passed the just-roasted, steaming beans around the room so that everyone could enjoy their sweet, black smoke, cooled them on a small straw mat, ground them in an electric grinder (at home in Eritrea she would have used a large mortar and pestle, but she explained that the pounding disturbed her downstairs neighbors!), brewed the coffee in a traditional clay pot, and served it in tiny cups. The entire event was an opportunity to talk and gossip while basking in the smell and spectacle of the preparation of the beverage whose consumption consummated the morning.

Since then I have participated in many similar ceremonies with African friends, in living rooms, in roadside hotels, and, most memorably, in family compounds in the Ethiopian countryside, where coffee is celebrated, not only as catalyst for community, but as the crop on which the villagers' livelihood depends. Occasionally the ritual was cut short for reason of time and one step or other was omitted, but I always felt that saturating every gesture was an unpretentious but genuine reverence for the gift of coffee, for the pleasure it brings us, and for the encouragement to community its gentle intoxication generates.

If American intellectuals had turned to the horn of Africa or Arabia rather than to Japan for their philosophy of art early in this century, the coffee ceremony might well rival the tea ceremony in influence. Though less formal, it is every bit as moving and elegant.

A World of Coffee Ceremonies

On a less literal level, a multitude of coffee ceremonies take place simultaneously all over the world: in office lunchrooms, in espresso bars, in Swedish parlors, in Japanese coffeehouses, wherever coffee drinkers gather to stare into space, to read a newspaper, or to share a moment, outside time and obligation, with their friends. Ritual is further wrapped up in the smell and taste of coffee. Certain aromas, flavors, gestures, and sounds combine to symbolize coffee and suggest a mood of contemplation or well-being in an entire culture. This, I am convinced, was the reason for the persistence of the pumping percolator in American culture in the 1940s through '60s. To Americans of that era, the gentle popping sound of the percolator and the smell the popping liberated signified coffee and made them feel good before they even lifted a cup.

Other cultures have similar associations. To people from the Middle East and parts of Eastern Europe, the froth that gathers in the pot when brewing coffee is an indispensable part of the drink, not only because it tastes good but because it symbolizes the meditative glow that comes with brewing and consuming coffee. Italians put a comparable, if somewhat less ceremonial, emphasis on the froth produced by espresso brewing. An Italian will not take a tazzina of espresso seriously if it is not topped with a layer of what to a filter-coffee drinker may look like gold-colored scum. Yet this golden scum, or crema, is what marks espresso as the real thing. Similar satisfaction resides in the milk froth that tops such drinks as caffè latte and cappuccino. The froth has almost no flavor, but a cappuccino is not a cappuccino without it.

Ritual is what gives validity to the extraordinary variety of cups, pots, and paraphernalia that human beings have developed to transport coffee from the pot to the palate. Practical issues are involved, notably keeping the coffee hot on the way, but most design variations are refinements that answer the need for the satisfaction of ritual. Of course, there is nothing to stop people from buying new gadgets or fancy pots as Christmas presents or to make an impression, but purchases made for the wrong reasons usually carry a roundabout retribution. Call it garage-sale karma. If you do not really care about espresso, for example, your new machine may end up in your driveway some Sunday selling for $5.

Coffee Anticeremonies

A comedian recently advanced the idea of drive-through communion as a way of counteracting declining church attendance.

For many of us what has happened to the public ritual of coffee in recent years is almost as grotesque. Rather than a hearty ceramic mug of drip coffee or elegant demitasse of espresso, we buy caffè lattes dispensed into cardboard with all the finesse of pumping gas. Rather than coffee as a catalyst for a brief moment alone with our thoughts, or a chat with a friend, or a round of banter with a waiter or waitress, that cardboard-encased latte is one element in a multitasking drive to work combining lukewarm coffee, a Danish lifted off a napkin on the lap, and a series of cell phone calls to clients.

Nothing to be done about this latest subversion of pleasure, of course, except exhort one another to slow down and sniff the coffee occasionally and perhaps replace the cardboard cup with a stainless steel, insulated mug.

But I often with I could transport some of the local baristas and their overcaffeinated, underserved customers to Italy, where they could experience a coffee ritual as elegant as it is brief and efficient. No one is in as much of a hurry as Italians, yet they always take a couple of minutes to give themselves to coffee and the moment that surrounds it: the tiny cup, always delivered with a small saucer and spoon, always half filled with rich, perfumy espresso, placed with economy of gesture on a clean bar. For a few seconds, nothing intrudes between the tiny pool of fragrant coffee and drinker. Then the cup is returned to the saucer with a definitive clack, the customer is on her or his way, carrying a respite, however momentary, from the press and clutter of obligation.

KEEPING IT HOT

The only absolutely practical contribution that serving paraphernalia can make to coffee-drinking pleasure is keeping the coffee hot. This contribution is an extremely important one, however. It involves a delicate balance between too much heat, which bakes the coffee, and too little, which leaves the coffee lukewarm and our senses ungratified. One way to keep coffee warm is to brew it in, or into, a preheated, insulated carafe. The other way is to apply some heat under the coffee as it is brewed.

An insulated carafe is by far the best approach technically. Any external heat, no matter how gentle, drives off delicate flavor oils, cooking the coffee and hardening its flavor.

Fortunately, there is no lack of brewing devices

that protect coffee heat in insulated receptacles during and after brewing. Automatic, filter-drip machines that brew directly into insulated carafes are available in a variety of styles and prices, and several designs of French-press brewer replace the usual glass brewing decanter with an insulted metal or plastic decanter. Designs incorporating insulated carafes typically cost a bit more than those that brew in or into conventional glass decanters, but for anyone who cares about coffee quality it is money well spent.

As for the less desirable expedient of keeping coffee hot by putting some heat under it, solutions range from the familiar hot plates on automatic drip machines to gentler approaches like candle warmers and insulated cloth wraps for French-press pots. Filter-drip purists who pour the water over the coffee by hand have the option of keeping their coffee hot by immersing their brewing decanters in a bath of warm water. Simply gently heat some water in any kitchen pan or pot large enough to accommodate both water and brewing decanter, and leave the combination over a very low flame as you enjoy the coffee. Of all of the heat-applying approaches to keeping coffee hot, this one is probably the least destructive to flavor.

SERVING PARAPHERNALIA

Covered serving pots have been in vogue since the Arabs started drinking coffee. At import stores you can find the traditional Arabian serving pot, with its S-shaped spout, Aladdin's lamp pedestal, and pointed cover. You can also occasionally find an ibrik, or Middle Eastern coffeemaker, with an embossed cover for keeping coffee hot. The changes in English coffeepot design are fascinating. On one hand stands the severe, straight-sided pewter pot of the seventeenth century, which suggests a Puritan in a stiff collar; on the other, the silver coffeepot of the Romantic period, which takes the original Arabian design and makes it seethe with exotic squiggles and flourishes.

Coffee-server design has continued to swing between these extremes. Although in the past two decades the coffeepot and matching sugar dish and creamer have been out of fashion, they are making a modest comeback, right next to the martini pitcher and cocktail shaker. Always favored by an esoteric few, the continental-style coffee server is an excellent choice for the coffee ritualist. Smaller than the English-style pot, it has a straight handle that protrudes from the body of the pot. The French often serve the coffee portion of the café au lait in this kind of pot and put the hot milk in a small, open-topped pitcher. You pick up the coffee with one hand, the milk with the other, and pour both into the bowl or cup simultaneously, in a single, smooth gesture. The straight handle, which points toward you and allows you to pour by simply twisting your wrist, facilitates this important operation. These pots are available in copper for around $25.

The coffee thermos, the space-age contribution to coffee serving, works like the old thermos jug but has design pretensions and is much easier on flavor than reheating. The cheapest (about $15 to $20) are plastic and embody a bright, postmodern chic. Bauhaus classicists can choose from clean-lined, stainless steel designs (around $25), while crystal-and-silver types can find thermoses ($60 and up) that rework traditional nineteenth-century designs in brass or silver-plate.

Mugs, Cups, Saucers

Coffee is probably best served in ceramic mugs or cups that have been warmed first with a little hot water. There are many stylistic directions to take: fancy china, deco and moderne revivals, new-wave whimsy, hand-thrown earthenware, inexpensive machine-made mugs that look hand-thrown, classic mugs and cups from restaurant suppliers, and contemporary imported restaurant ware from Europe. I prefer the restaurant-supply cup; it looks solid, feels authentic, reflects the hearty democratic tradition of coffee, and bounces when you drop it.

Straight espresso and after-dinner coffees brewed double strength are traditionally served in a half-size cup, or demitasse. It seems appropriate to drink such intense, aromatic coffee from small cups rather than from ingratiatingly generous mugs. You should have the small demitasse spoons that go with the cups; an ordinary spoon looks like a shovel next to a demitasse.

You can save considerable money on such gear at restaurant-supply stores.

The half-size cups used in the Middle Eastern and North African cuisine traditionally do without the little ceramic handle and sometimes are mounted on elegant metal stands. Most large North American cities today harbor neighborhoods of Middle Eastern or Ethiopian and Eritrean immigrants where specialty stores carry a broad range of goods from back home, including an assortment of traditional cups and coffee gear.

Nearly every traditional espresso specialty has its specialized style of cup, mug, or glass: unadorned espresso or espresso macchiato, a heavy demitasse cup and saucer; cappuccino, a heavy 6-ounce cup and saucer; mocha, a substantial mug; caffè latte, a 12- or 16-ounce glass or bowl; latte macchiato, an 8- or 10-ounce glass.

German and Scandinavian tradition calls for paper-thin porcelain cups for the water-thin coffee served at the traditional Kaffeeklatsch. Andres Uribe, in his book *Brown Gold,* claims that women at the original German Kaffeeklatsch called their coffee *Blumenkaffe,* "flower-coffee," after the little painted flowers that the thin, tealike beverage permitted them to see at the bottom of their Dresden cups.

MILK AND SWEETENERS

When I was a teenager in the Midwest, drinking coffee any other way than black was suspect. People would leer patronizingly at you and tell you that you

could not possibly like coffee if you had to add cream and sugar to it. I assume that they did not like beef, because most of them ate it seasoned. Perhaps the midcentury preference for thin, black coffee went along with an equivalent love of characterless white wines, dry martinis, and lager beer. It was as though to admit to liking sweet, heavy drinks was tantamount to confessing some unpardonable moral weakness.

Milk and Coffee

Today, of course, people have no problem whatsoever dousing espresso with kindergarten quantities of milk, not to mention an ounce or two of flavored syrup. The change may be partly owing to the contemporary tendency to brew stronger coffee, which stands up better to milk and sweetener than did the thin, underflavored beverage drunk in America in the years before the advent of specialty coffee. All of the great rich, full-bodied coffees of the world, brewed correctly, carry their flavor through nearly any reasonable amount of milk. And a great, rich, full-bodied

coffee brought to a moderately dark roast (not a thin, burned French roast) will carry through milk even better.

Too much milk, of course, cools the coffee, unless you heat it or, better yet, heat it and froth it with the steam wand of an espresso machine. As everyone knows, milk heated conventionally tends to congeal unpleasantly, an aesthetic turn-off avoided by heating and frothing milk with steam. Anyone who enjoys milk in coffee might consider purchasing an inexpensive countertop espresso machine (Category 2, page 179) simply to froth and heat milk.

Demon Sugar, Other Sweeteners, and Coffee

The debate over sugar in coffee has raged almost as long as the caffeine controversy, though with considerably less rancor. The inhabitants of the Arabian Peninsula, the first recorded coffee drinkers, apparently drank their coffee black and unsweetened, adding only spices. The Egyptians are given credit for having first added sugar to coffee, around 1625, and for having devised the traditional Middle Eastern mode of coffee brewing, in which powdered coffee is brought to a boil together with sugar to produce a sweet, syrupy beverage. The dairy-shy Egyptians still did not think to add milk to their sweetened coffee, however. Although the Dutch ambassador to China first experimented with milk in his coffee in 1660, this innovation did not become widely accepted until Franz George Kolschitzky opened the first Viennese café in 1684 and lured his new customers away from their beer and wine by adding both milk and honey to strained coffee.

Now that granulated sugar is a dietary villain in many circles, people who like to sweeten coffee resort to a variety of alternatives. Artificial sweeteners using saccharine like Sweet'n Low are unsatisfactory; coffee exaggerates their flat, metallic flavor. Aspartame-based sweeteners like Equal resonate with coffee much better, although the aftertaste still may be a touch tinny. To my palate, honey fades away in coffee, but the molasses in dark brown and raw or demerara sugars actually reinforces the rich, dark tones of coffee flavor. You are still consuming sugar, but you are adding some iron and B vitamins. The Japanese recognize the flavor symbiosis of raw sugar and coffee by calling the former coffee-sugar.

13 GROWING IT

How coffee is grown
processed, and graded
Growing your own

To imagine an arabica coffee tree, think of a camellia bush with flowers that resemble jasmine. The leaves are broad, shiny, and shaped like an arrow or spearhead. They are three to six inches long and line up in pairs on either side of a central stem. The flowers—small, white, star-shaped blossoms borne in clusters at the base of the leaves—produce an exquisite, slightly pungent scent. The white color and nocturnal aroma of the flowers may suggest that the coffee plant is pollinated by moths or other night-flying insects, but in fact the plant largely pollinates itself. In freshly roasted coffee, a hint of the flowers' fragrance seems to shimmer delicately within the darker perfumes of the brew, and some coffees, Ethiopia Yirgacheffe for example, are spectacularly floral.

The arabica plant is an evergreen. In the wild it grows to a height of 14 to 20 feet, but when cultivated it is usually kept pruned to about 6 to 8 feet to facilitate picking the beans and to encourage heavy bearing. It is self-pollinating, which accounts for the stability and persistence of famous varieties of the arabica species like *typica* and *bourbon*.

Flowering and Fruiting

In such regions as Brazil, where one or two rainy seasons each year are followed by dry seasons, the hills of the plantations whiten with blossoms all at once. In areas with sporadic rainfall the year around, like Sumatra, blossoms, unripe fruit, and ripe fruit may cohabit the trees simultaneously. Most coffee-growing regions fall somewhere between these two extremes, with a broad season of flowering provoked by rain and a longish, relatively dry season of fruiting and harvest.

The scent of an entire coffee plantation in bloom can be so intense that sailors have reported smelling the perfume two or three miles out to sea. Such glory is short-lived, however; three or four days later, the petals are strewn on the ground and the small coffee berries, or cherries as they are called in the trade, begin to form clusters at the base of the leaves.

In six or seven months, the coffee cherries have matured; they are oval, about the size of your little finger. Most varieties turn bright red when ripe; a few varieties ripen to a golden yellow. Inside the skin and pulp are nestled two coffee beans with their flat sides together. Occasionally, there are three seeds in one cherry, but a more common aberration is cherries that contain just one seed, which grows small and round, and is sold in the trade as peaberry coffee. Each tree can produce between one and twelve pounds of coffee per year, depending on soil, climate, and other factors. The plants are propagated either from seed or from cuttings. If propagated from seed, a tree takes about three years to bear and six to mature.

Shade vs. Sun

Coffee arabica grows wild in the mountain rain forests of Ethiopia, where it inhabits the middle tier of the forest, halfway between the brushy ground cover and the taller trees. It grows best wherever similar conditions prevail: no frost, but no hot extremes; fertile, well-watered but well-drained soil (soil of volcanic origin seems best). Heavy rainfall can cause the trees to produce too much too fast and exhaust themselves; inadequate rain prevents the trees from flowering or bearing fruit. The tree requires some but not

Coffee planted in managed shade. The coffee trees under the much taller shade trees are about three years old. Antigua Valley, Guatemala.

The tendency of growers in regions where shade growing is traditional to replace shade-grown coffee groves with new hybrid trees that grow well in sun and bear quickly and heavily is controversial, since these new fields of sun-grown coffee reduce diversity and require more artificial chemical inputs than shade-grown trees.

The Higher the Better (Usually)

Whereas arabica trees planted at low altitudes in the tropics overbear, weaken, and fall prey to disease, trees grown at high altitudes, 3,000 to 6,000 feet, usually produce coffee with a "hard bean." The colder climate encourages a slower-maturing fruit, which in turn produces a smaller, denser, less porous bean with less moisture and more flavor.

Beware, however, of easy distinctions. Some of the world's most celebrated coffees are softer bean, including Hawaii Kona, Sumatra Lintong, and Jamaica Blue Mountain.

Traditional vs. Hybrid Varieties

Researchers working in growing countries continue to develop new varieties of arabica that begin to bear fruit more quickly after planting than traditional varieties of arabica, bear more fruit, and are more disease-resistant. Often these hybrid varieties have in their heritage a bit of robusta, the coffee species that

too much direct sunlight; two hours a day seems ideal. The lacy leaves of the upper levels of the rain forest originally shaded the coffee tree.

In many parts of the world, including Central America, Mexico, Colombia, Ethiopia, and other regions, arabica coffee is traditionally grown in shade, which can range from dense thickets of native plants to careful, uniform plantings of imported shade trees. In other parts of the world—Hawaii, the Mandheling region of Sumatra, the Blue Mountain region of Jamaica, and many other places—coffee is not grown in shade because the weather is too rainy and wet and the trees need all the sun they can get. In other places—Yemen, Brazil—coffee is traditionally grown in sun.

is much hardier than arabica but which is (at best) neutral in the cup.

Hybrids and Taste. These hybrid varieties, whether or not they incorporate robusta, often do perform as intended, but many importers and roasters feel that this performance is at the cost of cup quality. For example, they attribute the fall-off in quality of Colombian coffees in recent years to the efforts of the Colombian government to replace "old arabicas," mostly of the respected *bourbon* and *typica* varieties, with the newer, faster- and heavier-bearing Colombia or Colombian variety.

As with generalizations connecting high, growing altitude and superior cup quality, the contention that traditional varieties of arabica are better tasting than newer hybrid varieties can be overstated. Traditional varieties usually display more character in the cup than hybrid varieties, but not invariably.

Genetically Engineered Coffees. Bear in mind that the "new" arabicas are not genetically engineered. They have been developed using traditional methods of cross-pollination and selection. However, two genetically engineered varieties have been developed by technicians in Hawaii.

At this writing they have not yet been released. They may never be, given current public resistance to genetically engineered crops. One variety is designed to simplify machine picking by producing fruit that ripens all at once rather than sporadically. The other variety is a favorite story of the media: It is a variety that grows naturally without caffeine. The chromo-somes that cause the plant to produce caffeine apparently have been inverted, neutralizing them. At this writing the first crop from both sets of test trees is on its way, at which point we will have some idea of how these engineered coffees actually taste.

Estates, Plots, and Plantations

The best coffees of the world are grown either on medium-size farms, often called estates, or on peasant plots. Processing of estate coffees is usually done on the farm itself or by consignment at nearby mills. The best peasant-grown coffees are generally processed through well-run cooperative mills. The farmer grows food crops for subsistence and some coffee for exchange. The cooperatives, often government sponsored, attempt to maintain and improve growing practices and grading standards.

In parts of the world with advanced economies and high labor costs, farms may be very large so as to facilitate economies of scale and the efficient use of technology. Mainly in Brazil, but also in Australia and parts of Hawaii, coffee trees may stretch for miles in groves as perfectly tended and monotonous as Iowa corn fields. Coffees from these large farms can range from mass-produced and mediocre (many Brazil coffees) to splendid products of exquisite technical sophistication (the best Brazil coffees).

The poorest-quality coffees of the world are peasant-grown coffees that are not properly picked or handled. In these cases the governments involved usually have failed to provide leadership in encouraging quality and establishing the kind of well-run processing facilities that make the small-holder coffees of

Left, selective coffee picking in East Africa. Right, strip picking in Brazil. In strip picking, the middle part of the branches are stripped of (mostly ripe) coffee fruit, which falls onto sheets laid on the ground beneath the trees. Done properly, as it is being done here, strip picking can be remarkably effective at harvesting only ripe fruit.

Kenya and the Yirgacheffe region of Ethiopia, for example, among the finest origins in the world.

Ripe Is Best

Harvesting is one of the most important influences on coffee quality. Coffee processed from ripe cherries is naturally sweet and shimmering with floral and fruit notes. Coffee processed from unripe cherries may taste grassy, green, thin, or astringent. Coffee processed from overripe, shriveled cherries (sometimes called raisins) runs the risk of tasting fermented, musty, or moldy.

Harvesting coffee is particularly challenging because coffee fruit typically does not ripen uniformly. The same branch may simultaneously display ripe red cherries, unripe green cherries, and dry, past-ripe black cherries.

In regions where labor is inexpensive or where families pick their own small plots, trees may be picked repeatedly, and only ripe fruit harvested during each pass through the trees. In part of the world where labor is scarce or expensive, coffee may be stripped from the trees in a single picking. Ripe, unripe, and overripe cherries are all gathered together, along with some leaves and twigs. Although sophisticated sorting methods can compensate to some degree for mass picking, no expedient is quite as effective as repeated, skillful hand picking.

Mechanical coffee harvester at work on a large farm in Hawaii. Fiberglass rods vibrate the branches, shaking ripe fruit loose but leaving most unripe fruit still attached to the branches. These machines are used only on flat terrain in regions with relatively high labor costs: large farms in Hawaii (not Kona), in the Cerrado and Bahia regions of Brazil, and in Australia.

Machines have been developed that selectively pick ripe cherries by vibrating the tree just vigorously enough to knock loose the ripe fruit, while leaving the unripe fruit still attached to the tree. Such machines do not approach the selectivity of a good hand picker, and are used only in regions of the world—Brazil, Australia, and parts of Hawaii—where labor is too costly to support hand picking. Almost all fine coffee is still picked selectively by hand.

Fruit Removal and Drying

How the fruit is removed from the coffee and how it is dried are extraordinarily important to how it finally tastes. If the fruit removal and drying, collectively called processing, is done carefully, the coffee will taste clean and free of distracting off-tastes. Furthermore, the various processing methods—dry, wet, and semidry—influence the cup character of coffee in fascinating and complex ways.

The Dry Method. In this, the oldest of processing methods, the coffee fruit is simply picked and put out into the sun to dry, fruit and all. It is spread in a thin layer and raked regularly to maintain even temperatures from top to bottom of the layer. Drying takes anywhere from ten days to three weeks, and, on larger farms, occasionally may be accelerated by putting the coffee into mechanical driers. The hard, shriveled fruit husk is later stripped off the beans by machine. In the marketplace, coffee processed by the dry method is called dry-processed, unwashed, or natural coffee.

The Wet Method. Here the fruit covering the seeds/beans is removed before they are dried. The wet method further subdivides into the classic ferment-and-wash method and a newer procedure variously called aquapulping or mechanical demucilaging. Regardless of which of the procedures is used, coffee processed by the wet method is called wet-processed or washed coffee.

In the classic ferment-and-wash version of the wet method, the fruit that covers the beans is taken off gingerly, layer by layer. First, the outer skin is gently slipped off the beans by machine, a step called pulping. This leaves the beans covered with a sticky fruit residue. The slimy beans then are allowed to sit in tanks while natural enzymes and bacteria loosen the sticky residue by literally beginning to digest it. This step is called fermentation. If water is added to the fermentation tanks, it is called wet fermentation; if no water is added and the beans simply sit in their own

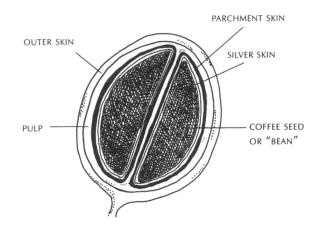

Cross-section of a coffee fruit. In the wet-processing method of fruit removal, the outer skin and pulp are removed immediately after harvesting. The parchment skin and silver skin are removed later, after drying. In the dry-processing method, the entire fruit is dried after harvesting and the various shriveled layers of fruit removed from the bean in a single operation after drying.

juice, it is called dry fermentation. The fermentation step is one of the main ways coffee-mill operators can nuance the taste of the coffees they process. Dry-fermented coffees usually are more complex and sweet than wet-fermented coffees, which tend to be brighter and drier in taste.

After the fermentation step, the coffee is gently washed and then dried, either by the sun on open terraces, where the thin layer of beans is periodically raked by workers, or in large mechanical driers, or in a combination of the two. This leaves a last thin skin covering the bean, called the parchment skin or pergamino. If all has gone well, the parchment is thoroughly dry and crumbly and easily removed. Coffee occasionally is sold and shipped in parchment or *en pergamino,* but most often a machine called a huller is used to crunch off the parchment skin before the beans are shipped. A last, optional step is polishing, which gives the dry beans a clean, glossy look important to some specialty roasters. Other roasters condemn polishing as pointless and detrimental to taste owing to the friction-generated heat it applies to the beans.

Machine-Assisted Wet-Processing. The mechanical demucilage or aquapulp variation of the wet method is essentially a short-cut approach that removes the sticky fruit residue from the beans by machine scrubbing rather than by fermenting and washing. This mechanized short cut is increasingly popular for two reasons, one admirable and one not so admirable.

The admirable reason: Mechanical demucilaging cuts down on water use and pollution. Ferment and wash water stinks, and communities downstream from coffee mills understandably object to having stinky water injected into their fisheries and water supply.

The not so admirable reason: Removing mucilage by machine is easier and more predictable than removing it by fermenting and washing. Unfortunately, machine demucilaging has been accused of limiting the taste palate of coffee by prematurely separating fruit and bean. By eliminating the fermentation step, the practice definitely robs mill operators of the most important expressive option they have at their disposal to influence coffee flavor. Furthermore, the eco-

Picking defective beans from coffee drying on raised racks in the Yirgacheffe region of Ethiopia. In most parts of East Africa coffee is dried on raised platforms, which allow air to circulate under and through the drying coffee.

logical criticism of the ferment-and-wash method increasingly has become moot, since a combination of low-water equipment plus settling tanks allows conscientious mill operators to carry out fermentation without polluting.

The Semidry or Pulped Natural Method. This procedure is practiced regularly in only two regions of the world, Brazil and certain parts of Sumatra and Sulawesi. The outer skin is removed as it is in the wet process, but the troublesome sticky fruit residue is allowed to dry on the bean and later removed by machine along with the parchment skin.

Keeping the Methods Straight. To summarize, the main technical difference among the various processing methods is how and when the outer skin and the sticky mucilage are removed from the beans. In the dry method, both skin and mucilage remain on the beans throughout the drying process to be removed later by machine. In the semidry or pulped natural method, the outer skin is removed immediately after picking but the sticky mucilage is allowed to dry on the beans and removed later. In the washed method, both outer skin and mucilage are removed immediately, either by controlled fermentation and washing or by machine scrubbing.

Careless Processing and Taste Taints

Regardless of method, there are many moments of truth in processing coffee, and many points when expedience may tempt the mill operator to cut corners.

There are two main categories of flavor taints caused by careless fruit removal and drying. The first is inadvertent fermentation of the sugars in the fruit (not to be confused with the deliberate, controlled fermentation that is part of the ferment-and-wash method). When sugars in the fruit ferment, they impart a taste to the coffee ranging from disturbingly overripe to outright, compost-pile rotten.

The second threat poor processing poses to coffee flavor is a harsh, flavor-dampening taste caused by molds or microorganisms that invade the fruit and/or the bean during drying and storage. These organisms attack the coffee during interruptions in the drying process (the drying coffee may be rained on, for example) or during storage and transportation (the coffee may be too moist when put into shipboard containers, where it develops molds). These tastes are often divided by coffee cup testers into categories—moldy, musty, baggy, medicinal, etc.—but all of these taints share a common sensation, a sort of taste-deadening hardness or harshness.

Flavor and Processing Method

However, if all goes well, each processing method accentuates certain aspects of coffee flavor. Generally, coffees processed by the mechanical mucilage wet method will be brightest, driest, and cleanest tasting. Those processed by the ferment-and-wash wet method will be next brightest and driest, though often a bit fruitier and more complex. Coffees processed by the semidry and the dry methods tend to be fruitiest, most complex, and heaviest in body owing to longer contact with fruit residue during drying.

Most fine coffees are processed by the classic ferment-and-wash wet method. A few, like Jamaica Blue Mountain and some Cost Rica coffees, are not processed by the mechanical mucilage method. A handful of coffees from Brazil and from Sumatra and Sulawesi are processed by the semidry or pulped natural method. Only three of the world's premium coffees are processed by the dry method: the finest coffees of Brazil and the splendid coffees of Yemen and the Harrar region of Ethiopia.

Why is the wet method used to process most of the finest coffees: Mainly because so much more can go wrong during dry-processing than during wet-processing. Since drying the entire coffee fruit takes so much longer than drying washed beans, there are more opportunities for the fruit to attract mold, ferment, or even rot. Most dry-processed coffee is also picked carelessly, which means there will always be some contamination of flavor by green or overripe fruit. Processed with care, however, dry-processed coffees can be as good as washed coffees, if not better, owing to their complexity and fruit-toned sweetness.

Cleaning and Sorting

The final steps in coffee processing involve removing the last layers of dry skin and remaining fruit residue from the now dry coffee, and cleaning and sorting it. These steps are often called dry milling to distinguish them from the steps that take place before drying, which collectively are called wet milling.

Removal of Dried Fruit Residue. The first step in dry milling is removing what is left of the fruit from the bean, whether simply the crumbly parchment skin in the case of wet-processed coffee, the parchment skin and dried mucilage in the case of semidry-processed coffee, or the entire dry, leathery fruit covering in the case of dry-processed coffee. The machines that do this range from simple millstones in Yemen to sophisticated machines that gently whack at the coffee.

Sorting by Size and Density. Most fine coffee goes through a battery of machines that sort the coffee by density of bean and by bean size, all the while removing sticks, rocks, nails, and miscellaneous debris that may have become mixed with the coffee during drying. First machines blow the beans into the air; those that

Drying coffee on patios. Top, concrete patio in the Cerrado region of Brazil. Bottom, brick patio in the Antigua Valley of Guatemala. As coffee dries on patios it must be almost constantly raked to prevent the moist beans from clumping and attracting molds or other flavor-inhibiting microorganisms.

fall into bins closest to the air source are heaviest and biggest; the lightest (and likely defective) beans plus chaff are blown in the farthest bin. Other machines shake the beans through a series of sieves, sorting them by size. Finally, an ingenious machine called a gravity

211

Coffee showing the dried parchment skin torn and partially removed, revealing the coffee beans inside. Coffee processed by the wet method is dried and conditioned inside this parchment skin "en pergamino." The parchment skin later is removed in a step called dry milling.

separator shakes the sized beans on a tilted table, so that the heaviest, densest, and best vibrate to one side of the pulsating table, and the lightest to the other.

Sorting by Color. The final step in the cleaning and sorting procedure is called color sorting, or separating defective beans from sound beans on the basis of color rather than density or size. Color sorting is the trickiest and perhaps most important of all the steps in sorting and cleaning.

Color Sorting by Eye and Hand. With most high-quality coffees, color sorting is done in the simplest possibly way—by hand. Teams of workers, often the wives of the men who work the fields, deftly pick dis-

colored and other defective beans from the sound beans. The very best coffees may be hand cleaned twice (double picked) or even three times (triple picked). Coffee that has been cleaned by hand is usually called European preparation. Most specialty coffees, since they are whole bean and consumers see what they get, are European preparation.

Color Sorting by Machine. Sophisticated machines can now mimic the human eye and hand. Streams of beans fall rapidly, one at a time, past sensors that are set according to parameters that identify defective beans by value (dark to light) or by color. A tiny, decisive puff of compressed air pops each defective bean out of the stream of sound beans the instant the machine detects an anomaly.

These delicate machines are not widely used in the coffee industry for two reasons. First, the capital investment to install them and the technical support to maintain them is daunting. Second, and perhaps most important, sorting coffee by hand supplies much-needed work for the small rural communities that cluster around coffee mills. The vision of huge rooms filled with women and a scattering of teenage boys patiently picking through piles of green coffee may offend urbanites, but the economic suffering caused by replacing these women with machines and a highly paid technician from the city is not a comfortable alternative either, particularly in small rural communities with strong communal values.

On the other hand, computerized color sorters are essential to coffee industries in regions with relatively high standards of living and high wage demands, places like Brazil and Hawaii. Readers who have seen television depictions of the slums of Rio may doubt that a labor shortage exists in rural Brazil, but it does. The main areas of coffee production in Brazil are quite prosperous, with a per capita income approximately equal to that of Belgium.

At the other extreme of the coffee economic spectrum is Yemen, where even the usual battery of machines that sort coffee by density and size are unknown, and hand sorting and cleaning is the only sorting and cleaning this wonderfully idiosyncratic coffee receives.

Grading and Beyond

The last step in coffee's complex, labor-intensive trip to market is grading, the procedure whereby agricultural products are categorized to facilitate communication between buyer and seller. Approaches differ from country to country, but there are four main grading criteria: how big the bean is, where and at what altitude it was grown, how it was prepared and picked, and how good it tastes, or its cup quality. Coffees also may be graded by the number of imperfections (defective and broken beans, pebbles, sticks, etc.) per sample.

As the finest coffees move from the status of commodities sold by description to specialty products sold by specific lot, grading becomes less important, and origin (farm or estate, region, cooperative) more important. Growers of premium estate or cooperative coffees may impose a quality control that goes well beyond conventionally defined grading criteria because they want their coffee to command the higher price that goes with recognition and consistent quality.

Even with fine coffee, however, government agencies in growing countries may impose grading standards to encourage and support quality and to attract and reassure foreign buyers. Coffee-growing countries like Kenya, for example, simultaneously promote high standards through imposing strict grading criteria while supporting growers by providing agricultural and social assistance. In many cases, governments may extend their support efforts to the consuming countries, where they promote their growers' coffees either behind the scenes or directly through media campaigns, like the famous and successful Colombian effort featuring Juan Valdez and his donkey.

Coffees may be subject to still another grading or sorting after they reach the United States. The San Francisco broker Mark Mountanos runs several already premium coffees through additional sophisticated machine sortings to further eliminate defects and sells these ultraselected beans for a premium as "San Francisco Preparation" coffees. Coffee-handling facilities and warehouses elsewhere may provide similar services. As sorting devices increase in sophistication and decrease in price, the industry may see more such regrading of coffees by importers in consuming countries.

Organically Grown Coffees

The issues surrounding coffee and chemical-free or organic agriculture are detailed in Chapter 6. A good deal of the coffee appearing in specialty stores is probably close to chemical-free, simply because the small peasant farmers who grow it cannot afford to purchase chemicals. They raise vegetables, keep some chickens and goats, and grow coffee to supply (a little) cash. The certified Latin America, Timor, and Papua New Guinea organic coffees now appearing in specialty coffee stores may have been grown in chemical-free conditions for years; the certification process simply confirms their chemical-free status for the consumer, while helping the growers understand, systematize, and improve their traditional agricultural processes. The certification movement has thus far reached only Latin America, Timor, and parts of Indonesia and Papua New Guinea. I am certain, however, that virtually all coffees raised in Ethiopia, Yemen, and the Mandheling region of Sumatra are also grown by traditional means, without chemicals.

People, Environment, and Coffee Growing

I outline the social, economic, and environmental issues surrounding coffee growing in Chapter 6 and show how those issues are reflected in the marketing of organic, bird-friendly, fair-trade, and other niche coffees in North American retail stores and web sites. In the larger picture, anyone who buys a specialty coffee by country of origin rather than by supermarket brand name is helping create better economic, social, and environmental conditions in growing countries, since the selling of coffee as an anonymous, price-driven commodity is at the heart of the oppression of the many millions of people in growing countries whose toil and passion go into the long, arduous process of bringing coffee from seedling to market.

Growing Your Own

Some enthusiastic readers may want to begin growing their own coffee. Unfortunately, for most of us this is a dream that is difficult to realize. A true devotee would need a commercial-size greenhouse or a large backyard in or near the tropics. The environment must be frost-free, which eliminates most yards in the United States. Then assume that one mature tree trimmed to about six feet tall will produce an average of two to four pounds of coffee a year. Obviously, a very substantial coffee orchard, a dozen trees at least, would be needed to keep the average coffee lover happy.

Growing It Indoors. If you want just a small specimen, the *Coffea arabica* is easy to grow indoors, makes a very attractive house plant, and may bear flowers and fruit. You can start a coffee plant in one of three ways. The easiest is to buy a seedling. Although *Coffea arabica* is not an extremely popular house plant, indoor nurseries occasionally carry it, and most will accept special orders. The next-easiest method is to take a cutting from a friend's plant and root it. Finally, you can plant some green coffee beans and wait for them to sprout in about three or four weeks. Obviously, the green beans that reach the coffee store are at least a couple of months old, and most will never germinate at all, but if you plant enough beans you should eventually be rewarded with a sprout.

Beans should be planted a little over a half inch deep in good, well-drained potting soil, and kept moist at all times, but not wet. Once the plant has sprouted, treat it as you would a camellia. Keep the soil moist but never wet, and provide plenty of bright indirect or diffused sunlight. Fertilize every other month. If something goes wrong, look up camellia in a good indoor gardening manual for the appropriate advice.

In order to coax your mature coffee plant to flower and bear fruit, you may need to mimic nature by providing a few weeks of "dry" weather (underwater the plant just to the point of allowing its leaves to droop) then giving it plenty of water for a few more weeks. Particularly if you make the heavy-watering part of the cycle correspond to the longer days of spring, you should provoke a flowering and, since *Coffea arabica* self-pollinates, a tiny but gratifying crop of coffee fruit a couple of months later.

Outdoor Growing. If you live in a frost-free area, you may want to plant some arabica in your yard. Temperatures should not be lower than 60°F normally or lower than 50° for short periods only. Parts of Hawaii are unsurpassed for coffee. It has long been held that coffee could be grown commercially along the southern California coast, but this has never been tried because of high labor costs. Remember, however, that you need to duplicate the conditions of the Ethiopian rain forest: moist, fertile, well-drained soil and partial shade. This last condition is especially important during the long summers in southern California. For more advice on growing, pruning (very important if you wish your tree to produce more coffee), and caring for coffee trees, try to find a copy of A. E. Haarer's *Coffee Growing* in the Oxford Tropical Handbooks series, published by Oxford University Press.

14 CELEBRATING IT

Public ceremonies and ritual conviviality
Coffee places

.

Every social lubricant has its home away from home, its church, as it were, where its effects are celebrated in public ceremonies and ritual conviviality. The café, caffè, or coffeehouse is as old as the beverage itself. The first people to enjoy coffee as a beverage rather than to use it as a medicine or an aid to meditation did so in coffeehouses in Mecca in the late-fifteenth century. The nature of the coffeehouse was established early in history and has changed remarkably little in five hundred years.

A UNIQUE IDENTITY

Jean de Thévenot describes a Turkish coffeehouse of 1664 in *Relation d'un voyage fait au Levant:*

> There are public coffeehouses where the drink is prepared in very big pots for the numerous guests. At these places guests mingle without distinction of rank or creed; nor does anyone think it amiss to enter such places, where people go to pass their leisure time. In front of the coffeehouses are benches with small mats, where those sit who would rather remain in the fresh air and amuse themselves by watching the passersby. Sometimes the coffeehouse keeper engages flute players and violin players, and also singers, to entertain his guests.

The "very big pots" of de Thévenot's café became the espresso machines or coffee urns of today; the "benches with small mats," outdoor terraces. And although the café shares many qualities with the bar, saloon, and *boîte* beloved of drinkers of wine and spirits, it has maintained a subtly unique identity.

Coffeehouse Culture and Caffeine

The customs of coffeehouse and café appear to be intimately connected to the effect of coffee and caffeine on mind and body. Coffee stimulates conscious mental associations, whereas alcohol, for instance, provokes instinctual responses. In other words, alcohol typically makes us want to eat, fight, make love, dance, and sleep, whereas coffee encourages us to think, talk, read, write, or work. Wine is consumed to relax, and coffee to drive home. For the Muslims, the world's first coffee drinkers, coffee was the "wine of Apollo," the beverage of thought, dream, and dialectic, "the milk of thinkers and chess players." For the faithful Muslim it was the answer to the Christian and pagan wine of Dionysus and ecstasy.

From the inception of the coffeehouse in Mecca to the present, customers in cafés tend to talk and read rather than dance, play chess rather than gamble, and listen contemplatively to music rather than sing. The café usually opens to the street and sun, unlike bars or saloons, whose dark interiors protect the drinker from the encroachment of the sober, workaday world. The coffee drinker wants not a subterranean refuge but a comfortable corner in which to read a newspaper and observe the world as it slips by, just beyond the edge of the table.

The café is connected with work (the truck stop, the coffee break) and with a special brand of informal study. A customer buried in reading matter is a common sight in even the most lowbrow café. The Turks called their cafés "schools of the wise." In seventeenth-century England, coffeehouses were often called "penny universities." For the price of entry—one penny; coffee cost two, which included newspapers. One could participate in a floating seminar that might include such notables as Joseph Addison and Sir Richard Steele.

As a matter of fact, aside from the Romanticists, who temporarily switched to plein-air, it is hard to find too many European or American intellectuals of the eighteenth and nineteenth centuries who did not spend the better part of their days in cafés or coffeehouses. Recall that the Enlightenment not only gave Europe a new worldview but coffee and tea as well. It must have been considerably easier revolutionizing Western thought after morning coffee than after the typical medieval breakfast of beer and herring.

PUT-DOWNS AND PERSECUTIONS

The first persecutions of coffee and coffeehouses were undertaken on religious grounds, but subsequent attacks were more explicitly political. In 1511, the governor of Mecca tried to repress the very first coffeehouses because "in these places men and women meet and play violins, tambourines . . . chess . . . and do other things contrary to our sacred law."

Similar attempts followed in Cairo, and the grand vizier of Constantinople ordered the coffeehouses of that city closed in the 1600s because, he said, they encouraged sedition. Caught drinking your first illegal cup of coffee, you got beaten with a stick; for the second, you got sewn in a leather bag and dumped in the Bosporus. Even such rigor failed to stop the coffee drinkers. Floating coffeehouses developed; enterprising people carried pots of the brew to serve secretly in alleys and behind buildings.

Charles II, Potency, and Politics

In 1675, King Charles II of England published an edict closing coffeehouses. The apparent pretext was an extraordinary document titled "The Women's Petition Against Coffee, representing to public consideration the grand inconveniences accruing to their sex from the excessive use of the drying and enfeebling Liquor." Conscientiously supporting their thesis with abundant examples of plentiful details, the authors contended that since becoming coffee drinkers, men had become "as unfruitful as the deserts from whence that unhappy berry is said to be brought," and that as a consequence "the whole race is in danger of extinction." The men rose to the occasion, however, with "The Men's Answer to the Women's Petition . . . vindicating their liquor from the undeserved aspersion lately cast upon them, in their scandalous pamphlet."

However concerned he may have been with questions of virility, Charles II revealed his true preoccupation in the wording of his proclamation: "In such Houses . . . divers False, Malicious and Scandalous Reports devised and spread abroad, to the Defamation of his Majestie's Government, and to the Disturbance of the Peace and Quiet of the Realm."

The reaction among coffee lovers was pronounced and immediate, and only eleven days later Charles II published a second edict withdrawing his first: "An Additional Proclamation Concerning Coffee Houses," which declared that he had decided to allow coffeehouses to stay open out of "royal compassion." Some observers cite this turnaround as a record for the most words eaten in the shortest time by any ruler of a major nation, unsurpassed until modern times.

A WORLDWIDE TRADITION

The tradition of the coffeehouse has spread worldwide. Australia is paved with Italian-style caffès and Japan has evolved its *kisatens,* an elegant interpretation of American 1950s-style coffee shops and coffeehouses. In Great Britain, the espresso-bar craze of the 1950s came and went but is in the midst of a Starbucks style comeback. Other parts of Europe and the Middle East have their own ongoing traditions. In Vienna, the home of some of the first European coffeehouses, the café tradition has undergone a renaissance.

In the United States, the 1930s and '40s brought the classic diner, and the 1950s and '60s the vinyl-boothed coffee shop, together with the coffeehouse—haunt of rebels, poets, beboppers, and beatniks. All of these incarnations are still with us. The classic diner is enjoying a revival, coffee shops still minister to the bottomless cup, and in American cities hundreds of new coffeehouses cater to a fresh generation of rebels, complete with funky furniture, radical posters, jazz, and folksingers.

But the 1970s and '80s appear to have produced still another North American café tradition. Classic Italian-American caffès of the 1950s, like Caffè Reggio in Manhattan and Caffè Trieste in San Francisco, appear to have influenced the development of a style of café or caffè that takes as its starting point an im-

migrant's nostalgic vision of the lost and gracious caffès of prewar Italy. From that vision come the light and spacious interiors of the new North American urban café, together with the open seating, the simple and straightforward furnishing, and an atmosphere formal enough to discourage customers from swaggering around and putting their feet on chairs, yet informal enough to mix students doing homework and executives having business meetings. Add an espresso machine and some light, new American cuisine, and the latest version of the American café is defined.

15 STAYING HEALTHY DRINKING IT

Poison vs. panacea
Science weighs in
Decaffeinated coffees

When Sir William Harvey, the seventeenth-century physician credited with discovering the circulation of the blood, was on his deathbed, he allegedly called his lawyer to his side and held up a coffee bean. "This little Fruit," he whispered, eyes doubtless still bright from his morning cup, "is the source of happiness and wit!" Sir William then bequeathed his entire supply of coffee, fifty-six pounds, to the London College of Physicians, directing them to commemorate the day of his death every month with a morning round of coffee. To those who hang out in health food stores, this anecdote may strike a sinister note. Did Sir William die young? How much coffee did he drink, and did he have any enemies in the College of Physicians?

PANACEA OR POISON

Contradictions run throughout the history of coffee. Coffee was first consumed as medicine and graduated to serving simultaneous roles as panacea and poison. Early in its history, coffee was adopted by Arabian dervishes to fortify religious meditation. Yet no more than fifty years later, in Mecca, it was the subject of vehement religious persecution on the grounds that it encouraged mirth and chess playing among the faithful. Religion still cannot make up its mind about coffee; Mormons and some fundamentalists reject it, whereas most Muslims and many Christians consider it a sober and wholesome alternative to wine and spirits.

In seventeenth-century Europe, as religion began to give way to science and priests to doctors, the debate continued. One physician claimed coffee re-

lieved dropsy, gravel, gout, migraine, hypochondria, and cured scurvy outright, whereas another declared that coffee drunk with milk caused leprosy. "The lovers of coffee used the physicians very ill when they met together," says one wonderfully detached French observer, "and the physicians on their side threatened the coffee drinkers with all sorts of diseases."

The Virility Issue

One of the most famous accusations leveled against coffee came in a tale by a seventeenth-century German traveler, Adam Oelshlazer, in his *Relation of a Voyage to Muscovie, Tartary, and Persia.* The story concerns the king of Persia, who "had become so habituated to the use of coffee that he took a dislike for women." One day the queen saw a stallion being emasculated; upon asking the reason, she was told the animal was too spirited and was being gelded to tame it. Whereupon the queen suggested a simpler solution would be to feed it coffee every morning. This story, when introduced into southern France, was said to have virtually ruined the coffee trade there for fifty years. On the other hand, a tale from a Persian saga reports that after the prophet Mohammed had his first cup of coffee (delivered by the archangel Gabriel), he "felt able to unseat forty horsemen and possess fifty women."

Rumsey's Cure

It was in England of the seventeenth century that coffee's career as medicine reached its apex and, possibly, its nadir. The most extravagant claims were launched for its medicinal value, and the most extraordinary accusations were leveled against it. One Englishman named Walter Rumsey invented an "electuary" of coffee, to be applied internally with the aid of an instrument called a *provang*. The electuary was prescribed for intestinal disorders and hysteria. First, you prepared the electuary, which consisted of heated butter, salad oil, honey, and ground coffee. Next, you introduced the provang, a thin, bone rod about a yard long with a little button on the end, into the intestinal tract by way of the rectum and manipulated it vigorously. Finally, you swallowed the electuary and concluded the treatment with a second energetic application of the provang. Perhaps it was at this point in history that tea began to replace coffee as England's favorite beverage.

THE VILLAIN UNCOVERED: CAFFEINE

Out of all this confusion and debate came the world's first scientific analysis of coffee. In 1685, Dr. Philippe Sylvestre Dufour described the chemical constituents of coffee with some accuracy and, apparently through numerous experiments on human beings, arrived at the same conclusion every other researcher has come to since: Some people can drink coffee comfortably and some cannot. Dufour even found a few who slept better after drinking coffee than they had before, probably because, in Dufour's words, the coffee "relieved their disquiet, and removed their feeling of anxiety."

Dufour also helped the critics of coffee identify for the first time their true enemy: the odorless, bitter alkaloid called caffeine. The average cup of American-style coffee contains about 100 to 150 milligrams of caffeine; a properly prepared demitasse or single serving of espresso 80 to 120 milligrams. The average cup of tea delivers about 40 milligrams; the average chocolate bar about 20 to 60. A 12-ounce bottle of cola drink contains 40 to 60 milligrams, about half as much as a cup of coffee.

The current conclusions about the short-term psychological and physiological effects of caffeine are not so different from the first conjectures by Arab physicians or the findings arrived at by Dufour in the seventeenth century. But the long-term effects are not nearly so well understood and remain the subject of a vigorous, confusing, and thus far inconclusive medical debate.

Short-Term Effects of Caffeine

The short-term effects of caffeine are well agreed upon and widely documented. A good summary appears in *The Pharmacological Basis of Therapeutics* by Dr. J. Murdoch Ritchie. On the positive side, caffeine produces "a more rapid and clearer flow of thought" and allays "drowsiness and fatigue. After taking caffeine one is capable of greater sustained intellectual effort and a more perfect association of ideas. There is also a keener appreciation of sensory stimuli, and motor activity is increased; typists, for example, work faster and with fewer errors."

Such effects are produced by caffeine equivalent to the amount contained in one to two cups of coffee. According to Dr. Ritchie, the same dosage stimulates the body in a variety of other ways: heart rate increases, blood vessels dilate; movement of fluid and solid wastes through the body is promoted. All this adds up to the beloved "lift."

On the negative side are the medical descriptions of the familiar "coffee nerves." The heavy coffee drinker may suffer from chronic anxiety, a sort of "coffee come-down," and may be restless and irritable. Insomnia and even twitching muscles and diarrhea may be among the effects. Very large doses of caffeine, the equivalent of about ten cups of strong coffee drunk in a row, produce toxic effects: vomiting, fever, chills, and mental confusion. In enormous doses, caffeine is, quite literally, deadly. The lethal dose of caffeine in humans is estimated at about 10 grams or the equivalent of one hundred cups of coffee. You would have to drink the hundred cups in one sitting, however, which doubtless accounts for the unpopularity of caffeine as a means of taking one's own life.

Simple Moderation

It would seem that the resolution to the caffeine debate, at least in terms of short-term effects, is simple moderation. Drunk to excess, coffee literally verges on poison; drunk in moderation, it is still the beloved tonic of tradition, a gentle aid to thought, labor, and conversation.

But just how much is enough and how much is too much? No study will commit itself. I can only offer an estimate based on inference. I have never found a study reporting negative effects from doses of caffeine under 300 milligrams a day. Since the average cup of coffee (or single serving of espresso) contains about 100 milligrams of caffeine, we would infer from this

One way coffee can contribute to healthy, strong bodies: Workers load coffee in the port of Medan, Sumatra.

evidence that anyone should be able to drink about three cups of coffee a day and enjoy the benefits of caffeine with none of the drawbacks. Such a figure assumes, of course, that you do not also consume quantities of cola drinks, chocolate bars, and headache pills. This is a conservative estimate, however. We could infer from other studies that five cups a day is safe for most people. Furthermore, reaction to caffeine varies greatly from individual to individual; some people cannot consume any amount comfortably.

Long-Term Effects of Caffeine

So much for the short-term effects. Researchers in the last thirty years or so have tried to implicate coffee, specifically the caffeine in coffee, in heart disease, birth defects, pancreatic cancer, and a half-dozen other less publicized health problems. So far, the evidence is, at most, inconclusive. Clinical reports and studies continue to generate far more questions than answers, and for every report tentatively claiming a link between caffeine and disease, there are several others contradicting it.

If anything, the medical evidence currently is running in favor of exonerating caffeine rather than further implicating it in disease. Some evidence even points to modest, long-term health benefits for coffee drinkers.

A Warning Withdrawn. One example of the way the medical establishment has tended to seesaw on caffeine, condemning on partial evidence then backing off on further evidence, is the purported connection between heavy caffeine intake by pregnant women and birth defects. In the mid-1970s, experiments indicated that the equivalent of 12 to 24 cups of coffee (or equivalent bottles of cola) per day may cause birth defects—in rats. Although human beings metabolize caffeine differently from rats (and other researchers had questioned some of the conditions of the experiments), the United States Food and Drug Administration issued a widely publicized warning about the possible ill effects of caffeine on the fetus. Subsequently, an analysis by Harvard researchers of coffee drinking among 12,000 women early in their pregnancies failed to find a significant link between coffee intake and birth defects. The upshot of the debate? The official position, if there is one, came from a committee of the National Academy of Sciences, which recommended what common sense dictates, what this book recommends, and what coffee lovers through the ages have argued: pregnant women, according to the NAS committee, should exercise "moderation" in their intake of caffeine.

Reassuring Results. Similar controversies have accompanied the purported links between coffee and fibrocystic breast disease, high blood pressure, and pancreatic and lung cancer. On the positive side, an eleven-year study of nearly 17,000 Norwegian men and women found that, once the effect of smoking had been eliminated from the data, people who drank coffee had lower than normal rates of cancers of the colon, kidney, and skin. Norwegian researcher Erik Bjelke's report to the 13th International Cancer Congress concluded, "While we cannot exclude the possibility that high coffee intakes may enhance carcinogenesis under special circumstances, overall, the results are reassuring." Two similar long-term studies of large samples of individuals, the kind of studies medical researchers call "population" studies, indicated no consistent association between coffee drinking and blood cholesterol levels (a study of 6,000 men and women reported by the Framingham Heart Study researchers) or between caffeine intake and heart attacks and stroke (a study of 45,000 men aged forty to seventy-five by Dr. Walter Willett and colleagues of the Harvard School of Public Health).

As for the possibility that coffee, in modest ways, may actually help us live healthier and longer, one population study reports that those among a group of 87,000 female nurses who drank two cups of coffee per day were 66 percent less likely to take their own lives than those who drank no coffee whatsoever or, curiously, those who drank equivalent volumes of tea.

Those who drank more than two cups of coffee per day were even less likely to kill themselves. And, something for male readers: A study conducted by researchers at Harvard University found that men who drank two to three cups of coffee per day had a 40 percent lower incidence of gallstones than those who did not drink coffee regularly. Men who drank four or more cups per day had a 45 percent lower incidence.

Nevertheless, Talk to Your Doctor. However, opinions on how to interpret the medical evidence on coffee differ, and important new studies appear regularly. Anyone who drinks regular caffeinated coffee and also is pregnant—or takes tranquilizers, or suffers from ulcers, high blood pressure, or heart complaints, or is experiencing benign breast lumps (fibrocystic breast disease)—should certainly bring his or her coffee-drinking habits to the attention of a physician for evaluation.

COFFEE AS SCAPEGOAT

In light of the continuing conflicts in the medical evidence, why have so many people, at least until recently, been so eager to pin blame on coffee? Partly, I think, because of the frustrations of dealing with degenerative diseases with multiple causes, such as heart failure.

There is a tendency in the face of our impotence before certain diseases to cast about for dietary scapegoats. Coffee is ideal for such a role, not only because it has no food value, but because it makes us feel good for no reason when we drink it. When we get sick, I suspect we tend to fix the blame on something we already feel guilty about: coffee, wine, chocolate cake, or whatever.

The ease with which the early persecutions of coffee on religious grounds modulated into condemnations on medical grounds makes the motivation behind popular attacks on the healthfulness of coffee doubly suspect. Every culture or religion has its dietary taboos as well as its sacraments. Certain foods are holy, and others are forbidden. A group that wishes to define its own identity must establish taboos.

Caffeine Was Not Holy. In the late 1960s, for example, an entire generation was busy trying to define itself as a culture distinct from the larger Western tradition. It was inevitable that coffee, as a social drug firmly identified with the establishment, should come under attack. I recall, for instance, visiting a commune where, in the late 1960s, ingesting caffeine was a spiritual and dietary sin almost as bad as closing the door to undress. Yet these same puritans, so critical of caffeine, regularly reduced themselves to monosyllabic incoherence with marijuana. Caffeine was taboo; marijuana was close to holy.

Dietary choices, particularly of nonnutritive, mood-altering frills like coffee, are arbitrary choices driven by culture and habit rather than by reason. But since we live in an ostensibly rational society, no one feels comfortable justifying dietary prejudices on religious or cultural grounds. Instead we elevate some very tentative medical evidence into dogma, which we then defend as "scientific." One upon a time foods were bad for the soul; now they are bad for our health.

Virtually every element in our diet is currently suspect on some medical grounds or another. At a time when the average glass of drinking water is suspected of harboring carcinogens, a once country-pure herbal tea like sassafras was taken off the market because it contains a proven carcinogen, and large doses of vitamin C have been suspected in birth defects, I see little medical reason for not drinking moderate amounts of a beverage against which nothing concrete has been proven, which has been consumed for centuries without decimating the population, and which is one of the few widely consumed modern foods that contains no multisyllabic preservatives, additives, or other adulterants.

Loving Attention. For the ordinary coffee drinker, the real solution to the coffee and health issue may be treating coffee with the love and attention it deserves.

If you are aware of what you are doing when you buy and make coffee and take a moment to appreciate the results, many of the alleged negative effects of coffee drinking might vanish. If anyone suffers from coffee, it is the unconscious coffeeholic who wanders around all day holding a half-filled cup of cold, tasteless instant or a badly prepared, lukewarm triple latte.

DECAFFEINATED COFFEE

Technology is always trying to give us back the garden without the snake. So you like coffee and not caffeine? Well, then, we will take out the caffeine and leave you your pleasure, intact.

Decaffeinated coffee is indeed without venom. It contains, at most, one-fortieth of the amount of caffeine in untreated beans. Nor should the removal of caffeine alter the taste of coffee. Isolated, caffeine is a crystalline substance lacking aroma and possessing only the slightest bitter taste. Its flavor is lost in the heady perfumes of fresh coffee. So if you hear people say, "Coffee doesn't taste like coffee without the caffeine," they are wrong. The only real problem is how to take out the caffeine without ruining the rest of what does influence coffee flavor. But technology has triumphed, more or less. The best decaffeinated coffee, freshly roasted and ground and carefully brewed, can taste so nearly the equal of a similar untreated coffee that only a tasting involving direct comparison reveals the difference.

Unfortunately, fine decaffeinated coffees are the exception rather than the norm. Decaffeinated beans are notoriously difficult to roast, so even the best decaffeinated beans may produce a thin-bodied, half-burned cup once they are roasted. Still, for the coffee devotee, even listless decaffeinated coffee is better than mint tea, and you can always compromise and spruce up a caffeine-free coffee by adding a little full-bodied caffeinated coffee before grinding it, or by creating your own low-caffeine blend.

Most caffeine-free coffee sold in specialty stores is shipped from the growing countries to decaffeinating plants in Europe or Canada, treated to remove the caffeine, then redried and shipped to the United States.

DECAFFEINATION METHODS

Coffee is decaffeinated in its green state, before the delicate oils are developed through roasting. Hundreds of patents exist for decaffeination processes, but only a few are actually used. They divide roughly into those that use a solvent to dissolve the caffeine, those that use water and charcoal filters, and those that use a special form of carbon dioxide.

Decaffeination Methods Using Solvents

The direct-solvent method is the oldest and most common decaffeination process. On coffee signs and bags it is typically not identified at all or called by various euphemisms such as European or traditional process. The beans are first steamed to open their pores, then soaked in an organic solvent that selectively unites with the caffeine. The beans are then steamed again to remove the solvent residues, dried, and roasted like any other green coffee.

A more recently developed process called the indirect-solvent method starts by soaking green beans in near boiling water for several hours. The water is transferred to another tank, where it is combined with a solvent that selectively absorbs most of the caffeine. The caffeine-laden solvent is then skimmed from the water, with which it is never really mixed. The water, now free of both caffeine and solvent, still contains oils and other materials important to flavor. In order to restore these substances to the beans, the water is returned to the first tank, where the beans reabsorb the flavor-bearing substances from the water.

What About the Solvents? The joker in the process is still the solvent. People concerned about the effects of coffee on their health obviously are not going to feel comfortable purchasing a product containing even minute traces of solvent. In 1975, one of the most widely used solvents, trichloroethylene, was named a probable cause of cancer in a "Cancer Alert" issued in 1975 by the National Cancer Institute.

The alert addressed the potential health hazards trichloroethylene posed to people who work around it rather than to consumers of decaffeinated coffee, since only extremely minute traces of the solvent remain in coffee. The Unites States Food and Drug Administration, for example, permits the solvent in quantities up to 10 parts per million in ground coffee. By comparison, the doses that the National Cancer Institute administered to laboratory animals were gargantuan. To match them in equivalent terms, a human being would have to drink 20 million cups of decaffeinated coffee a day over a lifetime.

Also, no one knows how much of the solvent residue—if any—is retained in the brewing process and ends up in the cup. Given the volatility of the solvent and the relatively minuscule amount left in the bean after roasting, I suspect that none whatsoever ends up in the coffee we ultimately consume.

A New and Better Solvent: Methylene Chloride. Nevertheless, the news that the caffeine that some feared caused heart disease was being replaced by a solvent that actually did cause cancer provoked understandable consternation among health-conscious consumers.

The coffee industry promptly responded by replacing trichloroethylene with methylene chloride, a solvent not implicated in the National Cancer Institute study. So far tests of methylene chloride have not linked it to any known disease, and given its volatility (it vaporizes at 104°F; coffee is roasted at over 400° for at least fifteen minutes then brewed at 200°) it seems hardly possible that any of the 1 part per million occasionally found in the green beans could end up in the consumer's cup or stomach.

An Even Newer and Better Solvent: Ethyl Acetate. Now in use in some European decaffeination plants, ethyl acetate, like methylene chloride, has not been implicated in any diseases, and environmentalists consider it more benign than methylene chloride. Because ethyl acetate is derived from fruit, some publicists and brochure writers have taken to calling coffees decaffeinated using ethyl acetate "naturally decaffeinated," and you may see them so advertised.

The Solvent-Free Swiss Water Process

In the 1980s, the Swiss firm Coffex S.A. developed a commercially viable decaffeination process using water only—no solvents whatsoever. As in the direct solvent or solvent/water process described earlier, the various chemical constituents of the green coffee, including the caffeine, are first removed by soaking the beans in very hot water.

In the Swiss Water Process, however, the water is stripped of its caffeine, not by a solvent, but by percolation through activated charcoal. (It really ought to be called the Swiss Charcoal Process.) The beans are returned to the hot water, where they reabsorb the remaining, caffeine-free flavor constituents from the water.

This process is more costly than the solvent process because the separated caffeine cannot be recovered from the charcoal and sold separately, as it is with the two solvent methods. It is also controversial in terms of flavor. Many coffee professionals contend that the Swiss Water Process blurs flavor more than the competing solvent processes. However, the management of the Canadian plant that currently produces all of the Swiss Water Decaffeinated coffees sold in North America continues to make determined efforts to refine and improve the process.

Decaffeination Methods Using Carbon Dioxide

Decaffeination processes using carbon dioxide (CO_2) differ in their details. All take advantage of the fact that carbon dioxide, when compressed, behaves partly like a gas and partly like a liquid and has the property of combining selectively with caffeine. In the most widely used CO_2 process, the steamed beans are bathed in the compressed carbon dioxide and the caffeine is removed from the carbon dioxide through charcoal filtering, just as it is in the water-only process. However, the flavor components remain in the bean throughout the process, rather than being soaked out and then put back in again, as they are in both the Swiss Water and the indirect solvent processes.

Since carbon dioxide is the same ubiquitous and undisputably "natural" substance that plants absorb and humans produce, and since, in most versions of the CO_2 method, the flavor components remain safely in the bean throughout the process rather than being removed and put back in again as they are in the Swiss Water Process, carbon dioxide methods would seem to be the decaffeinating wave of the future. However, coffees decaffeinated by the CO_2 method have been slow to come onto the specialty market, and reviews have been mixed.

Buying Decaffeinated Coffees

If you are concerned only about health issues, I suggest that you buy the decaffeinated coffee that tastes good to you, regardless of process. Given the temperature at which all currently used solvents evaporate, I do not think that enough of the chemical could possibly survive the roasting and brewing processes to be anything more than the tiniest pea under the health-conscious consumer's mattress.

If, however, you are concerned about the environment, there is good reason to avoid coffees decaf-feinated by methods using methylene chloride. Choose instead coffees decaffeinated by the Swiss Water method, by solvent methods using ethyl acetate, or by CO_2 processes. Coffees decaffeinated by the Swiss Water method are always so labeled. If no decaffeination method is indicated, or if the method is called European or traditional, you will have to make inquiries.

Decaffeination Method and Flavor

Which decaffeination method produces better tasting coffees? It is difficult to say for certain for two reasons. First, it is virtually impossible to turn up the identical coffee decaffeinated by a range of different methods, and the quality of the original coffee obviously influences the quality of the final cup. Second, decaffeinated coffees are difficult to roast properly, and subtle differences in decaffeination method may be overwhelmed by differences in the quality of the roast.

Nevertheless, my own experience clearly and consistently indicates that the Swiss Water Process tends to emphasize body, deemphasize acidity and high notes, and occasionally (but not always) alter or blur flavor, whereas the European or solvent method tends to preserve acidity, nuance, and high notes, but may reduce body and dimension. As for coffees processed using the CO_2 method, I have tasted some excellent samples but not enough of them to generalize.

Other Alternatives for Caffeine-Shy Coffee Drinkers

Of course, if you simply want to cut down on your caffeine intake, rather than eliminating caffeine from your diet completely, there are alternatives other than decaffeinated coffees.

One is to drink less coffee while focusing on enjoying it more. This is a good tactic for people who consume too much coffee at work out of habit or reflex. Rather than drinking the coffee from the automatic coffeemaker or urn, for example, make your own coffee carefully in a small plunger pot, focusing your attention on the act of brewing and drinking.

You can also buy coffees that are naturally low in caffeine. As I indicated earlier, specialty and other high-quality coffees contain considerably less caffeine than cheaper commercial coffees. Most inexpensive commercial blends are based on robusta coffees, which contain almost double the amount of caffeine as arabica. So if you drink a specialty coffee, you are probably consuming considerably less caffeine per cup than if you were drinking a cheap, canned coffee.

Or you can brew your coffee differently. The cold-water concentrate method (see pages 138–39) reduces caffeine, acidity, and fats. Unfortunately, it also reduces flavor. Coffee brewed with paper filters may contain slightly less caffeine than coffee made by other methods and definitely less fatty oil.

Lastly, you can amuse yourself making low-caffeine blends by combining decaffeinated coffees with varying amounts of distinctive, full-bodied, untreated coffees. Kenyas, Yemens, the best Ethiopias, and Guatemalas, for example, all pack enough flavor and body to spruce up even the drabbest of decaffeinated beans.

ANOTHER SUSPECT: ACID

Caffeine is only one of the villains in the coffee controversy. Another is certain chemicals often lumped together under the term "acid." Some people do not like the acid or sour note in coffee and claim it upsets their stomachs. Others say it causes jitters. I suggest that you experiment. Does that sourness in coffee make your tongue or stomach feel uncomfortable? Then you have three alternatives:

- Try to find a coffee with the acid reduced through a process much like the ethyl acetate solvent decaffeination process. These coffees, treated in Germany, are marketed under the name "special mild coffees." They are hard to find, do not offer much choice, and suffer from the same potential for flavor diminution as decaffeinated beans.
- Buy a moderately dark to dark-roast coffee. Dark roasting reduces the acidity in coffee.
- Buy a lower-altitude, naturally low-acid coffee brought to a moderately dark roast (full city, Viennese, light espresso). To me, this is by far the best solution for acid-shy coffee drinkers. Naturally low-acid coffees include Brazils, most India and Pacific (Sumatra, Timor, Hawaii) coffees, and most Caribbean coffees.

It also helps to buy very good coffee because the best coffee has been processed from ripe coffee fruit, and coffee from ripe fruit is naturally sweet and lacks the sharp, astringent sensation of cheaper coffee processed from less-than-ripe fruit.

COFFEE AND HEALTH CONCERNS

Concern	Where discussed	Comments	Possible Responses
Fears concerning the long-term negative impact of caffeine on health	Pages 227–29	Studies of long-term health risks associated with moderate consumption of caffeine range from inconclusive to reassuring.	Drink less coffee and enjoy it more; drink less coffee and drink higher quality coffee; drink coffee brewed by the cold-water concentrate method; drink decaffeinated coffee.
Fears that solvent residues from decaffeination processes may contaminate brewed coffee	Pages 231–32	Amounts of residue detected in green coffee decaffeinated by current solvent methods are so low that they hardly bear consideration. The possibility that any of these very volatile substances survive the roasting and brewing processes is highly unlikely.	Stop worrying and enjoy your decaffeinated coffee; go back to caffeinated coffees and practice one or more of the expedients listed above; drink water-only, Swiss Water Process decaffeinated, or CO_2-process decaffeinated coffees.
Fears that dioxin residues from bleached filter papers may contaminate brewed coffee	Page 133	Most filter manufacturers have switched to whitening methods that do not use dioxin.	Trust that whitening processes currently in use are dioxin-free; switch to a brewing method that does not use paper filters; buy brown, unbleached filters.
Fears that residues of agricultural chemicals may contaminate brewed coffee	Page 237	Given the cumulative impact of the roasting and brewing processes, it is extremely unlikely that any of the small amounts of residue legally allowable in green coffee actually reach the cup. Environmental concerns are much more significant than health concerns.	Drink coffees that have been certified organically grown; drink traditionally grown coffees from Yemen, Ethiopia, and the Mandheling region of Sumatra.
Fears that propylene glycol used in flavored coffees is not natural and may pose a health threat	Page 237	Propyline glycol has long been on the generally recognized as safe list of the U.S. Food and Drug Administration; it is used in numerous other foods.	Stop drinking artificially flavored coffees and start either adding natural flavorings to coffees yourself or drinking distinctive-tasting, single-origin coffees like Yemen, Kenya, or Ethiopia Yirgacheffe.

PESTICIDES, FILTER PAPERS, AND FLAVORINGS

We have met the enemy and he is us, the once-famous comic strip possum Pogo declared. Coffee is one of the few widely consumed contemporary foods and beverages that contain absolutely no additives, adulterants, or preservatives. Unfortunately, we have not been able to leave well enough alone. Through our own fussing with coffee we have added a few more health-related issues to the heap.

One is the solvent used in some decaffeination processes, which I discuss earlier in this chapter. Another is the dioxin formerly used in bleaching some paper filters, discussed on page 133. A third consists of health and environmental issues raised by the use of pesticides, fungicides, herbicides, and chemical fertilizers in growing coffee. Finally, some consumers have questioned the healthfulness of the chemical agents used in artificially flavored whole-bean coffees.

All of the various health issues raised in relationship to coffee are summarized in a sort of rogue's gallery of suspects on page 235. Most of the accusations appear unfounded or overstated, but in a world where newly identified multisyllabic health threats rear their carcinogenic heads from newspaper pages almost daily, concern seems justified. Since I treat the other suspects elsewhere, I am confining my final remarks in this chapter to the agricultural-chemical and coffee-flavoring issues.

Agricultural Chemicals and Organic Coffees

The concerns raised by those apprehensive about the use of agricultural chemicals in coffee growing are twofold. First is the health issue for the consumer: whether harmful chemical residues may reach our systems when we drink coffee. Second are the related environmental and social issues: Whether buying coffees that may be grown with the help of potentially harmful chemicals contributes to the destruction of the environment and threatens the health of the rural poor who raise coffee.

Agricultural Chemicals and Consumer Health. The consumer health issue is simplest to address. Coffee is not eaten raw like lettuce or apples. The bean is the seed of a fruit. The flesh of this fruit is discarded. Along the way the seed is soaked, fermented, and subjected to a thorough drying process. Later it is roasted at temperatures exceeding 400°F and finally broken apart and soaked in near boiling water. This savage history concludes when we consume only the water in which the previously soaked, fermented, dried, roasted, and infused seed was immersed. Given this history of relentless attrition, it hardly seems possible that much if any of the small amounts of pesticide/fungicide residue permitted by law in green coffee ever make it into the cup.

Agricultural Chemicals and the Environment. The environmental and social issues merit more attention. It would seem that only someone exceedingly isolated or stubborn could fail to grasp how dangerous the widespread use of agricultural poisons has become, both to our environment and to the workers who handle these substances. I discuss the environmental and social issues impacting coffee buying in Chapter 6.

Chemical-free Alternatives. In brief, coffee drinkers concerned about the impact of agricultural chemicals on environment and society or those unwilling to accept my reassurances on the consumer health issue have essentially three alternatives:

- Buy a traditional coffee, grown as coffee was grown from its inception, before agricultural chemicals were invented. All Yemen, almost all Ethiopia, and most Sumatra Mandehling coffees are grown in such a state of innocence, and all are among the world's finest.
- Buy a certified organic coffee, a coffee whose growing conditions and processing have been thoroughly monitored by independent agencies and found to be free of pesticides, herbicides, fungicides, chemical fertilizers, and other potentially harmful chemicals. The monitoring agencies visit the farm and verify that no chemicals have been used on the farm for several years and then follow every step of the processing, preparing, transporting, storage, and roasting. Such careful monitoring is of course expensive, which is one reason certified organic coffees cost more than similar uncertified coffees. Many such certified organic coffees are the product of socially and environmentally progressive cooperatives. See pages 96–97 for more on organically grown coffees.

- Buy a coffee labeled "sustainable." At this writing sustainable is a rather loose term meaning that, in the view of the importer or roaster, designated farmers are doing everything within reason to avoid the use of agricultural chemicals and to pursue enlightened environmental and socially progressive practices in the growing and processing of their coffees. See pages 97–98 for more on sustainable, "Bird-Friendly," and other recently coined terms for environmentally and socially progressive coffee-growing practices.

Artificial Flavorings and Flavored Coffees

It may seem odd that consumers who choose to buy an obviously artificial product like chocolate mint– or French vanilla–flavored coffee should also want it to be a natural product, but some do. Not only are many of the flavoring components used in flavoring whole bean coffees artificial by Food and Drug Administration definitions, but the substance that carries the flavorings into the pores of the bean and maintains their integrity throughout the stress of storing, transporting, and brewing is another substance with a spooky multisyllabic name that is technically classified as a solvent. But propylene glycol is a solvent only in the sense that it dissolves flavorings and preserves them. It is not a solvent in the sense that it dissolves stomachs or any other part of the anatomy. Nor is it antifreeze, that is ethylene glycol. Propylene glycol has long been on the Food and Drug Administration's GRAS (Generally Recognized as Safe) list, and is used in many other food products.

Flavoring Your Own Coffee. If you do not like consuming flavors that are technically artificial and that use propylene glycol as a medium, yet still enjoy flavored coffees, you probably need to start doing the flavoring yourself. You can add flavors before you grind and brew whole-bean coffee or in the cup after you brew the coffee.

Some flavored coffees are available that use only all-natural ingredients like chunks of vanilla bean or cinnamon, for example, but you will have more variety if you add these kinds of ingredients to whole-bean coffees yourself. I give an assortment of recipes that combine vanilla bean, citrus zest, and various whole spices to whole-bean coffee in my book *Home Coffee Roasting: Romance & Revival,* also published by St. Martin's Press.

Another approach is simply to add flavorings to the cup after you brew the coffee. Most good vanilla and almond extracts sold in markets are natural products in an alcohol and glycerin base, and can be added to brewed coffee a few drops at a time. Completely natural flavorings presented without propylene glycol or alcohol are available in some natural food stores. The Frontier brand of natural flavorings is a good one, although only the berry and brandy flavors seem to work well with coffee. Italian-style, flavored syrups of the kind used to flavor espresso-milk drinks will add both flavor and sweetness to regular brewed coffee as well. See pages 154–56. Of course, you could always try an unflavored coffee with low acid and a distinctive taste—an Ethiopia Yirgacheffe or Yemen, for example.

WORDS FOR IT

A Glossary

AA. Capitalized letters are grade indicators usually describing the size of the bean. In Peru, for example, AAA is the largest bean; in Kenya, Tanzania, and New Guinea, AA is the largest; in India, A is the largest.

Acidity, Acidy, Acid. Usually, the pleasant tartness of a fine coffee. Acidity, along with *flavor, aroma,* and *body,* is one of the principal categories used by professional tasters in *cupping,* or sensory evaluation of coffee. When not used to describe cup characteristics, the term acidity may refer to pH, or literal acidity, or to certain constituents present in coffee that may produce indigestion or nervousness in some individuals.

After-Dinner Roast. See *Espresso Roast.*

Aged Coffee, Vintage Coffee. Traditionally, coffee held in warehouses for several years, sometimes deliberately, sometimes inadvertently. Such aging reduces acidity and increases body. Aged coffee has been held longer than either *old crop* or *mature* coffee. Recently, some Indonesia coffee has been subject to a sort of accelerated aging involving deliberate exposure to moist air, much like India's *monsooned coffee.*

Alajuela. Market name for one of the better coffees of *Costa Rica.*

Note: Terms that appear elsewhere in the glossary are *italicized.*

Altura. Spanish for "heights"; describes *Mexico* coffee that has been high-grown.

American Roast. Coffee roasted to traditional American taste: medium brown.

Americano. See *Caffè Americano.*

Ankola. Seldom-used market name for arabica coffee from northern *Sumatra.*

Antigua. Market name for one of the most distinguished coffees of *Guatemala,* from the valley surrounding the old capital of Guatemala, Antigua.

Arabian Mocha, Yemen, Yemen Mocha, Mocha. See *Yemen.*

Arrabica, *Coffea Arabica.* The earliest cultivated species of coffee tree and still the most widely grown. It produces approximately 70 percent of the world's coffee, and is dramatically superior in cup quality to the other principal commercial coffee species, *Coffea canephora* or *robusta.* All fine, specialty, and fancy coffees come from *Coffea arabica* trees.

Aroma. The fragrance produced by hot, freshly brewed coffee. Aroma, along with *flavor, acidity,* and *body,* is one of the principal categories used by professional tasters in *cupping,* or sensory evaluation of coffee.

Arusha. Market name for coffee from the slopes of Mt. Meru in *Tanzania.*

Aquapulp. See *Demucilage.*

Automatic Filter-Drip Coffee Makers. Coffee brewers that automatically heat and measure water into a filter and filter receptacle containing the ground coffee.

Balance. Tasting term applied to coffees for which no single characteristic overwhelms others, but that display sufficient complexity to be interesting.

Bani. Market name for a good, low-acid coffee of the *Dominican Republic.*

Barahona. Market name for coffee from the southwest of the *Dominican Republic,* considered by many to be the best coffee from that country.

Barista. Italian term for skillful and experienced espresso bar operator.

Bar System. A complete system for producing espresso cuisine, usually including brewing and milk-frothing apparatus, specialized grinder and *doser,* accessories, and *waste tray* or *knock-out box.*

Batch Roaster. Apparatus that roasts a given quantity or batch of coffee at a time.

Bird Friendly. See *Shade Grown.*

Blade Grinder. Device that uses a propellorlike blade to grind coffee.

Blend. A mixture of two or more *single-origin* coffees.

Body. The sensation of heaviness, richness, or thickness and associated texture when one tastes coffee. Body, along with *flavor, acidity,* and *aroma,* is one of the principal categories used by professional tasters in *cupping,* or sensory evaluation of coffee.

Boiler. The tank in which water is heated for brewing and steam production in most espresso brewing apparatus.

Bourbon Santos. See *Santos.*

Bourbon. A botanical variety of *Coffea arabica. Var. bourbon* first appeared on the island of Bourbon, now Réunion. Some of the best Latin-American coffees are from *bourbon* stock.

Brazil. One of the world's most complicated coffee origins. Most Brazil coffee is carelessly picked and primitively processed, and is not a factor in the specialty trade. The best (usually dry-processed Bourbon *Santos*) can be a wonderfully deep, complex, sweet coffee particularly appropriate for espresso. Almost all Brazil coffee is relatively low-grown, but the variety of processing methods (*wet method, dry method,* and *semidry* or pulped natural method) makes Brazil a fascinating origin.

Brown Roast. See *American Roast.*

Bugishu, Bugisu. Market name for arabica coffee from the slopes of Mt. Elgon in Uganda. Considered the best *Uganda* coffee.

Burr Grinder, Burr Mill. Coffee grinder with two shredding discs or burrs that can be adjusted for maximum effectiveness.

Café au Lait. Coffee drink combining one-third drip-brewed coffee with two-thirds hot, frothed milk.

Caffè Americano, Americano. An espresso lengthened with hot water.

Caffè Latte. A serving of espresso combined with about three times as much hot milk topped with froth.

Caffeine. An odorless, bitter alkaloid responsible for the stimulating effect of coffee and tea.

Cappuccino. An espresso drink comprised of one serving of espresso topped with hot milk and froth.

Caracas. A class of coffees from *Venezuela,* ranging from fair to excellent in quality.

Caracol. See *Peaberry.*

Caturra. A relatively recently selected botanical variety of the *Coffea arabica* species that generally matures more quickly, grows more compactly, and is more disease resistant than older, traditional arabica varieties. Many experts contend that the caturra and modern hybrid varieties of *Coffea arabica* produce coffee that is inferior in cup quality and distinction to the coffee produced by the traditional "old arabica" varieties like *bourbon* and *typica.*

Celebes. See *Sulawesi.*

Chaff. Flakes of the innermost skin of the coffee fruit (the *silverskin*) that remain clinging to the green bean after processing and float free during roasting.

Chanchamayo. Market name for a respected coffee from South-Central *Peru.*

Cherry. Common term for the fruit of the coffee tree. Each cherry contains two regular coffee beans, or one *peaberry.*

Chiapas. Coffee-growing state in southern *Mexico.* The best Chiapas coffees are grown in the southeast corner of the state near the border with Guatemala, and may bear the market name Tapachula after the town of that name. At their best, Chiapas or Tapachula coffees display brisk acidity, delicate flavor, and light to medium body.

Chicory. The root of the endive, roasted and ground, it is blended with coffee in *New Orleans*–style coffee.

Chipinga. Region in eastern *Zimbabwe* near the border with Mozambique that produces the most admired coffees of that country.

Cibao. Market name for a good, generally low-acid coffee from the *Dominican Republic.*

Cinnamon Roast. See *Light Roast.*

City Roast. See *Full-City Roast.*

Clean. Coffee cupping or tasting term describing a coffee sample that is free from flavor defects.

Coatepec, Altura Coatepec. Market name for a respected washed coffee from the northern slopes of the central mountain range in Veracruz, *Mexico.*

Cobán. Market name for a respected, high-grown coffee from North-Central *Guatemala.*

Coffea Arabica. See *Arabica.*

Coffea Canephora, Robusta. See *Robusta.*

Coffee Oil, Coffeol. The volatile coffee essence developed in the bean during roasting.

Cold-Water Method. Brewing method in which ground coffee is soaked in a proportionally small amount of cold water for ten to twenty hours. The grounds are strained out and the resulting concentrated coffee is stored and mixed with hot water as needed. The cold-water method produces a low-acid, light-bodied cup that some find pleasingly delicate, and others find bland.

Colombia. The standard Colombia coffee is a *wet-processed* coffee produced by small holders, and collected, milled, and exported by the Colombian Coffee Federation. It is sold by grade (Supremo is the highest) rather than by market name or region. It can range from superb, high-grown, classic, mildly fruity Latin America coffee to rather ordinary, edge-of-fermented, fruity coffee. Coffees from some estates and cooperatives and from privately operated mills are sold by region as well as by botanical variety (*bourbon* is best). Narino State in southern Colombia is currently producing the most respected Colombia coffee. Mixed Medellín, Armenia, and Manizales Columbia coffees are often sold together as *MAMs*.

Commercial Coffees. Packaged preground (prebrewed in the case of instant or soluble) coffees sold by brand name.

Complexity. A tasting term describing coffees whose taste sensations shift and layer pleasurably, and give the impression of depth and resonance.

Continental Roast. See *Espresso Roast.*

Continuous Roaster. Large, commercial coffee roaster that roasts coffee continuously rather than in batches.

Costa Rica. The best Costa Rica coffees (San Marcos de Tarrazu, Tres Rios, Heredi, Alajuela) display a full body and clean, robust acidity that make them among the most admired of Central American coffees.

Crema. The pale brown foam covering the surface of a well-brewed *tazzina* of espresso.

Cúcuta. Market name for a coffee grown in northeastern Colombia but often shipped through Maracaibo, Venezuela.

Cupping. Procedure used by professional tasters to perform sensory evaluation of samples of coffee beans. The beans are ground, water is poured over the grounds, and the liquid is tasted both hot and as it cools. The key evaluative categories are *aroma, acidity, body,* and *flavor.*

Dark French Roast. A roast of coffee almost black in color with a shiny surface, thin-bodied, and bittersweet in flavor, with an overlay of burned or charcoal-like tones.

Dark Roast. Vague term; may describe any roast of coffee darker than the traditional American norm.

Decaffeination Processes. Specialty coffees are decaffeinated in the green state, currently by one of four methods. The direct solvent method involves treating the beans with solvent, which selectively unites with the caffeine and is removed from the beans by steaming. The indirect solvent or solvent-water method involves soaking the green beans in hot water, removing the caffeine from the hot water by means of a solvent, and recombining the water with the beans, which are then dried. Both processes using solvents are often called European process or traditional process. The water-only method, commonly known by the proprietary name Swiss Water Process, involves the same steps but removes the caffeine from the water by allowing it to percolate through a bed of activated charcoal. In the carbon dioxide method, which is only beginning to be established in the specialty coffee trade, the caffeine is stripped directly from the beans by a highly compressed semiliquid form of carbon dioxide.

Defects, Flavor Defects. Unpleasant flavor characteristics caused by problems during picking, processing (fruit removal), drying, sorting, storage, or transportation. Common defects include: excess numbers of immature or underripe fruit (unselective picking); inadvertent *fermentation* (careless processing); fermentation combined with invasion by microorganisms, causing moldy, hard, or *rioy* defects (careless or moisture-interrupted drying); and contact with excessive moisture after drying, causing musty or baggy defects (careless storage and transportation).

Degassing. A natural process in which recently roasted coffee releases carbon dioxide gas, temporarily protecting the coffee from the staling impact of oxygen.

Demitasse. "Half cup" in French; a half-size or 3-ounce cup used primarily for espresso coffee.

Demucilage, Aquapulp. Terms for a procedure in which the sticky fruit pulp, or mucilage, is removed from freshly picked coffee beans by scrubbing in machines. Mechanical demucilaging is gradually replacing the traditional *wet-processing* procedure of removing mucilage by *fermentation* and washing.

Djimah, Djimma, Jimma. A coffee from *Ethiopia*. Washed Djimah can be an excellent low-acid coffee. *Dry-processed* Djimah is a lesser coffee often exhibiting wild or medicinal taste characteristics and is not often traded as a specialty coffee.

Doppio. A double espresso, or 1½ to 3 ounces of straight espresso.

Dominican Republic, Santo Domingo. High-grown Dominican coffee is a fairly rich, acidy coffee with classic Caribbean characteristics. Lower-grown Dominican coffees tend to be softer and less acidy.

Doser. A spring-loaded device on specialized espresso grinders that dispenses single servings of ground coffee.

DP. Abbreviation for "double picked," meaning the coffee in question has been subjected to hand picking to remove imperfect beans, pebbles, and other foreign matter twice rather than once.

Drip Method. Brewing method that allows hot water to settle through a bed of ground coffee.

Drip Tray. In espresso brewing apparatus, the tray designed to catch the overflow from the brewing process.

Dry-Processed Coffee, Dry-Method Coffee, Natural Coffee. Coffee processed by removing the husk or fruit after the coffee fruit has been dried. When only ripe fruit is utilized and the drying is done carefully, dry-processed coffee can be complex, fruity, and deeply dimensioned. When the picking and drying are performed carelessly, as is the case with cheaper dry-processed coffees, the result is off-tasting, harsh coffee. The best and most celebrated dry-processed coffees are Yemen coffees, the Harrar coffees of Ethiopia, and the finest traditional Brazil coffees.

Earthiness. Either a taste defect or a desirable exotic taste characteristic depending on who is doing the tasting and how intense the earthy taste in question is. Apparently earthiness is caused by literal contact of wet coffee with earth during drying. Indonesia coffees from Sumatra and Sulawei are particularly prone to display earthy tones.

Ecuador. At best, Ecuador coffees are medium-bodies and fairly acidy, with a straightforward flavor typical of Central and South America coffees.

El Salvador. El Salvador coffees tend toward softer, less acidy versions of the classic Central American flavor profile. The best high-grown El Salvadors from trees of the *bourbon* and *pacamara* varieties can be fragrant, complex, lively, and pleasingly gentle.

En Pergamino, In Parchment. See *Parchment Coffee.*

Espresso Roast, After-Dinner Roast, Continental Roast, European Roast. Terms for coffee brought to degrees of roasting ranging from somewhat darker than the traditional American norm to dark brown. Acidity diminishes and a rich bittersweetness emerges. Among many newer American specialty roasters, roast styles once called by these names may in fact constitute the typical, "regular" roast of coffee.

Espresso. Used to describe both a roast of coffee (see *Espresso Roast*) and a method of brewing in which hot water is forced under pressure through a compressed bed of finely ground coffee. In the largest sense, an entire approach to coffee cuisine, involving a traditional menu of drinks, many combining brewed espresso coffee with steam-heated, steam-*frothed milk.*

Estate-Grown Coffee. Coffee produced by a single farm, single mill, or single group of farms, and marketed without mixture with other coffees. Many specialty coffees are now identified by estate name, rather than less specific regional or market name.

Ethiopia. Ethiopia is a very complex coffee origin. The best Ethiopia dry-processed coffee (*Harrar* or Harar) tends to be medium-bodied and brilliantly acidy with rough, fruity, berry, or winy tones. The best washed Ethiopian coffee (*Yirgacheffe, Sidamo,* some *Limu,* and some washed *Djimah*) is light-bodied but explosive with complex floral and citrus notes.

European Preparation. Used to describe coffee from which imperfect beans, pebbles, and other foreign matter have been removed by hand.

European Process. See *Decaffeination Processes.*

European Roast. See *Espresso Roast.*

Excelso. A comprehensive grade of Colombia coffee, combining the best, or supremo, and the second-best, or extra, grades.

Extra. Second-best grade of Colombia coffee.

Fair-Trade Coffee. Coffee that has been purchased from farmers (usually peasant farmers) at a "fair" price as defined by international agencies. The premium paid these farmers under fair-trade arrangements is quite modest, by the way.

Fermentation. An important but confusing coffee term with two main meanings. As a positive component of the *wet method* of coffee processing, fermentation is a stage in which the sticky pulp is loosened from the skinned coffee seeds or beans by natural enzymes while the beans rest in tanks. If water is added to the tanks, the process is called wet fermentation; if no water is added, it is called dry fermentation.

In sensory evaluation, or *cupping,* of coffee, fermentation is an important descriptor for a range of related taste defects set off when the sugars in the coffee fruit begin to ferment. Sensations described as ferment can range from sweet, composty, rotten-fruit tastes to harsh, moldy, musty, or medicinal tastes.

Filter Basket. The receptacle that holds the ground coffee during the brewing operation. In espresso brewing, a small metal filter basket fits inside the filter holder or *portafilter,* which in turn clamps onto the *group.*

Filter Holder. See *Portafilter.*

Filter Method, Filter-Drip Method. Technically, any brewing method in which water filters through a bed of ground coffee. In popular usage, describes drip-method brewers utilizing a paper filter to separate grounds from brewed coffee.

Finish. The sensory experience of coffee just after it is swallowed (or, in the professional *cupping* procedure, just after it is spit out). Some coffees transform from first impression on the palate to finish; others stand pat.

Flavored Coffees. Coffees that in their roasted, whole-bean form have been mixed with flavoring agents.

Flavor. In *cupping,* or sensory evaluation of coffee, what distinguishes the sensory experience of coffee once its *acidity, body,* and *aroma* have been described.

Flip Drip, Neapolitan Macchinetta, Macchinetta. A style of drip-method brewer in which the ground coffee is secured in a two-sided strainer at the waist of the pot between two closed compartments. The brewing water is heated in one compartment, then the pot is flipped over, and the hot water drips through the coffee into the opposite compartment.

Fluid Bed Roaster, Fluidized Bed Roaster, Air Roaster, Sivitz Roaster. A roasting apparatus that works much like a giant popcorn popper, utilizing a column of forced hot air to simultaneously agitate and roast green coffee beans. These devices are sometimes called Sivitz roasters, after their popularizer and first American manufacturer, inventor Michael Sivitz.

Fragrance. As a specialized term in *cupping,* or sensory evaluation of coffee, fragrance describes the scent of dry coffee immediately after it has been ground but before it is brewed.

French Press, Plunger Pot. Brewing method that separates spent grounds from brewed coffee by pressing them to the bottom of the brewing receptacle with a mesh plunger.

French Roast, Heavy Roast, Spanish Roast. Terms for coffee brought to degrees of roast considerably darker than the American norm; may range in color from dark brown (see *Espresso Roast*) to nearly black (see *Dark French Roast*) and in flavor from rich and bittersweet to thin-bodied and burned.

Frothed Milk. Milk that is heated and frothed with a steam wand as an element in the espresso cuisine.

Full-City Roast, Light French Roast, Viennese Roast, Light Espresso Roast, City Roast, High Roast. Terms for coffee brought to degrees of roast somewhat darker than the traditional American norm, but lighter than the classic dark roast variously called espresso, French, or Italian. In the cup, full-city and associated roast styles are less acidy and smoother than the traditional American "medium" roast, but may display fewer of the distinctive taste characteristics of the original coffee. Among many newer American specialty roasters, roast styles once called full-city, Viennese, etc., may constitute the typical, "regular" roast of coffee.

Gayo Mountain. Market name for coffee exported by a large processing center and mill in Aceh Province, northern *Sumatra.* Wet-processed Gayo Mountain tends to be a clean but often underpowered version of the Sumatra profile. Traditionally processed Gayo Mountain resembles similar coffees from the Mandheling region of Sumatra: at best displaying an expansive, quirky flavor and a low-toned, vibrant acidity.

Ghimbi, Gimbi. A *wet-processed* coffee from western *Ethiopia.*

Good Hard Bean (GHB). A grade designation based on growing altitude in some Central American countries, including *Costa Rica* and *Guatemala.* GHB is somewhat lower grown than the highest designation, *Strictly Hard Bean* (SHB).

Green Coffee. Unroasted coffee.

Group, Delivery Group, Brew Head. The fixture protruding from the front of most espresso machines into which the *portafilter* and filter clamp.

Guatamala. Guatemala is a complex coffee origin. *Strictly Hard Bean*–grade coffees from the central highlands (*Antigua,* Atitlan,) tend to exhibit a rich, spicy, or floral acidity. Coffees from mountainous areas exposed to either Pacific (San Marcos) or Caribbean (Cobán, Huehuetenango) weather tends to display a bit less acidity and more fruit.

Haiti. The best Haiti coffees are low-acid, medium-bodies, and pleasantly soft and rich. At this writing, virtually all Haiti coffees entering the United States are produced by a large group of cooperatives and marketed under the name Haitian Bleu.

Hard Bean. Term often used to describe coffees grown at relatively high altitudes; in the same context, coffees grown at lower altitudes are sometimes designated *soft bean*. The higher altitudes and lower temperatures produce a slower-maturing fruit and a harder, less porous bean. Hard-bean coffees usually make a more acidy and more flavorful cup than do soft-bean coffees, although there are many exceptions to this generalization. The hard/soft distinction is used most frequently in evaluating coffees of Central America, where it figures in grade descriptions.

Hard. Trade term for low-quality coffee, in contrast to *mild* coffee. In Brazil, hard is a grade name for coffee that has been tainted by microorganisms during drying and displays harsh, nuance-dampening flavor notes.

Harrar, Harar, Harer, Mocha Harrar, Moka Harar, Mocca Harar. The best of the *dry-processed,* or natural, coffees of Ethiopia. Grown in eastern Ethiopia near the city of Harrar. Usually rather light-bodied but fragrant with complex wine-, fruit-, or floral-toned acidity. Often substituted for *Yemen* in *Mocha Java* blends.

Hawaii. The traditional and classic coffee of Hawaii is *Kona,* grown on the west coast of the Big Island of Hawaii. On the other Hawaiian islands, however, sugar cane and pineapple plantations have been converted to premium coffee farms. Kauai (Kauai coffee), Maui (Kaanapali coffee), Molokai (Malulani Estate) and Oahu all now produce interesting and improving coffees.

Heavy Roast. See *French Roast.*

Heredia. Market name for a respected coffee of *Costa Rica.*

High-Grown. Arabic coffees grown at altitudes over 3,000 feet, usually higher. Such coffees are generally superior to coffees grown at lower altitudes. The term high-grown is also used in many Latin American grade descriptions.

High Roast. See *Full-City Roast.*

Huehuetenango. One of the better coffees of *Guatemala.*

India. India coffee is grown in the south of the country. The best is low-key, with moderate body and acidity and occasional intriguing nuance; at worst it is bland. *Mysore* is a market name for certain high-quality, wet-processed India coffees. Coffees from the Shevaroys and Nilgiris districts generally tend to display more acidity than coffees from other South India regions. Also see *Monsooned Coffee.*

Indonesia. Indonesia coffees are usually marketed under the name of the island of origin; see *Sumatra, Sulawesi, Java.* At best, most are distinguished by full body, rich flavor, and a low-toned, vibrant acidity. At worst, many display unpleasant hard or musty defects. Others display an *earthiness* that many coffee lovers enjoy and others deplore.

Ismaili. Market name for a respected coffee from Central *Yemen.* Also describes a traditional botanical variety of Yemen coffee with round, pealike beans and superior cup quality.

Italian Roast. A roast of coffee considerably darker than the traditional American norm. Usually dark brown in color and rich and bittersweet in flavor, but may range in color to almost black and in flavor to nearly burned.

Jamaica Blue Mountain Style. Various blends of coffee intended by their originators to approximate the qualities of authentic *Jamaica Blue Mountain.* These blends may contain no actual Jamaica coffee.

Jamaica Blue Mountain. Celebrated single-origin coffee from above 3,000-foot elevation in the Blue Mountain district of Jamaica. Can be exceptional: rich, complex, bouillonlike. More often a rather ordinary, balanced, low-toned, Caribbean coffee.

Jamaica. The best (*Jamaica Blue Mountain*) is, or was, a balanced, classic coffee with rich flavor, full body, and a smooth yet vibrant acidity. These characteristics and its relatively short supply have made it one of the world's most celebrated coffees. Whether it still merits this distinction is subject to debate among importers and roasters. Lower-grown Jamaica coffees (Jamaica High Mountain) tend to be less acidy and lighter in body. Other Jamaica coffees are undistinguished.

Java, Java Arabica. Unlike most other Indonesia coffees, which are grown on tiny farms and often primarily processed, Java coffees are grown on large farms or estates, most operated by the government, and are *wet-processed* using modern methods. The best display the low-toned richness characteristic of other *Indonesia* coffees, but are usually lighter in body and brighter. Old Java, Old Government, or Old Brown are specially processed coffees from Java, created to mimic the flavor characteristics of the original Java coffee, which was inadvertently aged in the holds of eighteenth- and nineteenth century ships during their passage to Europe.

Jimma, Djimma. See *Djimah*.

Jinotega. Market name for a respected *Nicaragua* coffee.

Kalossi. See *Sulawesi*.

Kenya. Kenya coffees are celebrated for their deep, winy acidity, resonant cup presence, and complex fruit and berry tones. Of the world's great coffees, Kenya probably is the most consistent in quality and most widely available.

Kilimanjaro. Coffee from the slopes of Mt. Kilimanjaro in Tanzania; also marketed as Moshi.

Knock-Out Box. In espresso brewing, a sturdy boxlike receptacle with a padded crossbar or edge. Spent grounds are dumped into the box by knocking the filter basket against the padded bar or edge.

Kona, Hawaii Kona. *Single-origin* coffee from the Kona coast of the island of *Hawaii*. The best Kona coffee displays classic balance, with medium body, good acidity, and rich, complex aroma and flavor.

Kopi Luak. Coffee from Sumatra, Indonesia, distinguished not by origin, but by the uniquely intimate way it is processed. A mammal called a luak, or civet, eats ripe coffee cherries, digests the fruit, and excretes the seeds, after which the seeds or beans are gathered from its dry droppings. Kopi luwak is one of the most expensive coffees in the world owing to obvious limitations on its production. Authorities differ on how much of the kopi luwak that arrives at coffee dealers is authentic and how much is ordinary coffee that has been "treated" in luwak manure, but samples certainly look authentic, smell authentic, and are pleasantly earthy, sweet, and full in the cup.

La Minita, La Minita Farm. Well-publicized estate in the Tarrazu district of *Costa Rica* that produces an excellent, meticulously prepared coffee.

Latte. See *Caffè Latte*.

Lavado Fino. Highest grade of *Venezuela* coffee.

Light Espresso Roast. See *Full-City Roast*.

Light French Roast. See *Full-City Roast*.

Light Roast, Cinnamon Roast, New England Roast. Coffee brought to a degree of roast of coffee lighter than the traditional American norm and grainlike in taste, with a sharp, almost sour acidity. This roast style is not a factor in specialty coffee.

Limu. Market name for a respected fragrant, floral- and fruit-toned *wet-processed* coffee from South-Central *Ethiopia.*

Lintong, Mandheling Lintong. Market name for the most admired coffee of *Sumatra,* Indonesia. From the Lake Toba area toward the northern end of the island.

Luak. See *Kopi Luak.*

Macchinetta, Neapolitan Macchinetta. See *Flip-Drip.*

Macchiato. Either a serving of *espresso* "stained" or marked with a small quantity of hot, *frothed milk* (espresso macchiato), or a moderately tall (about 8 ounces) glass of hot, frothed milk "stained" with espresso (latte macchiato). In North America, the term is more likely to describe the former than the latter.

Machine Drying. Coffee must be dried, either directly after picking (in the *dry method*) or after fruit removal (in the *wet method*). *Sun drying* is often replaced or supplemented by drying with machines, either in large, rotating drums or in cascading silos. Machine drying can be superior or inferior to sun drying in terms of promoting cup quality, depending on weather conditions, drying temperature, and other factors.

Malawi. Most Malawi (a small country west of Mozambique, Africa) coffee to reach the United States is grown on larger estates and distinguished by a rather soft, round profile.

Mandheling. The most famous of *Sumatra,* Indonesia. From the Lake Toba area toward the northern end of the island.

Maracaibo. A class of coffees from *Venezuela,* including many of the most characteristic and distinguished coffees of that country.

Maragogipe *(Mah*-rah-goh-*shzee*-peh), Elephant Bean. A variety of *Coffea arabica* distinguished by extremely large, porous beans. It first appeared in Maragogipe, Brazil, and has since been planted elsewhere in Latin America, particularly in Mexico and Central America. It is currently falling out of flavor owing to thinnish cup character and low-bearing trees.

Matagalpa. Market name for a respected coffee of *Nicaragua.*

Mattari, Matari. Market name for one of the most admired coffees of *Yemen.* From the Bani Mattar area west of the capital city of Sana'a. Usually a winier, sharper version of the Yemen style.

Mature Coffee. Coffee held in warehouses for two to three years. Mature coffee has been held longer than *old-crop* coffee but not as long as *aged* or vintage coffee.

Mbeya, Pare. Market names for coffee from the south of *Tanzania.*

Medium Roast, Medium-High Roast. See *American Roast.*

Mérida. Market name for one of the most respected and most characteristic *Venezuela* coffees, delicate and sweet in the cup.

Mexico. The best *Mexico* coffees (*Oaxaca Pluma, Coatepec, Chiapas*) are distinguished by medium body and a delicate, pleasant acidity. Highland Chiapas coffees can be bigger and more richly acidy.

Microwave Brewers. Brewing apparatus designed to take advantage of the unique properties of the microwave oven. Over the years microwave brewers have incorporated a variety of technical means, ranging from open pot through various approaches to filter drip. At this writing, none have made an impression on the market.

Middle Eastern Coffee, Turkish Coffee. Coffee ground to a powder, sweetened (usually), brought to a boil, and served grounds and all.

Mild. A trade term for high-quality arabica coffees. Often contrasted with *hard,* or inferior, coffees.

Milling. Mechanical removal of the dry *parchment* skin from *wet-processed* coffee beans, or the entire dried fruit husk from *dry-processed* beans.

Mocha, Moka, Mocca, Moca. *Single-origin* coffee from *Yemen;* also a drink combining chocolate and (usually espresso) coffee. The coffee, also called Arabian Mocha, Yemen, or Yemen Mocha, takes its name from the ancient port of Mocha. It is the world's oldest commercially cultivated coffee, distinguished by its distinctively rich, winy acidity and intriguing nuance. Coffee from the Harrar region of *Ethiopia,* which resembles Yemen coffee in cup character, is also sometimes called Mocha.

Mocha Java, Moka Java, Mocca Java. Traditionally, a blend of *Yemen Mocha* and *Java Arabica* coffees, usually one part Yemen Mocha and two parts Java Arabica. All commercial Mocha Java blends and many specialty versions no longer follow this recipe. Commercial blends may combine any of a variety of round, full coffees in place of the Java, and any of a variety of bright, acidy coffees in place of the Mocha. Versions offered by specialty roasters may blend a true Java with a true Yemen Mocha or may substitute another (often better) Indonesia coffee for the Java or an Ethiopia Harrar for the Yemen. Most specialty coffee variations probably do represent the classic blend accurately. In its traditional form, Mocha Java is the world's oldest coffee blend.

Monsooned Coffee, Monsooned Malabar. Dry-processed, *single-origin* coffee from southern *India* deliberately exposed to monsoon winds in open warehouses, with the aim of increasing body and reducing acidity.

Moshi. Market name for coffee from the slopes of Mt. Kilimanjaro in *Tanzania.*

Mysore, India Mysore. See *India.*

Nariño. Department in southern *Colombia* that produces certain particularly admired specialty coffees.

Natural Coffee. See *Dry-Processed Coffee.*

Neapolitan Macchinetta, Macchinetta. See *Flip Drip.*

Neapolitan Roast. Term for coffee brought to a degree of roast darker than the typical *espresso roast* but not quite black.

New Crop. Coffee delivered for roasting soon after harvesting and processing. Coffees are at their brightest (or rawest) and most acidy in this state. Also see *Old Crop.*

New England Roast. See *Light Roast.*

New Guinea. *Single-origin* coffee from *Papua New Guinea.* The best-known New Guinea coffees are produced on large, state-of-the-art estates that produce a very well-prepared, clean, fragrant, deeply dimensioned, moderately acidy coffee. Other organically grown New Guinea coffees are produced on small farms and processed by the farmers using technically simple means, producing quirky, full, complex coffees at best, off-tasting coffees at worst.

New Orleans Coffee. Traditionally, dark-roast coffee blended with up to 40 percent roasted and ground *chicory* root. Most New Orleans blends sold in specialty stores today contain no chicory, however. They are essentially dark-roast blends, heavy on dry-processed *Brazil* coffees.

Nicaragua. Nicaragua coffees (usually market names Jinotega and Matagalpa) are excellent but usually not distinguished coffees in the classic Central American style: medium-bodied, straightforwardly acidy, and flavorful.

Oaxaca (Wuh-*hAH*-kuh), Oaxaca Pluma. Market name for coffee from the southern *Mexico* state of Oaxaca.

Ocoa. Market name for one of the better-respected coffees of the *Dominican Republic.*

Old Arabicas. Botanical varieties or cultivars of the *Coffea arabica* species that were developed by selection relatively early in the history of coffee, such as *var. bourbon* and *var. typica,* as opposed to hybrid varieties that have been developed more recently in deliberate efforts to increase disease resistance and production. Many experts contend that the modern hybrid varieties of *Coffea arabica* produce coffee that is inferior in cup quality and interest to the coffee produced by the more traditional old arabica varieties.

Old Crop. Coffee that has been held in warehouses before shipping. Old crop differs from *aged* or vintage and *mature* coffees in two ways: It has not been held for as long a period, and it may not have been handled with as much deliberateness. Depending on the characteristics of the original coffee and the quality of the handling, old crop may or may not be considered superior in cup characteristics to a new crop version of the same coffee. See also *New Crop.*

Old Java, Old Government, Old Brown. Arabica coffee from *Java* that, like mature coffee, has been deliberately held in warehouses in port cities to reduce acidity and increase body. The purpose is to mimic the flavor characteristics of the original Java coffee, which was inadvertently aged in the holds of eighteenth- and nineteenth-century sailing ships during their passage to Europe.

Open-Pot Method. Brewing method in which the ground coffee is steeped (not boiled) in an open pot and separated from the brewed coffee by settling or being strained.

Organic Coffee, Certified Organic Coffee. Coffee that has been certified by a third-party agency as having been grown and processed without the use of pesticides, herbicides, or similar chemicals.

Parchment Coffee, In Parchment, En Pergamino. Describes *wet-processed* coffee shipped with the dried parchment skin still adhering to the bean. The parchment is removed prior to shipping and roasting, a step called *milling.*

Parchment. A final thin, crumbly skin covering *wet-processed* coffee beans after the coffee berries have been skinned, the pulp removed, and the beans dried.

Pare. See *Mbeya.*

Patio Drying. Drying coffee directly after picking (in the *dry-processed method*) or after fruit removal (in the *wet-processed method*) by exposing it to the heat of the sun by spreading and raking it in thin layers on open patios. A more traditional alternative to *machine drying.*

Peaberry, Caracol. A small, round bean formed when only one seed, rather than the usual two, develops at the heart of the coffee fruit. Peaberry beans are often separated from normal beans and sold as a distinct grade of a given coffee. Typically, but not always, they produce a brighter, more acidy, but lighter-bodied cup than normal beans from the same crop.

Percolation. Technically, any method of coffee brewing in which hot water percolates, or filters down through, a bed of ground coffee. The pumping percolator utilizes the power of boiling water to force water up a tube and over a bed of ground coffee.

Pergamino. See *Parchment.*

Peru. The best Peru coffee is flavorful, aromatic, gentle, and mildly acidy. Chanchamayo, from South-Central *Peru,*

250

and *Urubamba,* from a growing district farther south near Machu Picchu, are the best-known market names.

Piston Machine. An espresso machine that uses a piston operated by a lever to force brewing water at high pressure through the compacted bed of ground coffee.

Plunger Pot. See *French Press.*

Polishing. An optional procedure at the end of coffee processing and milling in which the dried, shipment-ready beans are subjected to polishing by friction to remove the innermost skin, or *silverskin,* and improve their appearance. Polishing does nothing to help flavor and may even hurt it by heating the beans, hence most specialty coffee buyers do not encourage the practice.

Portafilter, Filter Holder. In espresso brewing, a metal object with plastic handle that holds the coffee filter, and clamps onto the *group.*

Prima Lavado, Prime Washed. Middle grade of *Mexico* coffee.

Puerto Rico, Puerto Rico Yauco. Yauco coffees from *Puerto Rico* are a revived specialty origin that, at best, display the qualities that made Jamaica Blue Mountain famous: A deep, vibrant, yet restrained acidity and balanced, gently rich flavor. However, this potentially finest of Caribbean coffees is often marred by inconsistency.

Pull. In espresso brewing on a pump or piston machine, a single brewing episode. One pull may produce either a single serving of espresso if the single filter basket is used or a double serving if the double filter basket is used.

Pulping. Process of removing the outermost skin of the coffee cherry or fruit. See *Wet-Processed Coffee.*

Pump Machine. An espresso machine that uses a pump to force brewing water at high pressure through the compacted bed of ground coffee.

Pyrolysis. The chemical breakdown, during roasting, of fats and carbohydrates into the delicate oils that provide the aroma and most of the flavor of coffee.

Quakers. Defective coffee beans that fail to roast properly, remaining stubbornly light-colored.

Regular Roast. See *American Roast.*

Reservoir. In smaller pump-activated expresso brewing devices, the (usually removable) tank that holds water at room temperature before it is distributed to the *boiler* or *thermal block* for heating.

Richness. A satisfying fullness in *flavor, body,* or *acidity.*

Rio. A class of *dry-processed* coffees from *Brazil* with a characteristic medicinal, iodinelike flavor deriving from invasion of a microorganism during drying. The term rioy or rio-y has come to be applied to any coffee with similar taste characteristics. The rio taste is considered a rank defect by North American buyers but is sought after by some buyers from Balkan and Middle Eastern countries.

Rioy, Rio-y. See *Rio.*

Robusta, *Coffea Canephora.* Currently the only significant competitor to *Coffea arabica* among cultivated coffee species. Robusta produces about 30 percent of the world's coffee. It is a lower-growing, higher-bearing tree that produces full-bodied but bland coffee of inferior cup quality and higher caffeine content than *Coffea arabica.* It is used as a basis for blends of instant coffee and for less expensive blends of preground commerical coffee. It is not a factor in the specialty coffee trade except as a body-enhancing component in some Italian-style espresso blends.

Sanani. A comprehensive market name for coffees from several growing regions west of Sana'a, the capital city of *Yemen*. Usually a lower-toned, somewhat less acidy version of the *Yemen* style.

Santo Domingo. See *Dominican Republic*.

Santos, Bourbon Santos. A market name for a category of high-quality coffee from *Brazil*, usually shipped through the port of Santos, and usually grown in the state of São Paulo or the southern part of Minas Gerais State. The term Bourbon Santos is sometimes used to refer to any high-quality Santos coffee, but it properly describes Santos coffee from the *bourbon* variety of *arabica*, which tends to produce a fruitier, more acidy cup than other varieties grown in Brazil.

SCAA. See *Specialty Coffee Association of America*.

Semi-Dry-Processed Coffee, Pulped Natural Coffee, Semi-Wet-Processed Coffee. Coffee prepared by removing the outer skin of the coffee fruit (a process called pulping) and drying the skinned coffee with the sticky mucilage and the *parchment* and *silverskin* still adhering to the bean. This processing method, situated between the *dry method* and the *wet method*, has no consensus name. It is one of three processing methods practiced in Brazil, and is used sporadically on a small scale by farmers in Sumatra and Sulawesi, Indonesia.

Shade Grown, "Bird Friendly." Describes coffee grown under a shady canopy. Arabica coffee is traditionally grown in shade in many (but not all) parts of Mexico, Central America, Colombia, Peru, and Venezuela, and in some other parts of the world, including India and some regions of Indonesia and Africa. Elsewhere arabica coffee is traditionally grown in full sun or near-full sun. The importance of maintaining shade canopies to supply habitat for migrating song birds in Central America has led to a controversial campaign by researchers at the Smithsonian Institution and their supporters to define "shade grown" in rather narrow

terms (shade provided by mixed native trees) and label coffees grown under such a native canopy as "Bird Friendly."

Shot. A single serving of espresso, typically 1 to no more than 2 ounces.

Sidamo, Washed Sidamo. Market name for a distinguished light-to-medium-bodied, fragrantly floral or fruity wet-processed coffee from southern *Ethiopia*.

Silverskin. The thin, innermost skin of the coffee fruit. It clings to the dried coffee beans until it is either removed by *polishing* or floats free during roasting and becomes what roasters call chaff.

Single-Origin Coffee. Unblended coffee from a single country, region, and crop.

Sivitz Roaster. See *Fluid-Bed Roaster*.

Soft Bean. Sometimes used to describe coffees grown at relatively low altitudes. In the same context, coffees grown at higher altitudes are often designated *hard bean*. The lower altitudes and consequently warmer temperatures produce a faster-maturing fruit and a lighter, more porous bean. Soft-bean coffees usually make a less acidy and less flavorful cup than do hard-bean coffees, although there are many exceptions to this generalization. The hard/soft distinction is used most frequently in evaluating coffees of Central America, where it figures in grade descriptions.

Spanish Roast. See *French Roast*.

Specialty Coffee Association of America (SCAA). An important and influential association of specialty coffee roasters, wholesalers, retailers, importers and growers headquartered in Long Beach, California.

Specialty Coffee. Practice of selling coffees by country of origin, roast, flavoring, or special blend, rather than by brand or trademark. The term specialty coffee also suggests the trade and culture that has grown up around this merchandising practice.

Steam Wand, Nozzle, Pipe, Stylus. The small, protruding pipe on most espresso machines that provides live steam for the milk-frothing operation.

Straight Coffee, Varietal Coffee. See *Single-Origin* Coffee.

Strictly Hard Bean (SHB). The highest-grade designation based on growing altitude in some Central American countries, including *Costa Rica, Guatemala,* and *Panama.*

Strictly High-Grown. Highest grade of *El Salvador* and *Mexico* coffees based on growing altitude.

Sulawesi, Celebes. *Single-origin* coffee from the island of Sulawesi (formerly Celebes), *Indonesia.* Most come from the Toraja or Kalossi growing region in the southeastern highlands. At best, distinguished by full body, expansive flavor, and a low-toned, vibrant acidity. At worst, many display unpleasant hard or musty defects. Some display an *earthiness* that many coffee lovers enjoy and others avoid.

Sumatra. *Single-origin* coffee from the island of Sumatra, *Indonesia.* Most high-quality Sumatra coffee is grown either near Lake Toba (*Mandheling,* Lintong) or in Aceh Province, near Lake Biwa (Aceh, *Gayo Mountain*). At best, distinguished by full body, deep, expansive flavor and a low-toned, vibrant acidity. At worst, many display unpleasant hard or musty defects. Some display an *earthiness* that many coffee lovers enjoy and others avoid.

Sun Drying. Drying coffee directly after picking (in the *dry method*) or after fruit removal (in the *wet method*) by exposing it to the heat of the sun by spreading and raking it in thin layers on drying racks or patios. A more traditional alternative to *machine drying.*

Sun Grown. See *Shade Grown.*

Supremo. Highest grade of *Colombia* coffee.

Sustainable Coffee. At this writing, a contested and vaguely defined category of environmentally friendly coffees. A caucus in the *Specialty Coffee Association of America* (SCAA) is attempting to evolve reliable guidelines for what constitutes a genuine, sustainably grown coffee. Supporters of *organic* coffees currently object to the concept as dangerously fuzzy.

Swiss Water Process. See *Decaffeination Processes.*

Tamper. In espresso brewing, the small, pestlelike device with a round, flat end used to distribute and compress the ground coffee inside the filter basket.

Tanzania. The best and most characteristic Tanzanian coffees display a rich flavor and fully body, with a vibrantly winy acidity that makes them resemble the coffees of neighboring *Kenya.* Others are softer, gentler coffees.

Tapachula. See *Chiapas.*

Tarrazu, San Marcos de Tarrazu. Market name for one of the better coffees of *Costa Rica.*

Thermal Block. A system for heating water in espresso brewers that uses coils of pipe enclosed inside a heating element or hot water tank.

Timor. *Single-origin* coffee from East *Timor.* Timor coffee was a classic origin in the early years of the twentieth century. Recently it was revived with help from international assistance agencies. At best, distinguished by fullish body, expansive flavor, and a low-toned, vibrant acidity. At worst, may display unpleasant hard or musty defects.

Toraja, Kalossi. Market names for coffee from southwestern *Sulawesi* (formerly Celebes), Indonesia.

Traditional Process. See *Decaffeination Processes.*

Tres Rios. Market name for one of the more respected coffees of *Costa Rica.*

Turkish Coffee. See *Middle Eastern Coffee.*

Typica. A botanical variety of *Coffea arabica. var. typica* is one of the oldest and most traditional of coffee varieties. Some of the best Latin-American coffees are from *typica* stock.

Uganda. The finest Uganda arabica (Bugishu or Bugisu) displays the winy acidity and other flavor characteristics of the best East Africa coffees but is less admired than the finest *Kenya* or *Zimbabwe,* owing to generally lighter body and less complex flavor.

Vacuum-Filter Method. A brewing method that differs from other filter methods in that the brewing water is drawn through the ground coffee by means of a partial vacuum.

Varietal Coffee. As used by many people in the American specialty coffee industry, a term describing an unblended coffee from a single country, region, and crop. For example: Ethiopia Yirgacheffe, Kenya AA, or La Minita Costa Rica Tarrazu. However, to follow the California wine analogy more precisely, varietal coffees ought logically to come from a single predominant botanical variety of coffee tree; *var. bourbon,* for example, or *var. typica.* Increasingly, coffee writers use "single origin" rather than "varietal" to describe coffees from a single country, region, or crop.

Varietal Distinction, Varietal Character. A tasting or *cupping* term describing positive characteristics that distinguish a given coffee from coffee from other regions. Examples are the winy or berrylike acidity of *Kenya* coffees or the full, resonant character of the best *Sumatra.* See *Varietal Coffee.*

Venezuela. Some Venezuela coffees (Tachira, *Cúcuta*) resemble *Colombia* coffees. However, the most characteristic (*Mérida,* Caripe) are sweet and delicately flavored.

Viennese Coffee. Ambiguous term. Describes coffee brewed by the drip or filter method from a blend of coffee brought to a degree or darkness of roast called *Viennese Roast*; also refers to brewed coffee of any roast or origin topped with whipped cream.

Viennese Roast. Term for coffee brought to a degree of roast slightly darker than the traditional American norm, but lighter than degrees of roast variously called *espresso, French,* or *Italian.* In the cup, Viennese roast (also called full-city, light French, or light espresso roast) is less acidy and smoother than the characteristic American roast but may display fewer of the distinctive taste characteristics of the original coffee. Viennese roast may also refer to a mixture of beans roasted to a dark brown and beans roasted to the traditional American medium brown.

Vintage Coffee. See *Aged Coffee.*

Wallensford Estate Blue Mountain. At one time the most celebrated and best of *Jamaica* Blue Mountain coffee. Now simply any Blue Mountain coffee from the Wallensford mill, which makes it little different from any other Jamaica Blue Mountain.

Washed Coffee. See *Wet-Processed Coffee.*

Waste Tray. A small drawer in the base of espresso machines or bar units designed to facilitate the disposal of spent grounds during the brewing of multiple cups of espresso.

Wet-Processed Coffee, Wet-Method Coffee, Washed Coffee. Coffee prepared by removing the skin and pulp from the bean while the coffee fruit is still fresh. Most of the world's great coffees are processed by the wet method, which generally intensifies acidity. In the traditional wet process, the coffee skins are removed (pulping), the skinned beans are allowed to sit in tanks where enzymes loosen the sticky fruit pulp or mucilage (*fermentation*), after which the loosened fruit is washed off the beans (washing). In the shortcut *demucilage* or aquapulp method, the pulp or mucilage is scrubbed from the beans by machine.

Whole-Bean Coffee. Coffee that has been roasted but not yet ground.

Yauco, Yauco Selecto, Puerto Rico Yauco. See *Puerto Rico.*

Yemen, Yemen Mocha, Mocha, Arabian Mocha. *Single-origin* coffee from the southwestern tip of the Arabian Peninsula, bordering the Red Sea, in the mountainous regions of present-day *Yemen.* The world's oldest cultivated coffee, distinguished by its full body and distinctively rich, winy acidity.

Yirgacheffe, Yirga Cheffe, Yrgacheffe *(Yur-*ga-**shef-ay).** Market name for one of the most admired washed coffees of *Ethiopia,* distinguished by its fruitlike or floral acidity and high-toned, complex flavor.

Zambia. Some estate coffees from eastern *Zambia* (Zambia is located in South-Central Africa) appear in the North American specialty market. They tend toward the softer, less acidy version of the East Africa profile.

Zimbabwe. Zimbabwe coffee exhibits excellent cup presence and the vibrant, winy acidity characteristic of East Africa coffees. Some rank it second in quality only to *Kenya* among Africa coffees. Most is grown in the Chipinge region, along the eastern border with Mozambique.

SENDING FOR IT

A list of resources

The best place to buy coffee and brewing gear is at your neighborhood specialty coffee store. Look in the yellow pages under "Coffee Dealers–Retail." Excellent specialty coffees sometimes can be found in supermarkets as well.

However, if parking, freeways, isolation, or cocooning tendencies keep you at home, virtually everything described in this book is available via the Internet, catalogs, and telephone. In compiling the following list of Internet and mail-order resources, I have concentrated in particular on products that are difficult to find in person: green coffees, exotic equipment like piston espresso machines and home roasting devices, flavored syrups, etc.

Hard-to-Find Equipment by Internet or Telephone

Fante's
Philadelphia, Pennsylvania
www.fantes.com
800-878-5557

Fante's is a coffee-equipment fetishist's dream. Not only does it stock virtually every possible form of brewing and grinding equipment, exotic and otherwise (Neapolitan macchinetti, classic French ceramic drip pots, Middle Eastern brewing-and-serving paraphernalia, vacuum brewers, cast-iron, clamp-on hand grinders), but the helpful staff will research, find a source for, and special order any available piece of equipment that the store does not carry.

Sweet Maria's Coffee Roastery
Columbus, Ohio
ww.sweetmarias.com
888-876-5917

Sweet Maria's web site reviews and sells a small but carefully selected assortment of aficionado coffee gear.

Thomas Cara
San Francisco, California
415-781-0383

This old, family-owned business in San Francisco's North Beach is the source for the recommended Riviera Baby Lusso home piston espresso machine and the aficionado, spring-loaded, Riviera Bristol home piston machine, as well as high-end, home pump espresso brewers. Most importantly, it fully supports all of its machines with a knowledgeable staff and a basement full of replacement parts.

Mr. Espresso
Oakland, California
510-287-5200

Source for the recommended ECM Giotto, a handsome, rugged, romantic device on the cusp between small commercial and large home machine.

Coffee by Internet or Telephone

At this writing there appears to be no one-stop shopping for specialty coffee. In other words, there is no way to buy coffees from more than one roasting company without visiting or calling each company separately. One well-established site, www.coffeereview.com, does provide authoritative reviews of a wide range of coffees plus links to sites where those coffees can be purchased.

Single-Roaster Sites and Sources. At this writing there appears to be no one-stop shopping for specialty coffee. In other words, there is no way to buy coffees from more than one roasting company without visiting or calling each company separately. One well-established site, www.coffeereview.com, does provide authoritative reviews of a wide range of coffees plus links to sites where those coffees can be purchased.

Hence the following list of roaster-retailers who sell their coffee over the Internet and/or by catalog and newsletter. To help the armchair coffee shopper I have added some notes, in particular notes concerning the style or "darkness" of roast each company tends to emphasize when roasting its single-origin coffees. Keep in mind that companies that specialize in roast styles toward the medium range of the spectrum also produce dark-roasted coffees, whereas companies that specialize in dark roasts typically produce only varieties of dark roasts.

I have organized the list more or less geographically from east to west, and tried to name a selection of roasting companies from each part of the country.

Simply because a roaster does not appear on this list does not mean that that roaster does not produce excellent, well-roasted coffee. If you have a specialty coffee store in your neighborhood, try that store's coffee first before you begin punching keys and ordering over the Internet.

Green Mountain Coffee Roasters
Waterbury, Vermont
www.gmcr.com
800-545-bean

Traditional American roast styles. Wide range of origins, including sustainable coffees; full-color catalog.

Armeno Coffee Roasters
Northborough, Massachusetts
www.armeno.com
800-ARMENO-1

Wide range of origins and roast styles. Informative newsletter.

Gillies Coffee
Brooklyn, New York
800-344-5526

A specialty coffee treasure, Gillies is the nation's oldest continually operating roasting company. Traditional American roast styles. Wide range of origins.

Oren's Daily Roast
New York, New York
888-348-5400
orensdailyroast.com

Somewhat darker roast style than the traditional East Coast norm.

Willoughby's/New World Coffee
Branford, Connecticut
www.willoughbyscoffee.com
800-388-8400

Traditional American roast styles. Wide range of origins.

Bucks County Coffee
Langhorne, Pennsylvania
www.buckscounty.com
800-523-6163

Wide range of origins and roast styles. Try the premium blends.

Timothy's World Coffee
North York, Ontario, Canada
www.timothys.com
416-638-3333

Traditional range of roast styles. Wide range of origins.

J Martinez
Atlanta, Georgia
www.martinezfinecoffees.com
800-642-5282

Traditional range of roast styles. Wide range of origins. A source for the rare (and wildly expensive) Kopi Luak.

Counter Culture Coffee
Durham, North Carolina
www.counterculturecoffee.com
888-238-JAVA

Leader in sustainable, bird-friendly, and CO_2-decaffeinated coffees. Traditional range of roast styles.

Intelligentsia Coffee Roasters & Tea Blenders
Chicago, Illinois
www.intelligentsiacoffee.com
888-945-9786

Traditional range of roast styles; sound selection of origins.

Caribou Coffee
Minneapolis, Minnesota
www.caribou-coffee.com
888-227-4268

Somewhat darker roast styles than the traditional American norm.

Orleans Coffee Exchange
New Orleans, Louisiana
www.orleanscoffee.com
800-737-5464

Wide range of origins; excellent range of dark-roast blends, including an authentic New Orleans–style chicory blend.

The Roasterie
Kansas City, Missouri
www.theroasterie.com
800-376-0245

Traditional range of roast styles. Custom personal blending via web site.

Montana Coffee Traders
Whitefish, Montana
www.coffeetraders.com
800-345-5282

Wide range of origins.

Allegro Coffee
Boulder, Colorado
www.allegro-coffee.com
800-666-4869

Wide range of origins (including organics) and roast styles. Particularly informative newsletter. Try the Ethiopia and Yemen selections.

Arbuckle Coffee
Tucson, Arizona
www.arbucklecoffee.com
800-533-8278

Somewhat darker roast styles than the traditional American norm. Wide range of origins.

Alpen Sierra Coffee
South Lake Tahoe, California
www.alpensierra.com
800-531-1405

Small but sophisticated roaster.

Batdorf & Bronson Roasters
Olympia, Washington
www.batdorf.com
800-955-5282

Slightly darker roast styles than the traditional American norm. Wide range of origins.

Caffè Appassionato
Seattle, Washington
888-502-2333

Specializes in naturally low-acid coffees brought to roasts slightly darker than the traditional American norm.

Torrefazione Italia
Seattle, Washington
www.titalia.com
800-827-2333

Specializes in classic espresso blends. For straight espresso try the Perugia blend, for milk-heavy espresso drinks the Napoli.

Thanksgiving Coffee
Fort Bragg, California
www.thanksgivingcoffee.com
800-648-6491

Leans toward darker roast styles, but very respectful of the green coffees. Specializes in sustainable, organic, bird-friendly, and other cause coffees.

Peet's Coffee & Tea
Berkeley, California
www.peets.com
800-999-2132

The original, dark-roasting coffee company. Peet's manages to preserve an impressive range of green coffee character in its extremely dark, signature-roast styles. Catalog and newsletter.

Mr. Espresso
Oakland, California
510-287-5200

Specializes in espresso blends and smooth, moderately dark–roast coffees. Try the Gold Medal Blend.

Pasadena Coffee Roasters
Pasadena, California
www.thebestcoffee.com
626-564-9291

Small but sophisticated roaster.

Trader Joe's
Pasadena, California
www.traderjoes.com

Trader Joe's offers a line of whole-bean coffees packed in nitrogen-flushed fiberboard cans that may not be North America's finest specialty coffees but certainly are among the best values for the money. Wide variety of roast styles and origins.

Pannikin Coffee & Tea
San Diego, California
www.pannikin.net
800-232-6482

Generally darker roast styles than the traditional American norm. Try the Best of Africa blend.

Heritage Coffee
Juncau, Alaska
www.heritagecoffee.com
800-478-5282

Wide range of origins and roast styles. Espresso-with-milk drinkers should try the rich, rough, twisty espresso blend.

Café Del Mundo
Anchorage, Alaska
www.cafedelmundo.com
907-562-2326

Somewhat darker roast styles than the traditional American norm. Wide range of origins.

Home-Roasting Equipment and Green Coffees by Internet or Telephone

Hobbyist or home coffee roasting has developed its own grass-roots culture, which is easily accessed on the Internet.

Here are just two of many companies specializing in green coffees, home-roasting apparatus, and home-roasting information.

Sweet Maria's Coffee Roastery
Columbus, Ohio
www.sweetmarias.com
888-876-5917

Fante's
Philadelphia, Pennsylvania
www.fantes.com
800-878-5557

Italian-Style Syrups by Internet or Telephone

Torani Syrups
South San Francisco, California
www.torani.com
800-775-1925

Entertaining web site with extensive recipes and other information. Provides links to sites that sell Torani syrups online (select Online Torani Providers).

DaVinci Gourmet
Seattle, Washington
www.davincigourmet.com
800-640-6779

Offers three lines of syrups: conventional, all-natural, and sugar-free. Provides links to sites that sell DaVinci syrups online (select Order Online).

Stirling Foods
Renton, Washington
www.stirling.net
800-332-1714

Simple, serviceable site. Offers a full conventional line of syrups plus a few low-calorie selections.

Monin
Clearwater, Florida
www.monin.com
800-966-5225

Impressive site, but, at this writing, no links to retail sources. Monin syrups are assembled of all natural ingredients, without preservatives.

Stearns & Lehman
Mansfield, Ohio
www.stearns-lehman.com
800-533-2722

Impressive site and wide range of syrups and flavorings, but, at this writing, no links to retail sources.

Chicory by Internet or Telephone

Roast and ground chicory root, which is combined with darker roasted coffees in amounts of 10 to 40 percent to make New Orleans–style blends, can be purchased in bulk from:

Orleans Coffee Exchange
New Orleans, Louisiana
www.orleanscoffee.com
800-737-5464

Chai by Internet or Telephone

Chai, the spice and tea mix that is combined with frothed milk in the new American espresso cuisine, can be difficult to turn up in stores.

Chai Stall
www.chaistall.com

Currently this web site sells only one chai, but it is as pungently authentic as they come.

BuyChai.Com
www.buychai.com

A large selection of decaffeinated, herbal, green tea, and black tea chais, none fully authentic, but most tactfully crafted from natural ingredients.

Chai Land
www.chai-land.com
877-495-2421

Sells commerical chais from a variety of producers. None are authentic, and many are flat-out tacky.

Starbucks, the Coffee Store That's Always There

As Starbucks made its astonishing transformation from small Seattle specialty roaster to darling of the stock market, symbol of chain-store oppression, salvation of the coffee world, abomination of the coffee world, etc., its actual, useful place in the world of the coffee lover is sometimes overlooked: Starbucks is the coffee store that is always there. Almost always, anyhow. If you need access to fair-to-good, whole-bean coffee and a small but thoughtful selection of brewing equipment, and if you live in the suburbs and prefer to avoid both Internet commerce and freeway travel, you may want to visit your local Starbucks.

The extremely knowledgeable coffee leaders at Starbucks do an amazing job at maintaining quality, but apparently the company simply has become too big to produce a large range of really distinctive specialty coffee. At this writing Starbucks regularly features two or three single-origin coffees every few months or so. These featured selections are likely to be interesting and worthwhile. The Kenya is always excellent. But, of late, I have found Starbucks blends ordinary to drab.

Starbucks
Seattle, Washington
www.starbucks.com
800-STARBUC

Buying Kona and Other Hawaiian Coffees by Internet or Telephone

Given how much they cost, the celebrated coffees of Kona are best enjoyed as estate or special mill selections rather than as generic "Kona coffee." Thanksgiving Coffee and Green Mountain Coffee Roasters (see Coffee by Internet or Telephone) both sell good estate Konas, but the best approach is to order directly from Hawaii. Among the many excellent sources:

Pele Plantations
Honaunau, Hawaii
www.peleplantations.com
800-366-0487

Custom roasts and ships coffee from several tiny, boutique Kona farms.

Bayview Farms
Honaunau, Hawaii
www.bayviewfarmcoffees.com
808-328-9658

Bayview is a mill, not a farm, that custom roasts special mill selections.

Finding "Other Island" Hawaiis. The low-grown but interesting coffees from the large estates on Maui, Molokai, and Kauai also are hard to find retail on the mainland. Order directly from the farms:

Maui's Kaanapali Estate Coffee
Lahaina, Maui, Hawaii
www.kaanapalicoffee.com
800-99-MAUI-9

Malulani Estate
Coffees of Hawai'i
Kualapuu, Molokai, Hawaii
www.coffeehawaii.com
800-346-5051

Kauai Coffee
Eleele, Kauai, Hawaii
www.kauaicoffee.com
800-545-8605

THOSE WHO KNOW ABOUT IT

Acknowledgments

When a book has been living and growing and changing for over twenty-five years, the list of those who have generously contributed to that book becomes almost as long as those years. Given how generous coffee professionals have been with their time and information, the following list is, if anything, a short and stingy one.

Some cited here (Jim Reynolds and George Howell especially) deserve a gigantic gold star for having heard me out and answered my questions over almost every year of those twenty-five. Others were intensely helpful for the first edition of this book (Alfred Peet, Milt Mountanos, Thomas Cara, the late James Hardcastle), or for the latest (Micheal Glenister, Kevin Knox, Don Holly), or for those editions in between (Bob Barker, Michael Sivitz, Mark Mountanos, Kevin Sinnott, and many, many others). But everyone on the list has contributed something important along the way.

As long as it is, this list leaves out two important category of individuals: those in coffee countries who were not involved directly in coffee but helped me get to it, and those who have helped me write about it better by contributing their editorial skills and leadership to an increasingly sophisticated culture of coffee communication. In the coffee travel category, I have been helped by so many so well that I can only list a few: Tom Lyons, Mohammed Saif, and Mohamad Sheiban (Yemen), Pilar Masch (Guatemala), and Judy Barral (Ethiopia). As for those who have helped build a community of coffee communication:

Linda Yoshin (coffeereview.com), the redoubtable Jane McCabe (*Tea & Coffee Trade Journal*), Michael Segal (*Coffee & Cocoa International*), Ward Barbee and Rivers Janssen (*Fresh Cup Magazine*), Roger Sandon (*Café Ole* magazine), Susan Bonne (*Coffee Journal*), Laura Gorman (*Gourmet Retailer* magazine), Suzanne Brown (SJB Associates), Sue Gillerlain (*Specialty Coffee Retailer* magazine), Mike Ferguson (Specialty Coffee Association of America), Jamie Utendorf, Susie Spindler (SNS Communications), Kate LaPoint, my wonderful agents Claudia Menza and Richard Derus, my longtime illustrator-colleague Martha Wasik, the editors of past editions of this book, Jackie Killeen and Annette Gooch, and current editors Keith Kahla and Teresa Theophano of St. Martin's Press.

My deepest gratitude to:
Alemu Abayneh, Ethiopia Coffee & Tea Authority
Genel Abebe, Ethiopia Coffee & Tea Authority
Sotero Agoot, Kona Pacific Farmers Cooperative
Hammoud Al Hamadani, Yemen
Mané Alves, Coffee Lab International
Patrice Amani, BV Capital
Yehasab Aschalein, Ethiopia Coffee & Tea Authority
Dr. Oskari Atmawinata, Pusat Penelitian Kopi dan Kakao, Indonesia
Jerry Baldwin, Peet's Coffee & Tea
Robert Barker, coffee consultant
Chuck Beek

Doug Belling, Amcafe
Mark Berfield, Captain Cook Coffee
Ian Bersten, inventor and writer (*Coffee Floats, Tea Sinks*), Australia
H. C. Skip Bittenbender, University of Hawaii
Lindsey Bolger, Batdorf & Bronson Roasters
Ken Bollman, Torani Italian Syrups
Guilherme Braga Rosa, Fazenda Vereda, Brazil
Carlos Brando, P&A Marketing Internacional, Brazil
Scott Brant, Montana Coffee Traders
Gus Brocksen, Pele Plantations
Guy Burdett, InterAmerican Commodities
Christopher Cara, Thomas Cara, Ltd.
John Cara, Thomas Cara, Ltd.
Thomas Cara
Doug Carpenter, Ronnoco Importing Company
Robert Carpenter, Boyd Coffee
Angela, Caruso, Berardi's Fresh Roast
Michael Caruso, Berardi's Fresh Roast
Timothy Castle, Castle Communications
Catherine Cavaletto, University of Hawaii
Karen Cebreros, Elan Organic Coffees
Rodrigo Chacón, Anacafé, Guatemala
Sheree Chase, Kona Historical Society
Steve Colten, Atlantic Specialty Coffee
Milton Coreas, Sunrise Coffee
Dan Cox, Coffee Enterprises
Kenneth Coxen, The Coffee Beanery
David Dallis, Dallis Bros.
Tadele Darbie, Ethiopia Coffee & Tea Authority
Rogério Daros, Fazenda Cachoeira, Brazil
Syaufi Darus, PTP Commodities, Indonesia
Martin Diedrich, Diedrich Coffee
Stephan Diedrich, Diedrich Coffee Roasters
Carlo DiRuocco, Mr. Espresso
John DiRuocco, Mr. Espresso
Mary-Francis DiRuocco, Mr. Espresso
Sherman Dodd, Coffee/PER
Stefany Dybeck, Seattle Coffee Company
Jay Endres, Roastery Development Group

Jan Eno, Thanksgiving Coffee
Frederico Jose Fahsen, Anacafé, Guatemala
James Kimo Falconer, Kaanapali Coffee
Terry Fitzgerald, Kona, Hawaii
Jaimé Fortuño, Yauco Selecto, Puerto Rico
Robert Fulmer, Royal Coffee
Ambrogio Fumagalli, writer and collector, Italy
Yanni Georgalis, Moplaco Trading, Ethiopia
Elias Getahun, Ethiopia Coffee & Tea Authority
Roberto Giesemann, CALICAFE, Mexico
Danielle Giovannucci, Fante's
Jim Glang, Crossroads Espresso
Michael Glenister, Amcafe
Eduardo Gomez, Andina Cafe & Coffee Roastery
Karen Gordon, Coffee Holding Co.
Richard Grame, Western Flavors & Fragrance
David Griswold, Sustainable Harvest Coffee
Sri Haryati Hadi, Pusat Penelitian Kopi dan Kakao, Indonesia
James Hardcastle, co-founder of Hardcastle Coffee
Alice Harrison, Fante's
Hidetaka Hayashi, Hayashi Coffee Institute, Japan
Gary Heine, Heine Bros. Coffee
H. Hereth, Talben Café, Brazil
Bill Herne, Timothy's World Coffee, Canada
Don Holly, Specialty Coffee Association of America
Fred Houk, Counter Culture Coffee
George Howell, coffee cupper and writer
Cahya Ismayadi, Pusat Penelitian Kopi dan Kakao, Indonesia
Joseph John, Josuma Coffee
B. Philip Jones, Barnie's Coffee & Tea
Charles Jones, Doña Mireya Estate Coffee
Mireya Jones, Doña Mireya Estate Coffee
Phyllis Jordan, PJ's Coffee & Tea
Paul Kalenian, Armeno Coffee Roasters
Paul Katzeff, Thanksgiving Coffee Company
Frank Kiger, Kauai Coffee
Tom Kilty, M. P. Mountanos
Alberto Kishida, MC Coffee do Brasil, Brazil

Kevin Knox, Allegro Coffee
Erna Knutsen, Knutsen Coffees
Alf Kramer, Specialty Coffee Association of Europe
Dan Kuhn, Coffees of Hawaii
Randy Layton, Boyd Coffee
Silvio Leite, Agribahia, Brazil
Barry Levine, Willoughby's/New World Coffee
Ted Lingle, Specialty Coffee Association of America
Richard Loero, Kaanapali Coffee
William MacAlpin, La Minita Coffee
John Martinez, J. Martinez & Co
Hans Masch, Finca Pastores, Guatemala
Tim McKinney, Los Gatos Coffee Roasting
Becky McKinnon, Timothy's World Coffees, Canada
Francisco Mena, Deli Café, Costa Rica
Sunalini Menon, M/S Coffeelab, India
Perry Merkel, Café Del Mundo
Alf Mildenberger, Quantum Coffee
Sherri Miller, Miller & Associates
Bruce Milletto, Bellissimo Media Coffee Education Group
Ray Ming, Hawaii Agriculture Research Center
Mohamed Moledina, Moledina Commodities
Victor Allen Mondry, Victor Allen's Coffee & Tea
Mirian Monteiro de Aguiar, Fazenda Cachoeira, Brazil
Luis Fernando Montenegro, Anacafé, Guatemala
Kim Moore, Uncommon Grounds
Mark Mountanos, M. P. Mountanos
Michael Mountanos, Mountanos Bros. Coffee
Milt Mountanos, retired founder of United Coffee
Warren Muller, Interamerican Commodities
Bruce Mullins, Coffee Bean International
Chifumi Nagai, Hawaii Agriculture Research Center
Alan Nietlisbach, Holland Coffee
Desse Nure, Ethiopia Coffee & Tea Authority
Jonathan O'Bergin, Kona Kava Coffee
Danny O'Neill, The Roasterie
Alan Odom, Holland Coffee
Dave Olsen, Starbucks Coffee

Simeon Onchere, Coffee Board of Kenya
Robert Osgood, Hawaii Agriculture Research Center
Claudio Ottoni, Fazenda Vereda, Brazil
Rodger Owen, Bucks County Coffee
Norman Pearce, Pier 40 Roastery
Alfred Peet, retired founder of Peet's Coffee & Tea
Mark Pendergrast, writer (*Uncommon Grounds*)
José Pereira, Fazenda Monte Alegre, Brazil
Mark Perkins, The Earth's Choice
Mary Petitt, Colombian Coffee Federation
Rick Peyser, Green Mountain Coffee Roasters
John Pickersgill, Jamaican Coffee Industry Board
John Rapinchuk, Knutsen Coffees
Rick Ray, Melchers Flavors of America
Robert Regli
Alejandro Renjifo, Colombian Coffee Federation
Jim Reynolds, Peet's Coffee & Tea
David Roche, agriculture consultant
Washington Luis Alves Rodrigues, Ipanema Agrícola, Brazil
Liz Rodríguez-Dorey, Anacafé, Guatemala
Robert Rose, Kauai Coffee
Roslyn Roy, Bayview Farms
Andy Roy, Bayview Farms
Kazuo Sambongi, UCC Ueshima Coffee, Japan
Vincenzo Sandalj, Sandalj Trading, Italy
Leopoldo Santanna, Daterra, Brazil
Grady Saunders, Heritage Coffee
Les Schirato, Cantarella Group, Australia
Donald Schoenholt, Gillies Coffee
David Schomer, Espresso Vivace
Teshome Selamu, Ethiopia Coffee & Tea Authority
Joanne Shaw, The Coffee Beanery
Tom Shook, Gadsden Coffee
Bill Siemers, Orleans Coffee Exchange
Bob Sinclair, Pannikin Coffee & Tea
Kevin Sinnott, coffee pundit
Michael Sivitz, Sivitz Coffee
Tim Skaling, Fresh Beans
Linda Smithers, Susan's Coffee & Tea

Patrick Spillman
Carl Staub, Agtron
John Stiles, Hawaii Agriculture Research Center
Setiawan Subekti, Kali Bendo Estate, Indonesia
Leman Sulaiman, SKA Trading, Indonesia
Mustafa Sulaiman, Association of Indonesian Coffee
    Exporters
Peter Tausend, Kauai Coffee
Augie Techeira, Freed Teller & Freed
Steve Teisl, ANGCO
Paul Thornton, Coffee Bean International

Baskoro "T. J." Tjokroadisumarto, Association of
    Indonesian Coffee Exporters
Alex Twyman, Old Tavern Estate, Jamaica
Isidro Valdés, San Rafael Urias, Guatemala
Raúl Valdés, San Rafael Urias, Guatemala
Marcelo Vieira, Brazil Specialty Coffee Association
George Vukasin, Peerless Coffee
Sonja Vukasin, Peerless Coffee
Robert Williams, Willoughby's/New World Coffee
Christian Wolthers, Wolthers & Associates
Jeremy Woods, Atlantic Specialty Coffee

INDEX